RIGHTING THE BALANCE

Righting the Balance

How You Can Help Protect America

DANIEL SERWER

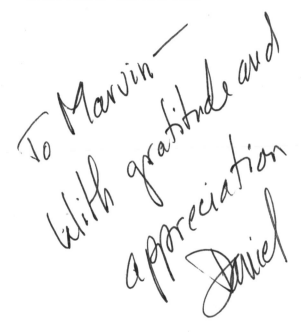

To Marvin—
With gratitude and
appreciation
Daniel

Potomac Books

AN IMPRINT OF THE UNIVERSITY OF NEBRASKA PRESS

Portions of chap. 9 originally appeared, in different form, as
"U.S.-EU Cooperation in Managing and Resolving Conflicts,"
by Daniel Serwer and Megan Chabalowski, in *Shoulder to
Shoulder: Forging a Strategic U.S.-EU Partnership*, ed. Daniel S.
Hamilton, 283–92 (Washington DC: Johns Hopkins University
Center for Transatlantic Relations, 2010). © Daniel S. Hamilton.

Library of Congress Cataloging-in-Publication Data
Serwer, Daniel Paul, 1945–
Righting the balance: how you can help protect America /
Daniel Serwer.
pages cm
Includes bibliographical references and index.
ISBN 978-1-61234-666-3 (cloth: alk. paper) 1. Peace-building—
United States. 2. National security—United States. 3. United
States—Foreign relations. I. Title.
JZ5584.U6S47 2013
327.73—dc23
2013025420

Set in Adobe Garamond by Hannah Gokie.

For Jacquelyn, Jared, and Adam

Contents

Preface

It is difficult for me to identify exactly when I became interested in international affairs: when my high school went to a model United Nations in the early 1960s playing the roles of the Soviet Union and Cuba, or was that a reflection of interests that had existed for some time? My mother, Blanche Luria, had spent a year in Palestine in the early 1930s and always talked fondly of the experience, even if her diary, discovered recently, betrays ambivalence. Was that what interested me in war and peace issues? My father, Zachary Serwer, worked to bring the Israel Philharmonic to the United States for the first time, in the early 1950s. Is that the origin of my conviction that cultural exchange really does matter?

Whatever its origins, my interest in international affairs took a long time to blossom. I was Sputnik generation, which meant a detour to science. I majored in chemistry at Haverford College, but even before graduation I knew I would not become a scientist. My treasured mentor, chemistry professor Colin MacKay, encouraged my nonscientific interests, in particular a healthy and realist appreciation for current affairs. I also studied a good bit of history, mostly with the masterful and dignified Wallace MacCaffrey. Thomas Kuhn, whom I met my senior year, urged me to get a master's degree in physical chemistry but then to come study history of science with him at Princeton. That is what I did.

War intervened. After a year at the University of Chicago and three semesters into my doctoral studies at Princeton, my birth date turned up in the draft lottery as number 23. A Vietnam War protester, I had been given conscientious-objector status by my local draft board, but I had no job with an approved agency. Oscar Schachter, the father of my Bryn Mawr friend Ellen Schachter (now Leventhal), was then director of research at the United Nations Institute for Training and Research in New York. He took me on to help with preparations for the first UN conference on the human environment, in June 1972 in Stockholm. After a year back at Princeton I returned to the UN with Peter Thacher, by then a UN Environment Programme representative in Geneva. I stayed through 1974 on a Rockefeller Foundation grant provided by Elmore Jackson and John Stremlau to help give birth to the International Register of Potentially Toxic Chemicals before heading back to Princeton to write my thesis.

Even then I did not understand that international affairs would be my profession, not a detour. But I chose a thesis topic that had important international dimensions: the origins of protection against ionizing radiation before World War II. Francesco Sella, the longtime secretary of the UN Scientific Committee on the Effects of Atomic Radiation, had told me that the International Congress of Radiology adopted the first international recommendations on protection against X-rays and radium in 1934. How had that happened?

The answers lay in international competition and cooperation among physicians and physicists in the preceding decades. War played its part there too: German physicists entered medical radiology during World War I to avoid military service and brought with them methods of measuring radiation dosage that would revolutionize the use of X-rays and radium to treat deep-seated cancers and to protect both patients and doctors from its effects. The International Commission on Radiological Protection, which still sets basic radiation protection standards for the world, is the direct descendant of this war-induced coupling of physicians and physicists. David Sowby, then its executive director, welcomed my historical inquiries.

The market for people with deep knowledge of the origins of radiation protection before World War II was not large in 1976, or any time since. Recalling my Haverford education, which had emphasized the "doctrine of transferable skills," I went to work for Leonard Hamilton at Brookhaven National Laboratory on contemporary energy and environment issues. I stayed less than a year and a half, leaving when Richard Gardner—already in Italy as President Carter's ambassador—asked me to come as his "science attaché" to handle scientific and technological issues. I jumped at the opportunity, managing somehow to pass muster with Allen Holmes, then deputy chief of mission (DCM) in Rome. My assignment there provided my first experience of physical danger in diplomacy: the Iraqi government put me on a list of people it would "hit" if anything bad happened to its nuclear program. When the Israelis bombed it in 1981, Assistant Secretary of State Tom Pickering ordered me into hiding.

The State Department moved me from Rome to Brasilia as science counselor in 1981, where Harry Kopp was DCM and Tony Motley was ambassador. Tony's concept of diplomacy—to get others to do what you want them to do—is one that undergirds this book. Harry has contributed enormously to my understanding of the State Department, which brought me back to DC in 1984 to handle "energy consuming country affairs" in the Economic Bureau. There E. Allan Wendt tasked me to lead the effort to convince American allies in the International Energy Agency that they needed larger "strategic" oil stocks that would be used early in a supply disruption to soften the economic damage, rather than the commercial practice of saving stocks for the last resort (see chapter 8).

By 1987 the State Department had forgotten that I was a science and technology specialist and sent me back to Rome as economic minister, where I succeeded John Holmes as DCM to Ambassador Peter Secchia in 1990. Leaving Rome as chargé d'affaires in 1993, I lobbied for the United States at the UN General Assembly, developed for Barbara Bodine a never consummated scheme to make Qaddafi's Libya pay compensation to Pan Am 103 victims, and organized a European chiefs of mission conference before Richard Holbrooke asked me to work on consolidating the Bosnian Federation in the fall of 1994.

Much of the rest of my life story appears in this book, from trips into war-torn and postwar Bosnia from November 1994 to June 1996, a year substituting for Bo Miller in Intelligence and Research at the State Department during 1996 and 1997, and my move to the United States

Institute of Peace (USIP) in 1998 and work there on Bosnia, Serbia, Kosovo, Macedonia, Iraq, Afghanistan, and other garden spots, as diplomats call them.

I am particularly indebted to two executive vice presidents at USIP: Harriet Hentges and Patricia Thomson, who seemed to know what I had to contribute before I did. But many colleagues there taught me things I have tried to incorporate in this book, among them David Smock, Bill Taylor, Abi Williams, Steve Hadley, Colette Rausch, Bob Perito, George Ward, Pamela Aall, Mike Lekson, Raymond Gilpin, Stephanie Schwartz, Jason Gluck, Qamar ul Huda, Barmak Pahzwak, Judy Barsalou, Steve Riskin, Sloan Mann, Alex Thier, Laurel Miller, Steve Heydemann, Joe Klaits, John Menzies, Neil Kritz, Mike Dziedzic, Rusty Barber, Paul Hughes, and many others whom I fear I am forgetting to mention. I had sterling assistants at USIP, now making brilliant careers in many different institutions, among them Kristine Herrmann, Jamie Baron, Matt Crane, Ylber and Yll Bajraktari, Samantha Williams, Megan Chabalowski, Courtney Rusin, Christina Parajon, Duke Lindsay, and Demis Yanco. Bless them all.

If this book is the product of a lifetime, it is also the product of the past two years, during which the Johns Hopkins School of Advanced International Studies (SAIS) provided generous space and support, including a very efficient and responsive library staff. My thanks in particular to Deans Vali Nasr and Jessica Einhorn and Associate Deans John Harrington and Amir Pasic as well as the Conflict Management program so ably led by Terry Hopmann and so kindly staffed by Isabelle Talpain-Long. It has been a privilege and an honor to get to know Professor Emeritus Bill Zartman. I have also enjoyed the devoted support on this book of unpaid assistants Emily Ohlsson, Adam Lewis, Geoffrey Curfman, Eric Shu, Gregor Nazarian, Ilona Gerbakher, Allison Stuewe, Ala' Alrababa'h, and Idon Natanzon, the last seven provided by the Middle East Institute. The students in my spring-term seminar on postwar reconstruction have been a constant source of stimulation. Eliot Cohen, Ruth Wedgwood, Eric Edelman, Tom Mahnken, Mary Habeck, Walter Andersen, Leila Austin, Christine Kunkel, and Stephen Wong—who sat nearby in the Rome Building of SAIS—have each contributed to my work, though they may be surprised to hear it. So too have my colleagues at the Center for Transatlantic Relations, especially Mike Haltzel and Dan Hamilton as well as their support staff Katrien Maes and Miriam Cunningham.

The Middle East looms large in this book, as it poses some of the greatest challenges of our time. Wendy Chamberlin has been kind to take me into the Middle East Institute fold as a scholar, where I have enormously enjoyed the company and support of Kate Seelye, Elisha Meyer, Deborah Jones, David Mack, Marvin Weinbaum, Sulaiman Wasty, and many other scholars and staff there. There are few more deserving, and less-well-endowed, institutions in Washington.

There are colleagues all over Washington—indeed all over the world—to whom I owe thanks for enriching my understanding of both war and peace, including Mort Abramowitz, Swanee Hunt, David Petraeus, Paul Forman, Veton Surroi, Jakup Finci, Ala Talabani, Cesare Merlini, Rob Satloff, Mike Eisenstadt, Michael Knights, Joost Hiltermann, Myron Brilliant, Heather Hurlburt, Antonella Caruso, Ejup Ganic, Hassan Cengic, Kresimir Zubak, Haris Silajdzic, Ed Joseph, Kresimir Zubak, Peter Ackerman, Jim Dobbins, Steve York, Srdja Popovic (the younger), Carl Gershman, Ken Wollack, Lorne Craner, Gerald Knaus, Zivko Budimir, Michael Steiner, Ylber Hysa, Sonja Biserko, Natasa Kandic, Enver Hoxhaj, Rend al Rahim, Randa Slim, Hal Saunders, Michael Abramowitz, Marina Ottaway, Bill Nash, John Menzies, Paul Stares, Michael Calingaert, Barbara Slavin, Carol Giacomo, Michael Gordon, Max Fisher, and James Ledbetter. I hope those whom I have somehow skipped will forgive me. My agent and friend of more than fifty years, Victoria Skurnick, has provided frank criticism, invaluable guidance, and unstinting encouragement. My cousin, Columbia Professor Emeritus Richard Brilliant, did me the favor of giving the manuscript a non-international affairs but critical reading, as did my treasured friend Marilyn Holmes. My Saturday running buddies of many years, Dan Edelman and Alan Schwartz, cheered me on, heard me out, sent me things to read, and lifted my spirits in difficult moments.

This book is dedicated to the three people who both inspired and encouraged it: my museum curator wife, Jacquelyn, and our two sons, architect Jared and journalist Adam, all three of whom suffered my absences, neglect, and distraction during years of service to the too often lost cause of peace with frequent good humor and only occasional (and merited) resentment. I swell with pride at the thought of the three of them. Each is helping to heal the world in ways different, but no less meaningful, than mine.

Washington DC

1. We Are All Diplomats

"Diplomats are born, not made," an Italian ambassador once told me. I begged to differ. "I was born in Brooklyn," I said, knowing all too well how déclassé that would sound to an aristocratic Italian. It was definitely a conversation-stopper. It served my purposes at the time that he should be ill at ease.

Making an adversary uncomfortable can be part of diplomacy, but I have gradually come to realize that I was wrong on the merits. We are all born diplomats: we spend our childhoods persuading, negotiating, cajoling, reframing, modeling, convincing—and continue to do it for the rest of our lives. As esoteric as the designation "diplomat" is to most Americans, diplomats do what most Americans do—try to get the best deal. Diplomats do it professionally for the country, not for themselves, though many are pretty good at that too.

Hard Questions

The country is today in serious trouble. It has more problems at home and abroad than it can handle. "America is broke," as House Speaker John Boehner likes to say, and needs to cut back on public expenditure, even as the retirement of baby boomers burdens the Social Security and Medicare rolls.[1] But it still has broad responsibilities and impact in a world that never runs out of problems. Europe relies on the United States as a critical partner in its defense, much of Asia looks to Washington to counterbalance growing Chinese power, Iran and North Korea have nuclear programs that could threaten America or its allies, rebellions against autocrats the United States once supported are roiling the Arab world, and peace between Israel and the Palestinians seems out of reach in the absence of American initiative. America has been the indispensable nation.[2] It is important that it remain that way.[3]

But with our troops out of Iraq and ending their combat role in Afghanistan by the end of 2014, we need to ask ourselves how we can defend vital American interests more cheaply and more effectively. We are a weary policeman.[4] What should our priorities be? Who and what threatens American national security? What instruments do we need to meet these threats and ensure the safety and security of our citizens and communities? How much are we going to have to spend? How can we spend it most wisely? These are questions people in Washington face every day. Those who do may find my treatment of them lightweight and even superficial.

This book is not intended for them. I wrote it for ordinary citizens who are puzzled about America's role in the world but do not face these questions professionally on a daily basis. The commonplace questions are good ones. Does America have to go to war as often as we do? Can't we do more to help people who are starving or being killed by their own governments? Is foreign aid a good idea? Why does everyone expect America to come to the rescue? Are we trying to do too much? Why don't others do more? Do we have the resources to be the world's policeman? If we don't stop mass atrocities, who will?

You are right to ask how and why your tax money is spent, and whether it is spent efficiently and effectively to protect and benefit Americans and improve the global context in which we live and work. Solid answers are often hard to come by, as the complexities are mind-boggling. But there is good evidence that civilian instruments of foreign policy, often wielded in combination with military instruments, produce tangible and cost-effective results. You may agree or disagree, but I hope you will find the discussion enlightening, the presentation entertaining, and the contents informative. Our country faces difficult decisions that can only be made well if its citizens demand clear and cogent explanations.

The World We Live In
These questions arise in a world where America, still the most powerful nation on earth economically and militarily, faces both challenges

and opportunities. People have been writing about the end of the American era for more than a decade.[5] Presidential candidates continue to promise that this will still be an American century, even if the mood of the country is more downbeat.[6] Both can be correct. American economic dominance is slowly eroding as other countries grow. The European Union (EU) of twenty-eight countries already has a larger economy than the American one. That did not deprive the United States of its unique position in the world—few even noticed when it happened. This is not only because the EU remains weak in military terms and divided politically, but also because of the alliance relationship that the United States maintains with a Europe that shares many of our concerns and objectives.

The so-called BRICs—Brazil, Russia, India, and China—have more ambiguous relations with the United States.[7] Their economies have been growing fast. China's will pass that of the United States within a few years, even though its per capita GDP will remain well behind and it will face increasing internal challenges.[8] Frictions between China and its neighbors, some allied with the United States, are becoming more heated and more frequent.[9] The long-term challenge is a diplomatic as well as a military one: to induce China to spend resources and evolve its economic and political system in ways we prefer as well as to manage a necessarily difficult relationship in a way that provides opportunities for both Washington and Beijing to benefit.[10] "We will be rivals and partners for the foreseeable future," writes Nina Hachigian. "In this way the U.S.-China relationship is more like an acrimonious marriage than it is like a one-off boxing match. We are interdependent, mutually mistrustful, and stuck with one another for good."[11] The Chinese challenge is one reason the United States will have to maintain a level of military expenditure, readiness, and force-projection capacity that otherwise would not make sense.[12] India, because of its economic liberalization and rivalry with China, has moved closer to the United States, as has Brazil, even as it tries to cultivate its own sphere of influence in Latin America. Russia remains an adversary on many issues, despite Hillary Clinton's "reset," but it is not the menacing enemy it once was.[13]

The BRICs are not alone among emerging powers. An economically vitalized Turkey, a secular country led by an Islamist government, is playing an increasing role in the Middle East.[14] Though hobbled by internal difficulties, South Africa is a key player in its region, as is South Korea not only in northeast Asia but also globally.[15] Nigeria, already a major oil producer, has enormous potential if it can resolve its violent internal conflicts. What we are seeing is widespread, relatively strong economic growth in large countries in Latin America, Africa, and Asia that manage to maintain domestic stability and stay out of serious internal conflict or conflict with their neighbors.[16] This is both a competitive challenge and an enormous opportunity for the United States—these "emerging markets" will want and need equipment, technology, and investment from the more developed world.

The rapid economic growth of other powers is also a political and military fact of enormous importance that raises difficult questions for America. It opens up the possibility of both competition and collaboration, which are not mutually exclusive. So far the benefits of collaboration have prevailed, even if the news of competition often grabs the lead, as it did two decades ago when the media portrayed Japan's rise as a challenge to the United States. The facts since then have proved that thesis wrong.[17] Still, American dominance of the world order is inevitably declining. Worry about the consequences is growing.[18] Will we be able to shape the rules of international relations as we have in the past?[19] Will our interests be closely enough aligned with those of other powers to allow for collaboration and burden-sharing?

"Burden-sharing" is a term diplomats use when several countries agree to divide responsibility. This they do either in an ad hoc coalition or a preexisting international organization like the UN, NATO, or the Arab League. After the 2010 earthquake in Haiti, for example, the U.S. Navy played a vital role in cooperation with a mainly Brazilian UN peacekeeping contingent that was already stationed on the island. The Brazilians stayed, enabling the Americans to withdraw to take care of other priorities. Turkey has played an important role during the Arab uprisings in the Middle East, especially in Libya and Syria, even while contesting American views on Israel and the Palestinians. The Arab League, an organization previously regarded as the quintessential talk shop, encouraged the NATO intervention in Libya and deployed human-rights observers to Syria in a well-intentioned but unsuccessful effort. These are important examples of burden-sharing with countries that only partly share American views but are doing things consistent with U.S. interests.

The United Nations, much criticized in some political circles in the United States, is one of the principal means by which America gets other people to carry burdens. I started my diplomatic career there, and I know how cumbersome and inefficient it is. Like it or not, many other countries regard the UN, in particular the Security Council, as author-itative. They recognize its legitimacy and respond—at times slowly and inadequately—to its calls for money, troops, trade embargoes, finan-cial sanctions, and other resources needed to manage world affairs. We might be expected to welcome this—after all, we have a veto in the Security Council, which cannot take action if the Americans object. Anyone who has seen the Security Council at work understands that the Americans also carry enormous weight there in getting interna-tional action. Congress complains about the bills, but UN troops cost much less than American ones. We pay only 27.1 percent of the cost, not 100 percent, as we do when the U.S. military deploys.[20]

Burden-sharing and collaboration with both traditional allies and emerging powers have become much easier in a world where transpor-tation and communication are much less expensive. Formal means of diplomatic communication—the *demarche, aide memoire, note verbale*—are still used, but more for the sake of form than content.[21] It is old news by now that diplomacy is done by e-mail, text messaging, phone calls, Skype, Twitter, and high-level visits. While restricted communication channels (hotlines, closed websites) are sometimes used, the distinguish-ing characteristic of the newer communication channels is that they are available not only to diplomats but to everyone else as well. This includes ordinary citizens as well as politicians, businesses, and nongovernmen-tal organizations (NGOs), not to mention terrorists, insurgents, drug traffickers, warlords, and the rest. Diplomats no longer have exclusive communication channels. International collaboration extends far beyond official channels to businesses, NGOs, and ordinary citizens.[22]

This is important because of a shift in the sources of power.[23] "Hard" power has traditionally been thought of mainly in terms of coercion, often but not necessarily of a military character. Sanctions that block the bank accounts of people committing war crimes, for example, are a form of civilian coercion. In today's world, persuasion and attraction, now termed "soft" power, are increasingly important. Soft power may also take a military form—the U.S. Navy does lots of port visits around the world every year, hoping that people will find it attractive to visit its ships and sometimes even get medical treatment or a Christmas present from the sailors. But soft power is also often exerted in civilian guise: President Obama's Cairo speech on America's relations with the Muslim world in 2009, for example, was an effort to persuade, attract, and set an agenda.[24] The combination of hard and soft power has been termed "smart" power, obviously reflecting the preferences of those who chose the term.

Experience Informs Perspective

That is my preference too. Experience suggests that combining civilian and military power, hard power and soft, is the most effective means of getting our way in the world. This book unabashedly aims for the "smart" power part of the spectrum. While I will be illustrating the limits of American military power and arguing for greater emphasis on what the State Department has termed "civilian power," it is really the combination of the two that is important for the future. It would be a mistake to think that civilians can be fully effective without military power behind them. But it would also be a mistake to think that military power acting alone is sufficient. The United States is uniquely well equipped with military power. But it lacks vital civilian counterparts needed today to meet our national security requirements.[25] These include relatively few military challenges, or even conventional diplomatic ones. We are in a new era and need new tools.

Apart from this introduction and the concluding chapter, which discusses institutional requirements for solving the problems identified here, there will not be much here of my ten years of experience in Rome as an American diplomat. Nor will you find much from my years in

Brasilia, or my work at the UN prior to the U.S. Foreign Service. Those were experiences of conventional diplomacy, years in which I worked in a secretariat preparing papers or in an embassy carrying messages to and from foreign governments, reporting on what I observed or was told and trying to convince others to back the American perspective on the issues of the day. Much of that work was done during the Cold War, when "containing" the Soviet Union and preventing it from undermining our allies and friends was the order of the day. It was an era when war was a constant threat but only occasionally a reality for Americans. In Korea the United States stopped Communist expansion; in Vietnam it failed. Nuclear holocaust was something we imagined and spent our lives trying to avoid, not something we experienced.

Traditional diplomatic tools remain important today. Dialogue and negotiation are vital in a world where new powers are rising and adjustments need to be made in the international balance, the division of labor, and the rules governing international behavior. But I will deal relatively little with the "talk" part of diplomacy in this volume, which is focused on less traditional challenges. My colleague William Zartman, the dean of negotiation studies in the United States, has published with Fen Osler Hampson a highly readable account of how negotiations can and do serve American national interests.[26] My own slim volume, edited with David Smock, of case studies on facilitating dialogue in conflict zones treats less formal efforts involving both government officials and civil society in postwar environments.[27] For international perspectives on many of the challenges discussed here, it is hard to do better than the writings of Kofi Annan and Lakhdar Brahimi.[28] I won't try to cover the ground explored in those writings in this book.

The Cold War ended suddenly in 1989, while I was economic minister at the U.S. Embassy in Rome. The Berlin Wall was only a few hundred miles to the north. Figuratively, it had extended even to Rome, where the embassy had focused for decades on keeping the Italian Communist Party out of government.[29] Suddenly, what had seemed paramount became irrelevant. Old certainties evaporated. New possibilities opened up. Serious risks arose. The Italian Communist Party soon changed its name and quickly completed its evolution to a normal "Democratic Party of the Left." Within a few years, it would be in power. Across the Adriatic, Yugoslavia flew apart into its component republics, bringing war to Europe for the first time in more than forty-five years. Ethnicity, once suppressed, trumped political borders. Unfrozen, the world changed incredibly fast with reunification of Germany and collapse of the Soviet Union.

I had become the deputy chief of mission in Rome—the ambassador's deputy and alter ego—in 1990 and plunged into support for U.S. forces as they deployed to Iraq. The defense attaché rushed into my office one day with a great sheaf of cables. "What's the problem?" "We need to get permission for all these aircraft to land," he said. That's pretty routine, so I wondered out loud why he was troubling me with something his office normally handled. "You don't understand," he exclaimed. "They've already taken off and the first planes are halfway across the Atlantic." We raced to the prime minister's office and convinced him to approve their transit. Five hundred thousand American soldiers and marines passed through Fiumicino airport before and after the first Gulf War without serious incident. The ambassador met one planeload on their way home with ice cream cones. None of us had imagined that such a thing was possible: American forces fighting a war in the Middle East backed by NATO and even Arab allies.

The succeeding years held many more surprises. I found myself arguing for international intervention in Bosnia at the UN General Assembly in New York, then unexpectedly on the ground in Sarajevo while the war was still going on. An American army major at the embassy showed me where I could run through the streets of the old city where snipers could not target me. Last summer, on a first trip back to the city in ten years, it was hard for me to believe that I could run safely across what had been the "confrontation line" between rebel Serb and loyalist forces during the war. Later I found myself in Belgrade meeting the students who would organize the street demonstrations that forced Slobodan Milosevic to step down, and in Kosovo talking with Kosovo Liberation Army fighters about their objectives in the struggle against Serb forces. I would visit Baghdad a dozen times to facilitate dialogue among Shias, Sunnis, and Kurds as well as Kabul in support of colleagues trying to build the rule of law there.

The enterprise I was involved with was no longer the conventional diplomacy of the Cold War era. That had not disappeared—there were still people in embassies all over the world carrying messages to foreign ministries and reporting the results. But increasingly many of us were engaged in something different: post–Cold War efforts to build free societies and states that would treat their own people well, preventing threats to American national security. Instead of dealing with well-established states, which is what diplomacy traditionally does, we were dealing with "ungoverned" spaces, partly built states, or weak, failed, and failing states. The vocabulary was varied and fluid. We were to stabilize, to reconstruct, to build institutions, to make peace. Unable to come up with the right words, some said we were conducting "complex operations."

This was uncharted territory. There were obvious gaps in our capabilities, and more subtle ones that we discovered only gradually. My colleagues and I at the United States Institute of Peace, where I moved in 1998 from the State Department, first focused on "filling the gaps." We published a series of papers trying to identify discrete problems that needed fixing in America's efforts to deal with conflict-affected states.[30] Later one of my bosses challenged us to take a more comprehensive approach and, following the military model, lay out a set of "end states" and a strategy for achieving them.[31] This "civilian doctrine" ("doctrine" is what the military calls "guiding principles") is still very much in use, not only in the U.S. government but also in NGOs, the UN, and other governments as well.

But proud as I am of these achievements, I have grown increasingly concerned about two things: our capacity to do things the way they should be done, and the focus inside government on what the government can do. We prefer a world in which states govern for the benefit of their people and behave peacefully toward each other. It is more than likely that our world will change in coming decades in ways that increase the call on our capacity to help them do this. New states—formed either from the breakup of existing ones or their fusion into new combinations—are becoming more the rule than the exception.[32] Our resources no longer permit the kinds of state-building efforts that we undertook, with some success, in Bosnia and Kosovo. Iraq and Afghanistan were far bigger and more complex challenges that arose in a period of tightening budgets. We tried to build states there while fighting was still ongoing. That took an enormous toll on American finances, not to mention the thousands killed and wounded. Neither is likely to come out as the stable democracy we would have liked. We cannot afford to end up trying to fix Iran, Pakistan, or even Syria in anything like the same way.

Just as important: a lot of the personnel and experience required simply do not exist within the U.S. government. It is common today for government officials to talk a blue streak about "whole of government" solutions, the "comprehensive approach," and "civilian-military cooperation" in "complex contingencies." But the problems we face today require skills that go far beyond what you will find in even good bureaucracies. We face a need to heal broken societies, not only repair states. I know how difficult and expensive this is. I would not want to be misunderstood as advocating that we do it except when U.S. interests are at stake. When they are, we need the capacity to respond with appropriate people and programs that are well planned and well executed, as well as suited to the local conditions.

Why Do We Need to Do It?

Many of my colleagues who worry about international affairs react to this situation by throwing up their hands in despair and declaring that we should never do these things. We have drones with which to kill anyone on earth we can find. We have a navy that can scare any other navy on earth back to port. No army on earth will care to meet ours on a conventional field of battle for at least several decades. Why not just leave other countries to their own devices? More often than not, they will find an equilibrium we can live with. Why should Americans worry about what happens in the Middle East, Pakistan, or Iran?

The answer is that what happens in these far-off places can affect us—our safety, our economy, our welfare. Terrorists who target Americans come from these places. You may kill them with drones, but in doing so you also make the ungoverned territory from which they come more likely to breed replacements. Much of the oil, gas, and minerals required to operate our economy comes from such unstable areas. When commodities are traded in a world market, turmoil anywhere affects prices everywhere. If you ask, as some politicians do, "Why should the federal government restrict my freedom on what type of light [bulb] I use?" the answer is clear: because it affects how much oil we use.[33] Even if we imported no oil at all, our economy would be vulnerable to world price spikes. Moreover, oil-producing countries now provide investment that sustains our banks, companies, and retirement plans. Globalization means that what happens over there affects us. There is nowhere to run, nowhere to hide.

I find that most Americans appreciate this but are mystified what to do about it. Sure, Iran's getting nuclear weapons will not be nice, and it could be catastrophic, but what precisely can you do about it? The most obvious answer is to bomb their nuclear program, but it does not take a nuclear scientist to understand that they will respond by redoubling their efforts. So we'll have to repeat the bombing, possibly at shortening intervals, with consequences that are impossible to predict.[34] Pakistan is also fraught: it supports Taliban insurgents in Afghanistan who attack Americans, even while we are financing the Pakistani army. Do we cut off aid to Pakistan, reducing our influence, or do we continue to provide aid while striking with drones in ungoverned parts of Pakistan's border with Afghanistan?

Are we condemned to perpetual war? Certainly there are some who think so and want to prepare accordingly. They want no further cuts in our defense budget.[35] They want to maintain eleven carrier strike groups and possibly add a few more.[36] They want to keep the eighty thousand American troops stationed abroad permanently. They want to modernize our nuclear weapons and maintain them at the ready, even if our main onetime nuclear adversary has disappeared.

I am as proud of today's U.S. military as any American. I have worked closely with U.S. troops in Bosnia, Kosovo, and Iraq. They are dedicated, energetic, and imaginative. I dread the day—nowhere in sight, fortunately—that the United States is not the world's strongest military power. We cannot be the world's policeman, but we do need to be its fireman, ready to move quickly to put out fires that may otherwise spread and burn down our American home or prevent it from getting the oil and gas it needs. But there must be better ways of dealing with the problems we face than spending a million dollars per year on every soldier deployed to a combat zone.[37]

There are often better ways, but they are not cost-free or easy to organize. We will require civilian capacities that we lack today and a willingness to anticipate problems that far exceeds our current practice. We will require Americans from "ordinary" walks of life—policemen, engineers, judges, city managers, politicians—to be ready to go abroad on short notice to dangerous places. We will require training and organization that today are lacking. We will need civilians willing to take risks, institutions to support them, and funding to make them effective. We will need citizens who understand these needs and are willing to fund the requirements to meet them.

We do not have these things today. What we have instead are institutions established for other purposes onto which we have grafted these responsibilities. The State Department was established in the late eighteenth century when America still hoped to avoid any but commercial engagement with the rest of the world. The U.S. Agency for International Development (USAID) was designed for the Cold War, when an enemy superpower threatened the United States with nuclear war. They have sometimes resisted adaptation and sometimes embraced it.

But they will never be what our current circumstances require and allow. Their legacy is too great, their habits too ingrained, their personnel too stuck in outmoded ways of doing things. First-rate leadership in recent years—by Colin Powell, Condoleezza Rice, and Hillary Clinton—has pushed the State Department and USAID in the right direction but has failed to transform them to meet today's needs. This book will end with a proposal to abolish both of them and grow, from new seeds, a foreign office committed to protecting American national security and equipped with the civilian instruments needed for that purpose.

Outline of This Book

I do not jump to that conclusion. I start in chapter 2 by taking a hard look at America's wars: How have they affected the country's evolution and its role in the world? To a degree most Americans do not recognize, the nation's wars have been fundamental to our history and have shaped our national government and its international responsibilities. The Iraq and Afghanistan wars, which have loomed large over the past decade, will do likewise. Only this time it will be our limits, not our capabilities, that are most clearly in focus.

Seeing the limits, we need to assess carefully our current and future national security requirements and how we can best achieve them. Many of the threats we face are not military, and using the military to confront them is neither effective nor economical. Chapter 3 will show that we are seeing diminishing returns from military investments in a period of extreme budgetary stringency.

Our relatively inexpensive civilian instruments are still too weak to pick up the burden, even when they are more appropriate to the tasks at hand. They need to reallocate their resources and acquire appropriate staff before they can begin to contribute on the scale required. Their needs are discussed in chapter 4. People are the heart of the matter, as discussed in chapter 5.

Civilians are less costly than troops, but still we cannot afford to continue to use them principally in postwar situations, which are frighteningly difficult, complex, and dangerous. We need foreign policy instruments that can anticipate requirements and act to prevent threats to American national security rather than cleaning up after war or state collapse. Prevention works, as discussed in chapter 6, but it will require civilian capabilities that do not today exist, or exist in unwieldy and ineffective forms, as discussed in chapter 7.

America cannot confront all the problems it faces on its own. Getting the energy the country needs to fuel its economy at reasonable prices will continue to require extensive international collaboration, as discussed in chapter 8. But this is not the only area in which partnership with others will be important. We can and should share burdens with selected others, as outlined in chapter 9.

The State Department and USAID as they exist today cannot meet future requirements (chapter 10). State is too committed to its legacy. Hollowed out, USAID has lost its way. Our two premier civilian institutions lack the flexibility and agility we now require. New requirements call for at least one new institution built over a three-year transition period: a foreign office that combines State and USAID. They also call for a greatly strengthened nongovernmental effort, using in part governmental resources. The funding required should come from within current allotments to the existing institutions. The result will be fewer, not more, official Americans stationed abroad, but more interconnectedness between Americans in many different walks of life and their counterparts in the rest of the world. Diplomacy in today's world is too important and too multifaceted to be reserved to diplomats.

Yes, my view is that we are all diplomats, or can be if we choose to engage internationally through the many means available today. Some will do it by signing up for tours as civilians working with the U.S. government or with NGOs helping to rebuild Afghanistan, but others will do it by joining the burgeoning "citizen diplomacy" movement that connects donors in the United States with microfinance organizations in developing countries or American city managers with mayors in "sister" cities abroad. We are far from reaching the limits of communication and interconnectedness that technology now provides, not to mention how much more will be provided in the future. Are you a teacher, a lawyer, a judge, a policeman, an architect, an entrepreneur, a politician? An engineer, a software geek, a web master, a labor organizer, a city manager, a business executive, a banker? Uncle Sam may not know it, but he needs you.

2. War Shapes the Nation and Its Role in the World

Americans think of their country as peaceful. The events of September 11, 2001, were shocking not only because of the loss of almost three thousand people in the country's largest city but also because no deadly enemy attack on America had occurred in the lifetimes of most of its citizens. The "homeland," as we have now become used to calling it, had been safe from large-scale foreign attack since Pearl Harbor. Home-grown terrorists, not foreign *jihadis*, committed the worst previous attack inside the United States—in Oklahoma City in 1995. The vast majority of Americans have had little directly to fear from war, international conflict, and terrorism throughout their lives.

Even during the past decade, when the country was fighting wars in both Iraq and Afghanistan, far more Americans were dying in automobile accidents on the nation's roads (almost 33,000 per year) and in criminal attacks (under 14,000 in 2009) than in international conflict. On Memorial Day 2012, fewer than 6,600 Americans had been killed in Iraq and Afghanistan over the previous decade, about 10 percent of the total number killed or still missing in Vietnam. The numbers dying in international terrorist acts—other than those directed against U.S. troops—are small. You have a better chance of being killed by a meteorite than by an international terrorist.[1] International terrorism killed seventeen private American citizens in 2011—fifteen in Afghanistan, one in Israel, one in Iraq, and none in the United States.[2]

International conflict is far from most Americans' minds. Asked in a CBS news poll in March 2011 what is the most important issue facing the United States, only 3 percent of Americans responded that it was the ongoing wars in Iraq and Afghanistan, well behind the economy/

jobs (51 percent), the budget deficit/national debt (7 percent), and health care (5 percent). While international terrorism brought death and destruction to the United States in 2001, a decade later few ordinary citizens had reason to worry about it, even if international terrorism remained a top priority for those who worry about national security. Few remember how and why the United States went to Iraq, and once Osama bin Laden, mastermind of the 9/11 attacks, was killed, many thought there was little reason to remain in Afghanistan. Nor has homegrown terrorism with international connections grown as anticipated.[3]

The U.S. military, which deployed 3.3 million troops to Iraq and Afghanistan from September 11, 2001, to December 2009 (a total of 2 million individuals), is among the most respected institutions in American society.[4] Amid a general decline in confidence in public institutions, confidence in the military and military leaders soared in the 1990s and again in the following decade, with particularly strong confidence among the young.[5] But they are less and less inclined to serve in the armed forces, which have become a kind of praetorian fraternity/sorority, drawn disproportionately from the South, that Americans respect but many do not want to join.[6] In June 2012, 77 percent of Americans had "quite a lot" or a "great deal" of confidence in the U.S. military, but the numbers of people serving, and their proportion of the general population, was at a post–World War II low.[7] War today is fought by a small, professional military in countries that few Americans have visited or care much about, unless they harbor terrorists who might threaten the United States.

The invisibility of our current wars should not mislead us. War is never unimportant. It affects not only those who serve and their families but the nation as a whole. The consequences of war are notoriously unpredictable. Today's wars in Iraq and Afghanistan, as well as the even less visible war on terror, will shape the American role in the world for decades to come. To paraphrase Professor Charles Tilly, America has made war throughout its history, and those wars have made America what it is today.[8] The United States has been at war for roughly 62 of the 237 years since its founding, not counting numerous expeditions against Native Americans and pirates, which were frequent in the eighteenth and nineteenth centuries. While America saw many years of relative peace in the twentieth century, it also participated in two world wars and two major conflicts with Communist states in Korea and Vietnam.

The relative peace we know as the Cold War gave way in 1989 to more than two decades of American military interventions abroad, starting in Somalia, Panama, Bosnia, and Kosovo and culminating in Afghanistan, Iraq, and Libya. While the overall level of deadly conflict in the world has declined, American troops have been in conflict zones virtually every year since the fall of the Berlin Wall.[9] No matter how distant, no matter how invisible, these wars will shape not only what we think we are capable of but what the rest of the world thinks of us for decades more into the future.

This is not new. From even before the Revolution, war has improved the country's technological capabilities, expanded its geographic reach, and enhanced its international role. The United States we know today is a global power equipped to project military force wherever and whenever its interests or values require. That America did not burst suddenly on the world scene. Rachel Maddow views today's military as unmoored from the founders' intentions, but what she views as "drift" is in fact the main current of American history.[10]

What do we know about the effect of war on the United States in the past? What can we expect in the future?

America's Wars and Their Consequences

The British defeat of the French in what our textbooks call the French and Indian Wars (1754–63) vastly expanded British (and Spanish) territory in North America—including present-day Canada and the United States—beyond the thirteen colonies, whose populations at the time still hugged the East Coast and the Saint Lawrence River. The war extended the claimed boundaries of the colonies to the Mississippi River, more than doubling their nominal land area and opening up the then "west" between the Appalachians and the Mississippi to exploration.

It was while fighting for the British in these wars that George Washington gained his first military experience and his reputation not only in the colonies but also in Europe. His officers said of him, "In you we place the most implicit confidence."[11] He would not be the last American military officer to receive this kind of accolade. Thirty-one of forty-four American presidents have had military experience, which has generally been regarded as a political asset.

America's independence from Great Britain was established in law by the Revolution (1776–83) and by what Americans call the War of 1812. At the very start of the Revolution, the Continental Congress appealed to French Canadians to join them in resisting the British Crown, inviting them to be "conquered into liberty," a phrase that foreshadows America's later commitments to war in the democratic cause.[12] The America that emerged from the Revolution was determined to avoid what Thomas Jefferson later termed "entangling alliances," generalizing on what Washington had said in his presidential farewell address: "it must be unwise in us to implicate ourselves, by artificial ties, in the ordinary vicissitudes of [Europe's] politics, or the ordinary combinations and collisions of her friendships or enmities."[13] Washington hoped that America's distance from Europe would allow it to pursue commercial relations while avoiding political connections.

This proved impossible. American commercial and territorial ambitions collided with British restrictions on trade and forced recruitment of American sailors, as well as British presence in Canada and the Northwest Territory. The War of 1812 (which ended in 1815) is little remembered in the United States except for the British burning of Washington DC and the composition of the Francis Scott Key's "Star-Spangled Banner," a poem celebrating the unsuccessful British attack on Fort McHenry in Baltimore. Canadians remember it for the burning of Toronto, then called York.

But the immediate impact of war, dreadful and inspirational as it may be, often proves less consequential than its longer-term consequences. The country developed its own technological capacities, especially in cotton manufacturing, to replace British goods. The United States came to recognize that it would continue to need military capabilities, including a substantial navy and professional army officers, provided by West Point. The formerly contentious issue of America's border with Canada was at least partly settled, and the conquest and expropriation of Indian lands in what we now term the Midwest was begun. Whether the War of 1812 was a victory or a defeat is still debated, but America was a much more self-confident and secure nation after the Treaty of Ghent that brought it to an end than it had been before.

From 1815 on, the United States undertook to explore, define, secure, and expand its territory while continuing to try to prevent Europe from maintaining its positions in the Western Hemisphere. In a lightning military expedition, Andrew Jackson seized Florida from the Spanish in 1818. Concern with British and Spanish use of Native Americans against the United States led to repeated military expeditions against them. The Monroe Doctrine (1823), which at the time was intended to lend support to Spanish colonies seeking independence, formalized America's intention to extend its reach and exclude Europeans from South America.

It was during the administration of Jackson (1829–37) that the American presidency took on a more modern form. Jackson was the first president elected by something resembling universal white male suffrage, and his popularity as a former military leader and advocate for ordinary citizens enabled him to assert far wider executive authority than previous presidents claimed. Among other things, he used this authority both to preserve the union from efforts by slave states to nullify federal law and also to force removal of Native Americans to west of the Mississippi River, he claimed for their own benefit. But removal also secured the white population of what were then twenty-four states from Native American efforts to enforce their rights under the treaties the United States had signed with them. The modern executive presidency had its origins in Indian removal and the resulting extension of control over territory.[14]

The Mexican War of 1846–48 and the Gadsden Purchase of 1853 settled America's southern border and opened up the West beyond the Mississippi to mass migration and railroads, which were vital to America's completion as a continental power. The Mexican War also marked the first successful projection of American ground forces into a foreign country, with the brief occupation of Mexico City and the cession to the United States (by the Treaty of Guadalupe Hidalgo) of California, Arizona, New Mexico, and parts of Colorado and Nevada.

The Civil War, though catastrophic in human and material losses, shaped an economically more powerful America. The North's war-stimulated manufacturing made the United States an industrial power for the first time, even as the first transcontinental railroad, started during the war but completed a few years later, consolidated its territorial ambitions. Saddled with debt and constrained by Congress, the federal government, which acquired an enhanced role during the war, did not retain it past the end of Reconstruction in the early 1870s. But gradually in the 1880s and 1890s, new technologies, the growing economy (as well as tax revenues), and increasingly national markets forced strengthening of the federal government, in particular the executive branch and the military.[15]

It was not until war with Spain in 1898 and the subsequent colonization of the Philippines, Guam, and Puerto Rico, as well as the less formal domination of Cuba, that the United States began to become a world power capable of serious international intervention. Its well-equipped navy was the essential instrument.[16]

While America hesitated to intervene in World War I, its eventual deployment on the side of the Allies was decisive. The American Expeditionary Force under General Pershing tipped the scales in favor of Britain and France, but President Wilson's efforts to extend America's diplomatic reach in the postwar period through the League of Nations failed. In World War II the United States likewise tilted the balance in favor of the Allies in Europe with both manpower and air supremacy, even as it used atomic bombs to end the Japanese challenge to American domination of the Pacific. In the postwar period, President Truman succeeded where Wilson had failed: the United Nations established a multilateral diplomatic framework that served U.S. purposes and provided a global governance structure for the superpower competition known as the Cold War. More than sixty-eight years later, the permanent seats and vetoes in the Security Council (which belong to the United States, the United Kingdom, France, Russia, and China) still reflect the global power configuration at the end of World War II, rather than the reality of the twenty-first century, to America's great advantage in world affairs.

America fought Communist powers twice during the Cold War: first in Korea, to a draw that allowed the South to remain non-Communist; then in Vietnam, where a similar effort at division of the country into Communist North and non-Communist South failed, as the United States faced a determined guerrilla struggle that viewed itself as fighting for independence and unity of the country. The Vietnam failure made the United States hesitant about international intervention and unwilling to fight guerrilla wars. Responding to domestic resistance to the war, especially strong among draftees, it was decided to professionalize the armed forces.

In the aftermath of the Vietnam War, Secretary of Defense Weinberger and later Colin Powell enunciated policies seeking to limit the conditions under which the United States would intervene militarily abroad. American military doctrine virtually erased guerrilla warfare and counterinsurgency operations.[17] Weinberger and Powell believed the American military should only be committed if vital U.S. interests (or those of its allies) were at stake, and then only wholeheartedly, with clear and achievable political and military objectives, and with a reasonable assurance of support from the American people and Congress. Force was explicitly a last resort. Powell also required a clear exit strategy once fighting ended.[18]

Restraint was short-lived. American victory in the Cold War dramatically changed the global balance of power. After 1989 the Soviet Union no longer presented an existential threat (one that threatens the very existence of the United States, the worst kind of threat to vital national interests). First Panama (Operation Just Cause, 1989) and then the expulsion of Iraq from Kuwait (Gulf War, 1990–91) demonstrated that successful intervention was feasible in the post–Cold War world, provided overwhelming force was used and goals were clear and limited. In Panama the United States acted unilaterally to remove President Manuel Noriega, who had falsified election results and was running drug-trafficking operations. In Kuwait the UN Security Council provided a clear mandate to use "all necessary means" to liberate Kuwait from Iraqi occupation. The United States assembled a broad international coalition for the purpose.

Both wars were fought in accordance with Powell's view that overwhelming force should be brought to bear and a clear exit strategy maintained. The Gulf War was fought with a combination of more traditional armor and massive manpower as well as with high-tech laser-guided bombs and other advanced weaponry, followed by a quick retreat once Kuwait was liberated and Iraq sued for peace, without taking Baghdad.[19]

The United States departed from the Powell doctrine in Somalia, where President George H. W. Bush embarked on Operation Restore Hope in December 1992. No vital American interest was at stake. The intervention was in response to a humanitarian crisis, one made severe by the collapse of the Somali state and the start of a civil war among tribal chieftains. The newly inaugurated Clinton administration passed off the operation to the UN as quickly as possible, and the UN withdrew in 1995. Efforts to rebuild the Somali state failed. Almost twenty years later the situation there remained unstable, with the Somali state weak and extremist Islamic forces waging *jihad*. The United States remained involved through proxy forces from Ethiopia, Kenya, and other African countries as well as through the use of drones. Only gradually has stability returned to some areas.

American intervention in Bosnia (1995) and Kosovo (1999) showed that "economy of force" operations conducted from the air, in support of local forces on the ground, are possible even without a strong international mandate, though the eventual outcomes were negotiated settlements that fell short of complete success. U.S. troops and civilians remained in both Bosnia and Kosovo postwar to maintain the peace and assist with reconstruction. Nominal exit strategies were in the end ignored.

The overall pattern is clear: American wars—even many of those that did not go well—have extended America's physical reach and technological capacity to project military power, enhanced its postwar role, and increased its weight in world affairs. The process has occasionally slowed but never stopped. By the end of the twentieth century the United States reigned as the sole superpower, with global military, political, diplomatic, and economic reach. The rest of the world together spent not much more than the United States alone on defense.

On the eve of 9/11, it seemed that nothing could stand in the way. The world was unipolar, America was the indispensable nation, the country whose leadership was essential to getting things done in the post–Cold War world.[20] It is not uncommon to find Americans who regard this role as divinely granted, and no American politician feels free to treat the United States as just one among the world's many equal sovereign states. America, they all agree, is exceptional.

Andrew Bacevich encapsulates this twenty-first-century American apotheosis in what he terms a credo and a trinity: "An abiding conviction that the minimum essentials of international peace and order require the United States to maintain a *global military presence*, to configure its forces for *global power projection*, and to counter existing or anticipated threats by relying on a policy of *global interventionism*."[21] These are what he terms the "Washington rules," which enable Washington to rule on a global scale but also condemn it to "permanent war," at least since the fall of the Berlin Wall.

Americans may not be much aware of international conflict, but their government is spending a good deal of their hard-earned money on ensuring that it has all the means necessary to pursue America's interests and values through military means, which have become the primary instrument of American foreign policy.

Iraq and Afghanistan Have Also Extended America's Reach

Have the wars in Iraq and Afghanistan followed this pattern? Have they extended America's physical reach, expanded its technological capacity to project power, shaped its postwar role, and increased its weight in world affairs? Is America still the indispensable nation?

At first glance, the answer is yes to all these questions. Certainly these recent wars have demonstrated astounding physical reach and technological capacity to project power. Baghdad and Kabul, respectively, stand more than six thousand and close to seven thousand miles from Washington DC. The army that invaded Iraq in 2003 was less than half the size of the one that fought the Iraqi army in 1991 but had equal if not greater "effect," as the military terms the impact on opposing forces. In Afghanistan the Americans fought the Taliban mainly from the air. One of my neighbors is a commercial pilot who did weekend bombing runs for the air force reserve, flying from the United States to his targets and getting back to his Jet Blue job by midweek. The Northern Alliance, Afghan fighters who had opposed the Taliban for the better part of a decade, carried the brunt of the action on the ground, with American advice and technology. This power projection by proxy was as successful in Afghanistan as it had been two years earlier in Kosovo, a far smaller and less forbidding place.

The main technological development associated with the Iraq and Afghanistan wars is the removal of human beings from some of the most perilous wartime situations.[22] This is apparent not only in the spectacular use of drones controlled by pilots in the United States against targets in Afghanistan and Pakistan but also in more mundane tasks like dealing with improvised explosive devices so common in Iraq. War robots, electronic countermeasures, and dogs, controlled by human beings at a distance from the greatest danger, significantly lower risks to U.S. troops, as well as the political threshold for their deployment. A president no longer has to deploy half a million Americans to go to war half a world away.

War can now become virtually invisible to the people in whose name it is conducted, like the drone wars against Islamic extremists in Somalia and Yemen as well as Afghanistan and Pakistan. Americans may read about them in the morning paper, and even see their clever technology and devastating impact on TV, but the pilots return home after a day at the joystick without any apparent risk to life or limb, except from traffic on the interstate. There is no need for a Pearl Harbor to justify going to war; all that is needed are a few declarations of intent to harm Americans, or maybe an electronic intercept revealing a plot to send explosive packages to the United States onboard commercial aircraft. Asserting the right to self-defense, we respond with Predator drones. The military calls this "counterterrorism," a term it contrasts with "counterinsurgency." The latter requires a much greater on-the-ground effort to clear insurgents from an area, establish control over it, and rebuild civilian life.

But there is good reason to expect that in both Iraq and Afghanistan America will be a major player for a long time into the future. Some are disappointed that the United States did not leave troops and bases behind in Iraq, but Americans are likely to be training the Iraqi air force and navy for the better part of the next decade, if not longer.[23] American equipment will keep Iraq tied to the United States for decades more.[24] The United States has agreed to support Afghanistan until 2024, ten years after it completes its transfer of primary war-fighting responsibility to Afghan security forces.[25] Negotiations for basing rights are ongoing. Afghanistan and Iraq, like other countries once invaded by the United States, are likely to remain tied to the United States for a long time to come.

As for America's weight in world affairs, these two twenty-first-century wars have underlined the importance of the United States as a military power, one that can kill anyone it can find half a world away. Almost three hundred drone strikes in Pakistan from 2004 to 2012 killed between 1,785 and 2,771 people, 83 percent of whom were described as "militants" in press accounts.[26] American ability to find people is also formidable, especially when it relies on its full array of intelligence methods, though identifying them can be extraordinarily difficult. Even the night he was killed, the Americans were not sure the person they had found was Osama bin Laden, who remained hidden only by avoiding the use of telephones and the Internet and by taking extraordinary measures to make his couriers hard to follow. He also likely had a support network reaching into Pakistan's military and intelligence services. Few terrorists can expect to hide as long as bin Laden if the Americans are serious about looking for them. America's military capabilities are far-reaching and precise, though not 100 percent accurate.

America remains indispensable. It appeared by the end of the first decade of this century to some that the difficulties of the Iraq and Afghanistan wars would render American intervention abroad much less likely in the future. Defense Secretary Gates said, "In my opinion, any future defense secretary who advises the president to again send a big American land army into Asia or into the Middle East or Africa should 'have his head examined.'"[27] Gates a few weeks later opposed American intervention in Libya, and he was successful in limiting its participation to enforcement of a UN Security Council–mandated no-fly zone and protection of civilians. But no one was under any illusions: U.S. participation was vital if Muammar Qaddafi was to be stopped when he threatened to murder his opponents en masse in Benghazi. Neither Europeans nor Arabs were prepared to act without the United States, or as expeditiously as the United States, but a reasonably broad "coalition of the willing" was assembled to act with the United States initially taking the lead, which it yielded over the next several weeks to NATO.[28]

America's leadership role is apparent elsewhere as well. American hesitation to use force against Bashar al-Assad's homicidal campaign against his Syrian opponents has made Turkey, Saudi Arabia, and Qatar hesitate to go further than arming the rebellion there. Even after years of obvious failure in the Israel/Palestine "peace process," a presidential speech on the Middle East in May 2011 drew a worldwide audience unequaled by any other world leader.[29] Arabs and Jews who agree on little else were disappointed in the speech, which offered nothing new but aroused a wide-ranging debate, including a pilgrimage to the U.S. Congress by Israel's prime minister to rally supporters against the administration. The Gaza war of November 2012 found a cease-fire agreement only with support from Egypt and the still indispensable United States.

Each of the regimes infected with rebellion during the Arab Spring has looked to the United States for support, as have protesters in the streets of Tunisia, Egypt, Syria, Yemen, Libya, and Bahrain. The Chinese focus on denying the United States access along its shores and targeting weak points like its satellites but do not contest superior American conventional firepower.[30] While Moscow is nostalgic for its superpower status, Washington's unique role is clear even there, as Russia tries to counter NATO's spread into former Soviet and Warsaw Pact countries. The Europeans complain about it, the Arabs bemoan it, the

Russians resist it, the Third World resents it, and the Chinese may in the future seek to counter it, but no one can afford to ignore the United States or its capacity for military action anywhere in the world. America is still indispensable and still exceptional, even if it is no longer as dominant as it was when the world lay in ruins in 1945.[31]

What Has Changed?

Still, something has changed. The decade between 9/11 and the death of Osama bin Laden on May 2, 2011, saw a profound shift in America's position in the world as well as the means available to sustain it.

The United States in 2000 was in champion condition. The 1990s dot-com boom was still in full swing. The federal government was looking forward to a future of budget surpluses. It would face big money decisions about whether to use them to improve the long-term viability of Medicare and Social Security, to pay off the national debt, or to give them back to the taxpayers, but these were a rich country's choices. Likewise, in foreign policy America faced sometimes difficult decisions, but nowhere on earth were its vital national interests—the term wonks use to describe something that threatens enough Americans to bother doing something about—at risk. Emblematic of the era was Tiger Woods, who that spring won all four major golf titles. The United States seemed likewise to have won all the world power competitions.

That would change quickly. Contested election results, a recession, and the 9/11 attacks followed over the course of 2001. The election of George W. Bush with a majority of electoral votes but without a majority of popular votes was not decided until January, after a bitter Supreme Court fight that left the country divided. Recession officially began in March, followed by sharp falls in the stock market. The September attacks made the economic situation markedly worse than it otherwise would have been. By 2003, America was running large budget deficits while it fought wars in two or three Muslim countries (depending on whether you count Pakistan in addition to Afghanistan and Iraq) and pursued a worldwide "war on terror" that required military, intelligence, and law enforcement operations in dozens of other countries. While the economy was recovering, fueled by a real estate bubble that then burst in 2008, the federal deficit was growing dramatically. The United States became dependent for financing the deficit on China's dollars, earned in a spectacular expansion of exports, much of them to the United States.[32]

Today, American politicians often debate who was to blame for the reversal of American fortunes, in particular for the sharp deterioration in the federal budget. It shifted from an expectation in 2001 of a $2.3 trillion surplus in 2011 to an actual deficit of $10.4 trillion. It would be difficult to tell from the political debates, but who was to blame can be settled with hard facts and figures. Not surprisingly, the answer is the politicians themselves. Congress put the country on the path to growing deficits by passing spending increases that account for 41 percent of the total and tax cuts that account for another 27 percent (the rest is mainly due to economic and technical factors beyond Congress' control). A relatively small percentage of the total "fiscal shift" is attributable directly to the wars in Iraq and Afghanistan: 10 percent. Easily 85 percent of the total was due to domestic policies and programs.[33]

That said, the military expenditures are still huge. American politicians proudly vaunt the country's extraordinary intelligence and military capabilities. They have been less anxious to talk about what they cost.

The "intelligence community," which includes dozens of agencies of the U.S. government, has also grown rapidly since 9/11. The *Washington Post* summarized its investigation of "Top Secret America" this way: "The top-secret world the government created in response to the terrorist attacks of Sept. 11, 2001, has become so large, so unwieldy and so secretive that no one knows how much money it costs, how many people it employs, how many programs exist within it or exactly how many agencies do the same work."[34] Or, for those interested in the numbers rather than the qualitative judgments:

An estimated 854,000 people, nearly 1.5 times as many people as live in Washington, D.C., hold top-secret security clearances.

In Washington and the surrounding area, 33 building complexes for top-secret intelligence work are under construction or have been built since

September 2001. Together they occupy the equivalent of almost three Pentagons or 22 U.S. Capitol buildings—about 17 million square feet of space.

Many security and intelligence agencies do the same work, creating redundancy and waste. For example, 51 federal organizations and military commands, operating in 15 U.S. cities, track the flow of money to and from terrorist networks.

Analysts who make sense of documents and conversations obtained by foreign and domestic spying share their judgment by publishing 50,000 intelligence reports each year—a volume so large that many are routinely ignored.[35]

The publicly disclosed budget for the civilian intelligence establishment was over $53 billion in fiscal year 2010.[36] Adding the military intelligence portion brings the total to at least $80 billion, which might be enough to support the extensive intelligence establishment the *Washington Post* describes.

Military expenditures have also grown rapidly. Not counting money for the wars in Iraq and Afghanistan, the Defense Department budget increased 81 percent between 2000 and 2010. This was well above the general rate of inflation and does not include $1.2 trillion in Afghanistan and Iraq war spending. The Bush administration from the first wanted to increase defense expenditure, but the increase that actually occurred was far greater than the administration had planned before 9/11, even without counting war expenditures. After 9/11, political opposition to defense expenditures virtually disappeared. As one critic put it, "September 11 provided the political cover for massive increases in military spending to furnish the martial muscle for a grand strategy premised on unprecedented military superiority."[37]

Attacked, the United States responded with a massive military and intelligence buildup aimed at forestalling, deterring, and responding to its enemies. There is nothing inherently surprising or wrong with that. In a democracy, any administration that failed to do the utmost to protect the nation after 9/11 would have found itself in deep political trouble.

The buildup nevertheless created problems. It came without a tax increase at a time when the United States was shifting rapidly from a budget surplus to a budget deficit. We borrowed all the money required. We never asked ourselves whether we were prepared to pay for the defense buildup with higher taxes, or if we preferred paying for prescription drugs for senior citizens or for invading Iraq. Entitlements, especially health expenditures, were a much bigger contributor to the overall deficit than increased defense expenditures, which hit, however, at a particularly bad moment.

The absolute numbers are staggering: $3 trillion for the war in Iraq even without macroeconomic costs (the broad impact on the economy), and $7 trillion for the Iraq and Afghanistan wars together, counting not only government expenditures but also macroeconomic and interest costs, since both wars were financed with borrowed money.[38] When the financial crisis hit in 2008, these extraordinary expenditures contributed to a weakened economy. As financial markets froze, bank stocks collapsed, and housing prices went into free fall, the U.S. government found itself locked into defense expenditures higher in real terms than at any other time in its history except for World War II. The "opportunity costs"—the other things we might have done with this money—were dramatic: whether you would have preferred tax cuts, reduced borrowing, or government programs, the enlarged defense budget was an important reason for not getting what you wanted during the financial crisis of 2008.

While timing of the post-9/11 defense buildup has damaged the American economy, the added value of what we are buying is declining. This law of diminishing returns is a natural phenomenon in many situations, familiar to anyone who looks seriously at the added performance associated with expensive cars, for example: it costs a lot more to buy demonstrably improved performance in luxury cars than it does in economy vehicles. Secretary Gates recognized this during his last year in office as he canceled new weapons systems, including a second engine for the Joint Strike Fighter, the air force's F-22 fighter, the army's Future Combat System, and the navy's next-generation destroyer. Each of these had its defenders, but on close examination none offered improvements over current weapons worth anything like their additional costs.

Gates also projected significant cuts in personnel, starting in 2015, in the planned aftermath of the war in Afghanistan.

The law of diminishing returns is evident in other ways too. Our military means are far less effective against adversaries who do not share our cultural predilections.[39] Tribal societies in particular have proven challenging for both our conventional and unconventional forces. The multiplier effect of defense expenditures on the economy—how much economic activity they generate—is less than one.[40] Spending money on defense is like shouting loudly in a soundproof room: you get back less sound than you put out. You also get less improvement in performance for every dollar spent. We have created an extraordinary, high-performance military machine, but it is just as extraordinarily costly. Military spending has reached well over $200,000 per person per year for active-duty personnel, an expenditure that has made the U.S. military highly effective and terrifically expensive. The evidence does not support those who claim that military hegemony yields economic benefits under present global conditions.[41]

There was a time when this was little to worry about. So long as the United States was running surpluses it could afford such expenditures, especially when it was under attack. No longer. While the legal authority is well established, it is far less clear that the United States can afford to continue its war on terror.[42] Predator drones are a relatively low-cost option, but they come with a price tag of upwards of $4 million each. How many more terrorists can we afford to kill at that price? How many more "surge" operations can we conduct when deployed troops cost $1 million each? Drones and other robotic weapons make it easier to go to war because fewer lives are put at risk. But the costs of war are not declining. It is getting easier and cheaper to get in, but if you are going to need thousands of troops on the ground it is harder and more expensive to get out.

Ten years ago, America was looking at budget surpluses and relatively few national security challenges. Its military establishment had developed through more than two hundred years to become the nation's main instrument of foreign policy. Forward-deployed around the world since World War II, it proved an effective deterrent during the Cold

War and a useful intervenor thereafter. In the absence of immediate threats to the United States, or even enemies meriting deterrence, American marines fed Somalis who were starving and imposed law and order in Haiti. America's air assets rescued Bosnians subjected to mass murder and Albanian Kosovars forced out of their homes by a Serbian government that claimed to be their own. These were not vital American interests and are properly described as wars of choice, not necessity.[43]

Things have changed a great deal. Today we face not only an urgent requirement to cut the budget deficit but also multiple national security challenges. Even as we have extracted ourselves from a war of choice in Iraq, we continue to fight a war most Americans once regarded as necessary in Afghanistan, manage a global effort against violent extremists as well as nuclear proliferation, and meet longer-term competition from China and other emerging powers. How are we going to respond to these and many other challenges with limited resources?

3. National Security Is More Than a Military Mission

National security is necessarily the federal government's top priority. It is the one function of government on which virtually all Americans can agree: if the feds do nothing else, they should at least ensure that Americans are safe from a foreign enemy ready to perpetrate mass violence, kill individual Americans, disrupt our economy, or destroy our democratic system. Our military exists for this purpose, whether it is deployed on air, land, sea, or most recently in cyberspace. This is the president's number one concern and a primary preoccupation among both Democrats and Republicans in Congress. This is what "We the people" sought in 1787: to "insure domestic Tranquility, provide for the common defence."[1]

What does this mean in the twenty-first century? Not, certainly, what it meant when European powers occupied Canada, or when settlers wanted the federal government to remove Native Americans from Florida. Not what it meant the day after Japan attacked Pearl Harbor, or when the Soviet Union was building its nuclear arsenal to ensure it could annihilate American cities. There is no absolute measure of security, which changes with the threats we face and the capacity we have to meet them. If we are going to spend our reduced means wisely, we need to consider national security goals in our current context and prospects for the next ten to twenty years.

I once asked a Brazilian diplomat what he had learned at the Rio Branco Institute, which trains Brasilia's foreign service officers. He looked at me with surprise and said, as if the answer were obvious, "We learn to think about what Brazil should be like and its role in the world in fifty years." Asked the same question about America's Foreign Service Institute, many of our diplomats respond, "How to empty an inbox quickly and distribute the work needed to others." I emptied a lot of in-boxes in the U.S. Foreign Service. Not once in more than two decades did anyone ask me to think about the country's role in the world decades hence. Out of practice, I'm going to rely not on my own views but rather those of the current president of the United States and his immediate predecessor.

President George W. Bush defined American national security interests broadly but with admirable clarity in 2002, shortly after the 9/11 attacks:

Champion aspirations for human dignity

Strengthen alliances to defeat global terrorism and work to prevent attacks against us and our friends

Work with others to defuse regional conflicts

Prevent our enemies from threatening us, our allies, and our friends, with weapons of mass destruction

Ignite a new era of global economic growth through free markets and free trade

Expand the circle of development by opening societies and building the infrastructure of democracy

Develop agendas for cooperative action with other main centers of global power

Transform America's national security institutions to meet the challenges and opportunities of the twenty-first century[2]

President Bush was clearly focused on countering terrorism, but not to the exclusion of other interests. This is a far-reaching agenda, one that emphasizes defeating terrorism but also includes preventing attacks and creating a world that is safe for democracy, in the Wilsonian tradition.

Eight years later, President Barack Obama defined American interests with less focus on terrorism and more succinctly but in remarkably similar, broad strokes:

Security: The security of the United States, its citizens, and U.S. allies and partners.

Prosperity: A strong, innovative and growing U.S. economy in an open international economic system that promotes opportunity and prosperity.

Values: Respect for universal values at home and around the world.

International Order: An international order advanced by U.S. leadership that promotes peace, security, and opportunity through stronger cooperation to meet global challenges.[3]

Obama skipped the sweeping statement about human dignity but included "universal values" no less explicitly.

Despite much talk of a growing partisan divide and many differences in the ways in which they have behaved, the main difference between our two most recent presidents, one a Republican and the other a Democrat, in defining national security interests is Obama's emphasis on "international order," whereas Bush preferred the less formal reference to allies and working with others. This difference is important—underlying it is a difference of view on the usefulness of international institutions, which Obama exploits and Bush at times shunned. But the difference concerns means more than ends. The objectives are essentially the same, as they were also in 2006.[4]

President Bush also advocated at times "preemptive action."[5] In 2002 he stated that "we will not hesitate to act alone, if necessary, to exercise our right of self defense by acting preemptively against such terrorists, to prevent them from doing harm against our people and our country."[6] President Obama has dropped talking about preemption, which the failure to find nuclear and other weapons of mass destruction in Iraq discredited. But many drone strikes—much more common under Obama than they were during Bush's presidency—are likely conceived as preemptive, taken against terrorists who are allegedly plotting, or might in the future plot, attacks on the United States or its citizens. We are back to publicly treating major military action as a late resort, if not always the *last* resort. There is more continuity between Presidents Obama and Bush than there is difference.

Whichever version you prefer, it is clear that these national security interests cannot be achieved exclusively by military means.[7] The Obama administration was more explicit and comprehensive in its assertion that strengthening national security will require a "whole of government" approach, but that notion underlay the Bush administration's national security strategy as well. Extremism will not yield to drones alone. Democracy and human rights require more than bayonets. Terrorism is a law enforcement as well as a military concern. Cooperative efforts with friends and allies will include diplomatic as well as military efforts. Economic prosperity depends on opening markets and investment opportunities as well as ensuring security. Support for human dignity and respect for universal values—which proved so important in inspiring the Arab Spring of 2011—require civilian institutions at least as much as military ones.

What of more immediate national security requirements? Are they mainly military, or do they have civilian dimensions as well? The Council on Foreign Relations publishes an annual survey of preventive priorities: issues that might threaten U.S. national interests, directly or indirectly. For 2012, more or less half the issues involved military threats, but half did not. The non-exclusively-military "Tier 1" priorities included the following:

> A highly disruptive cyberattack on U.S. critical infrastructure (e.g., telecommunications, electrical power, gas and oil, water supply, banking and finance, transportation, and emergency services)
>
> A significant increase in drug-trafficking violence in Mexico that spills over into the United States
>
> Severe internal instability in Pakistan, triggered by a civil-military crisis or terror attacks
>
> Political instability in Saudi Arabia that endangers global oil supplies
>
> Intensification of the European sovereign debt crisis that leads to the collapse of the euro, triggering a double-dip U.S. recession and further limiting budgetary resources

Military means might contribute to resolving some of these problems, just as civilian means might be useful in preventing or resolving some of the military contingencies in "Tier 1":

A major military incident with China involving U.S. or allied forces

An Iranian nuclear crisis (e.g., surprise advances in nuclear weapons/delivery capability, Israeli response)

A U.S.-Pakistan military confrontation, triggered by a terror attack or U.S. counterterror operations[8]

Even immediate national security threats do not sort out nicely into civilian and military categories. Few are purely "military" or purely "civilian." The bipartisan Project for a United and Strong America likewise found a mix of civilian and military challenges in setting out a national security strategy in early 2013.[9] A survey of potential political transitions between 1989 and 2010 demonstrates that U.S. response "favors nonintervention over intervention and civilian response over military response," even though the capacity for civilian response is limited."[10]

Soldiers, sailors, and airmen have no monopoly on national security in the twenty-first century, if ever they did. Diplomats think they are the nation's first line of defense. They certainly provide a good deal of its intelligence, as Wikileaks demonstrated.[11] They also keep relations with many countries on the friendly basis that prevents problems from arising unnecessarily. Aid workers think the assistance they provide reduces poverty, provides livelihoods, and decreases the temptations of violent extremism. Nonprofit organizations believe their efforts are vital to improving governance, establishing free media, and getting grievances heard and acted upon. Businesspeople are convinced that only a fool would go to war if there is prosperity. Certainly civilian efforts correlate with peace when focused on good governance, resource equity, equal rights, good relations with neighbors, free flow of information, education, and corruption, even if causality is hard to demonstrate.[12]

How Do We Decide What Gets Funded?

We have no objective way of comparing these disparate contributions to national security. They are incommensurable. Human dignity or free trade? Free trade or capturing terrorists? There is no common measure. Instead, the U.S. Congress makes judgments about what gets funded. Each year, Congress decides how much money will go to the

Department of Defense, the State Department, USAID, and other organizations that contribute to our national security goals. The president sends proposals to Congress, but he cannot easily transfer money from one agency to another, or even in many instances from one program to another within a given agency. The president proposes; the Congress disposes.

Even within the Congress, there is rigidity. It might seem simple to move money from one of these budgets to another. All dollar bills are green. That is not, however, true in Congress. Each subcommittee of the House and Senate Appropriations Committees on the Hill gets its own pot of money to "appropriate," or assign, to the government agencies it oversees. The Defense Department "belongs" to the defense subcommittee (except for military construction, which is handled by a separate subcommittee). The State Department and most foreign assistance providers belong to a different subcommittee, as does Homeland Security and other agencies like the Justice Department whose functions contribute to national security goals. All dollars are not green: it is as if the Defense Department can only spend red ones, State only yellow ones, USAID purple ones. Gordon Adams, a leading student of the defense budget, says, "Reforming the executive branch so it can do program and budget planning in a more integrated, interagency manner will be minimally effective if Congress remains stovepiped."[13]

National security is the top priority, but there is no national security budget of the United States, only the sum of bits and pieces of different national security functions spread among many government agencies.[14] Congressional oversight of national security policies and expenditures is also done on a piecemeal, agency-by-agency basis, though Defense, State, and USAID may sometimes testify together and their responses to congressional inquiries are coordinated. The White House does the coordination through the National Security Council, whose committees are also known, awkwardly, as "the interagency." But the system is stovepiped: the main direction in which money, decisions, and power flows is vertical, with each boss at every bureaucratic level trying to ensure that her money is spent to achieve her assigned mission.[15] Efforts to create an interagency cadre of "National Security Professionals" have petered out.[16]

The U.S. government behaves like a family that is used to living securely in a nice big house but parcels out responsibility for getting things done and paying the bills to different family members. One pays for water, another pays for cleaning, and another pays for heat, without the possibility of moving money from one account to another under normal circumstances. Most days this works well. But if one of these family members has more money than he needs, he tries to spend it on his particular responsibilities. If the money goes unspent, the amount provided next year may well be cut, so there is a premium on spending down to zero. If another family member runs short, she cannot readily get money transferred from someone else, even if it is not needed for the original purpose assigned. If suddenly there is a major project—a kitchen renovation, for example—coordination becomes exceedingly difficult, with each member of the family trying to ensure that his own commitments are minimized, or at least contained within the allocation provided, while scrambling for as large a percentage as possible of any new funding that becomes available. There is no consensus on how to fix this and related problems.[17]

Not only is the federal budget stovepiped, but different parts of it are tied to the districts of particular members of Congress, who promote the interests of those districts through their committee memberships. Defense expenditures are a particularly large prize. When an issue like modernization of nuclear weapons arises, the decision may depend as much on which members of Congress have companies or laboratories in their districts that will benefit as it does on whether more modern weapons are needed. This is true for many modern weapons systems. But it is far less true for the civilian agencies working on national security, which not only have less money to spend but also spend more of it overseas. USAID manages to use domestic U.S. companies and NGOs to do much of its work abroad, sometimes to the detriment of effectiveness, but that is much harder for the State Department, whose biggest expenses are associated with embassies in foreign countries.

We'll need to take a look at a few of these agency budgets to see what is happening on the national security front as the wars in Iraq and Afghanistan wind down.

The Defense Budget Is Big But Taking Some Hits

At $688 billion in fiscal year 2012 (October 1, 20011–September 30, 2012), the Defense Department's budget made up two-thirds of the federal government's budget other than "entitlements" (programs like Social Security and Medicare that are not subject to the normal budget discipline and represent most federal expenditure).[18] Defense expenditure overall is still a relatively small part of the U.S. economy (5 percent or less),[19] even counting the war expenditures. But no "discretionary" portion—the slice subject to congressional decisions, as opposed to "entitlements," which are driven by the numbers of eligible recipients—of the budget is larger.

It starts from a high level, but the defense budget is no longer immune from cuts. Before "sequestration" struck in 2013, proposals ranged from the radical to the modest.[20] The radical cut of $280 billion per year would require a dramatic downsizing of the U.S. military, withdrawal from virtually all its overseas bases, and dramatic cuts in hardware.[21] It is highly unlikely that anything approaching such cuts would pass the Congress.[22] The more modest effort proposed so far by the Obama administration would keep the growth in defense spending at the rate of inflation, requiring cuts from projected spending levels of $400 billion but over twelve years. The Republican proposal for 2012 cut defense less than 5 percent from the projected level, about the same amount as the president's proposals.

Defense Secretary Gates took a relatively easy $100 billion out of defense spending over the next four years by canceling lower-priority upgrades and eliminating unneeded personnel. He then proposed that additional cuts be based on a comprehensive review of national security priorities.[23] This is a reasonable proposition, but if the review is done only within the military context its results will be misleading and far from comprehensive. The last military review was done as recently as 2010 and set multiple and wide-ranging goals. As one critic put it: "Counterinsurgency (COIN), nation-building, counterterrorism operations, and stabilization and reconstruction are right up there with conventional deterrence, nuclear deterrence, forward presence, and humanitarian operations. They are all equal, and the stated intention is to reduce risks in all of them to as close to zero as possible."[24] The Defense Department wants to prepare for a formidable array of "full spectrum" goals requiring maintenance of America's overseas commitments and power projection capabilities. The "Quadrennial Defense Review" provides little real guidance as to what the military should prepare for.[25] The answer is "everything." Resistance to serious cuts at the Pentagon remains strong, though it appears that the need for fiscal discipline will force at least some cuts beyond what Gates decided.[26]

As the Pentagon acknowledges, it is unlikely that America's enemies will choose to meet its military forces on a battlefield, where American capabilities are unequaled.[27] Since the end of the Cold War, conventional military threats have been rare. The only ground force to contest the Americans directly during the past two decades was the Iraqi army, which suffered two quick defeats in American-led offensives. All other national security challenges have come in less conventional forms. Terrorism, insurgency, drug trafficking and other international crime, mass atrocities, nuclear and other proliferation of weapons of mass destruction, pandemics, and insecure energy sources have posed frequent threats to national security over the past twenty years. They arise more often from relatively weak (but not necessarily the weakest) states than from strong ones.[28] Military means are not always the right tool for dealing with these problems, or the most economical one.

But in today's America the military instrument is relatively well funded and ready to act. With more than 1.4 million people in uniform and another 1.1 million in the National Guard and Reserve forces, the U.S. military is ready to take on big or small responsibilities anywhere in the world on short notice. It is not only prepared for "kinetic" operations that kill and destroy but also for relief operations after an earthquake or tsunami that save lives and for "stabilization" operations to help install more effective governance in failed states.

The U.S. military is also extraordinarily expensive and not necessarily appropriate to all the national security challenges America faces. America has a proverbial hammer: when you have only a hammer, everything looks like a nail. But it is a lot easier to insert a screw with a screwdriver, modest though it may appear next to a hammer.

The Civilian Instruments of National Power Are Weak

What is the alternative? The United States, like other countries, has civilian instruments to project national power and influence as well as military ones. Americans are not always aware of these instruments. At a New York party years ago, a young lawyer—hearing that I was a diplomat serving abroad—asked me why it was that I had special parking privileges in the city's crowded streets. I explained that those privileges were for foreign diplomats serving in the United States, not for an American diplomat serving overseas (and certainly not while serving at home). "Really," she exclaimed. "Do we have diplomats overseas?"

Yes, we do. There are about twelve thousand Foreign Service members, at home and abroad, or one for every one hundred members of the active-duty armed forces.[29] In peacetime they may suffer more casualties from hostile action than the armed forces, since they are targets of assassins and terrorists. Their numbers presumably include a significant number of CIA officers, many of whom serve "under cover" in "stations" located within American embassies and some separately under non-official cover. There are another seventeen hundred Americans serving in USAID, and a scattering elsewhere in the U.S. government who contribute to foreign affairs.[30] The entire "international affairs" function of the U.S. government—including embassies, contributions to international organizations, foreign assistance, and the rest—amounts to about 10 percent of the Pentagon's budget.[31] What we have here is one very strong, well-exercised arm ready to defend U.S. national security anytime anywhere, and one rather weak arm struggling to hold up its end in meeting national security requirements.

The contrast is worse than the numbers suggest. "Diplomat" is a prestigious occupation and generally attracts some of America's "best and brightest" recruited through a highly competitive and open process. The secretary of state is in protocol terms the third-ranking official in the U.S. government, after the president and vice president, but the State Department is notoriously low in the bureaucratic pecking order in Washington. It is somehow fitting that it is located in, and known as, "Foggy Bottom." State is one of the smallest departments in terms of number of employees in the U.S. government, and its preoccupation with foreign affairs in a capital that only occasionally focuses on events abroad makes it seem elitist and irrelevant a good part of the time. If unfamiliarity has bred respect for the military, it has on the contrary bred disdain, bordering on contempt, for diplomacy. Cookie pushers in pinstripes is a wimpy image. Only the rare murder of an American ambassador in Benghazi, along with several of his supporting staff, attracts any positive attention to our diplomats abroad. Take a look at portrayals of American diplomats in movies like *Argo*. They are almost always weak, vacillating, mendacious, or worse.

The national security challenges we face today are precisely those that require more civilian capability, not less. If the war you are fighting is not with a foreign army but with insurgents, terrorists, or organized crime, civilian skills are vital. Soldiers and marines defeat few insurgencies. Law enforcement, economic development, and political settlements are far more effective.[32] Of the three stages of U.S. counterinsurgency strategy—clear, hold, and build—only the first is primarily a military responsibility. Holding and building require civilian capacity to impose law and order—something soldiers do reluctantly and not necessarily well.[33] Building requires government and economic development, which are not military strengths.

So it is not surprising that in recent years Defense Department officials have consistently supported increased funding for diplomacy and development. General David Petraeus testified on Afghanistan in March 2011: "I am concerned that levels of funding for our State Department and USAID partners will not sufficiently enable them to build on the hard-fought security achievements of our men and women in uniform. Inadequate resourcing of our civilian partners could, in fact, jeopardize accomplishment of the overall mission."[34] Secretary Gates called foreign affairs funding "a critical component of an integrated and effective national security program."[35] He also emphasized: "Where possible, what the military calls kinetic operations should be subordinated to measures aimed at promoting better governance, economic programs that spur development, and efforts to address the grievances among the discontented, from whom the terrorists recruit. It will take the patient accumulation of quiet successes over a long time to discredit and defeat extremist movements and their ideologies."[36] The U.S. military is acutely aware of its need for civilian partners. Bemoaning the limited capacities of the State Department and USAID, Gates said it bluntly: "The military and civilian elements of the United States' national security apparatus have responded unevenly and have grown increasingly out of balance."[37]

He had good reason to be concerned. Without adequate foreign affairs funding, the Pentagon ends up spending a good deal of its own money on business development efforts in Iraq and Afghanistan. Its Commander's Emergency Response Program is devoted mainly to civilian expenditures designed to win "hearts and minds." Pentagon money is fixing potholes, paying *imams* for Friday sermons, building schools, rehabilitating water supplies, and paying for agricultural advice.[38] Petraeus, who literally wrote the Pentagon's book on counterinsurgency warfare, thought that money is ammunition.[39] Whatever will win the loyalty of local communities is worth spending on when you are fighting a guerrilla war.[40] In a statement interpreted by the press as softening the military plea for civilian funding, U.S. Marine Corps general James Mattis put it more succinctly: "If you don't fund the State Department fully, then I need to buy more ammunition, ultimately."[41]

Congress has not shared the Pentagon's enthusiasm for the military's civilian partners. It has been particularly parsimonious with foreign assistance, which is less than 1 percent of the total federal budget and has been declining for twenty-five years. Many members of Congress think that cutting foreign aid will save *hundreds* of billions, but the total foreign aid budget—including those parts they would like to preserve, like assistance to Israel—totals *tens* of billions. At no point in the more than forty years since the UN General Assembly adopted 0.7 percent of GNP as the target for official development assistance has the United States met the recommendation.

This is not, however, what most Americans think. One poll shows half of Americans believe that foreign assistance represents 25 percent of the federal budget and that a more appropriate figure would be 10 percent, more than ten times the actual figure.[42] It is therefore not surprising that 72 percent of Americans would like to cut foreign assistance.[43] While many Americans are convinced the United States is overly generous in giving to the rest of the world, in fact it ranks among the lower donors relative to the size of its economy in providing *government* assistance abroad.

Generosity is not the issue. Private financial flows—investment, remittances by workers in the United States, and charitable donations—are larger than official government assistance, and have been since the early 1990s. These private financial flows are important: they feed and clothe a lot of poor people, improve the American image abroad, fund private investment, and create jobs. But they are not usually an instrument of foreign policy, except when the U.S. government decides that they should be cut off to put pressure on the country receiving them, as happens from time to time with countries like North Korea, Iran, or Cuba. Such sanctions are an important tool for diplomats.[44] But private money flows to most countries on most days freely and without government constraints, other than notification if the amount exceeds $10,000.

It should not be surprising that the civilian international affairs apparatus has difficulty increasing its budget—if I thought a quarter of my taxes were going to foreign aid, I would want to cut the amount too. In the budget battles of the summer of 2011, House Republicans proposed a 43 percent cut in the "150 account," which funds foreign affairs. This was the largest cut in a proposal that cut Defense Department funding by a mere 3.5 percent.[45] In the end, foreign affairs got cut 12 percent from fiscal year 2011, while Defense stayed flat.[46] But State got a big increase for "overseas contingencies," which is funding that is supposed to disappear within the next few years. It was mostly for Iraq, where State has taken over and Defense is largely out. The Republican House proposal for 2013 would have taken another 20 percent out of foreign affairs and restored a large chunk of defense spending.[47]

That, however, was not the end of the story. "Sequestration" intervened on March 1, 2013. This initially required a 13 percent cut in nonexempt discretionary defense spending and an 8.2 percent cut for civilian foreign affairs. That was done to make the cuts particularly unpalatable to Republicans, who, however, took the dare. These were across-the-board cuts not allowing transfers from one program to another.

So, ironically, the civilian side of national security, whose prospects had looked particularly bleak, came out relatively well in 2013, with a substantial cut but one smaller than the Pentagon's. It is unlikely though that this represents a real departure from the historical pattern: a strengthening military arm and a weakening civilian one.

Why Does This Matter?

This matters because the challenges to U.S. national security are shifting rapidly toward that weaker civilian arm, which will need to carry more weight in the future. Al-Qaeda's havens in Afghanistan and Pakistan, the insurgency in Iraq, North Korea's nuclear weapons program, and Mexico's traffickers in drugs and people cannot be solved exclusively with military means. The main national security challenge of our era is getting others to govern themselves and prosper well enough that they can (and will) prevent threats to the United States.

The idea that we need to be concerned about how others govern themselves is not a universally held view. One of my colleagues at Johns Hopkins University, Michael Mandelbaum, argues that "the enterprise of state-building, to which the post–Cold War interventions led, will disappear from the foreign policy of the United States . . . state-building has become a luxury the United States could no longer afford."[48] John Mearsheimer believes that the United States needs to give up on what he regards as imperial pretensions and return to a policy of "off-shore" balancing,[49] that is, playing one regional power off against another in ways that will enable the United States to avoid expensive commitments.[50] Others object to U.S. government efforts to intervene abroad because they suggest functions for the federal government that are unwelcome at home.[51] If the U.S. government is involved in improving educational systems in Mauritania, why should it not be involved in Chicago?

American presidents have often shared the skepticism about getting non-Americans to govern themselves better. While waxing eloquent about democracy, every American president since the fall of the Berlin Wall has tried to avoid getting too deeply involved in building up governing capacity in other countries. George H. W. Bush shunned getting involved in how Somalia governed itself—he wanted only to feed the hungry when he intervened there in 1989. Today Somalia is a chronic breeding ground for Islamic extremists, whom the United States tries to counter using drones and proxy military forces (not only Somali but also Ethiopian and Kenyan).

Bill Clinton wanted to send American troops to Bosnia for only a year but discovered that their withdrawal would collapse the Dayton peace agreements and create an Islamic state in central Bosnia that the Americans feared would become a platform for Iranian terrorism in Europe. They stayed for ten years to enable Bosnia to govern itself, a goal still not fully realized but passed off to Europeans. George W. Bush famously derided "nation-building" but launched the two biggest efforts the United States has undertaken, in Iraq and Afghanistan. Barack Obama has tried to avoid doing more than "killing al-Qaeda" in Afghanistan. He prefers to do nation-building at home.[52] But he has had to postpone the American withdrawal until 2014, fearing the Afghans can't handle the task, and is promising a substantial commitment after that date. He also quietly launched a major effort to help South Sudan govern itself after it declared independence in July 2011.[53]

The State Department, to its credit, has recognized the need for a stronger civilian arm to deal with national security issues. In the first Quadrennial Diplomacy and Development Review, Secretary Clinton called in 2010 for "leading with civilian power." This means, she said, "directing and coordinating the resources of all America's civilian agencies to prevent and resolve conflicts; help countries lift themselves out of poverty into prosperous, stable, and democratic states; and build global coalitions to address global problems."[54] None of this detracts from the importance of the U.S. military, which will remain a vital component of projecting American power abroad and protecting vital U.S. interests and values. But asking the armed forces to do the whole job means burdening them with political, economic and social issues they are not prepared to resolve. It also means using the most expensive instrument of national power where less expensive instruments might suffice.

Presidents try to duck it, professors regard it as a luxury, and libertarians rail against it, but there is no way of preventing many threats to

American security unless other countries can govern themselves in ways that prevent those threats from emerging.

Where Do the Answers Lie?

The questions are clear enough: How can the United States, the world's greatest military power but now and for the foreseeable future in difficult financial straits, best protect its interests in a world that presents us with many, often non-military challenges to our national security? How can we reduce dependence on oil from insecure sources and the associated civilian and military costs? How can we adjust our behavior and expectations to a world that no longer views us as bigger or better than the rest?

The answers do not lie in the direction that our history points. We are approaching the limits of military power. Drones are fine instruments with which to kill well-identified enemies, but they leave behind poorly governed spaces that will breed more.[55] The law of diminishing returns will guarantee that more investment does little to increase our military capabilities, which in any event are not appropriate to all our requirements.[56] We need a thorough reorientation, away from excessive reliance on a well-honed but expensive military instrument that has served us well for more than two centuries. The right direction is toward civilian instruments that remain unproven at best, failed at worst.

In the three chapters that follow we'll take a hard look at the civilian instruments of American foreign policy. We'll focus on those that seem most lacking. Chapter 4 will deal with what I prefer to call "state-building." What experience do we have in this much-maligned and sometimes expensive activity? How can it be made more effective, and cheaper? In chapter 5 we'll look at the merits of prevention strategies, because an ounce of prevention really is worth a pound of cure. In chapter 6 we'll look at vital areas of prevention in which the United States is surprisingly weak. These will include support for democracy (especially the kinds of mass movements that have brought us the promise of the Arab awakening in 2011–12), reform of security forces, and countering violent extremism.

4. Building States Requires Money, People, and Local Knowledge

Bosnia

I first heard war in Bosnia, November 1994. I say "heard" because the noise was much more apparent than the visual effects, as it often is in war zones. Mortars and machine guns make a racket that carries for miles, much farther than you are likely to see. As my colleague and I strolled down the ramp from our UN transport plane, we looked back to try to discern the holes in the tail—we'd been told that the plane had taken small-arms fire during the landing. The Swedish UN peacekeepers hustled us along with a warning that Serb forces were still firing. We did not hang around to find out whether it was true.

We collected our bags from a muddy hole that served as a luggage carousel. The airport terminal itself squatted, a dark empty ruin off to the side. Out front in the parking lot we found ourselves stranded—no pickup from the American Embassy, just a couple of French armored personnel carriers whose drivers explained that they were not going into town with the baguettes they had picked up from an incoming flight but out to Igman, the looming mountain that had served as a site of Sarajevo's Winter Olympics ten years earlier. A lone Italian *alpino*, a soldier from one of the north Italy regiments that wear feathers in their hats, came up to ask where the terminal was. He expressed no surprise when I responded in good Italian, though he had no reason at all to know that I spoke the language. We were already in the polyglot world of the international peacekeeping intervention.

The intervention in the Balkans had begun in 1992, when the UN deployed a small contingent of military observers. They would suffer through three and a half long years of war, first in Croatia between

Croats and Serbs; then in Bosnia between Bosniaks (the politically correct term for a group we in the United States usually call Bosnian Muslims), Croats, and Serbs who were loyal to Sarajevo against Serbs who were not; then between Bosniaks and Croats who wanted to secede from Bosnia; and finally between combined Bosniak and Croat forces and the Serb forces who wanted to secede from Bosnia. War can be extraordinarily messy and complicated, with shifting loyalties and slippery alliances that make even an egghead like mine spin dizzily.

I was a civilian, a diplomat, sent to Sarajevo by Dick Holbrooke to preserve the peace between Croats and Bosniaks, who had fought a war with each other in 1992 and 1993 in southern Bosnia even while they were fighting together against the Serbs in the center and north.[1] The Bosniak/Croat war ended in early 1993, when the Americans and the UN got them to sign up to a joint governing structure, the Bosnian Federation. The Federation would thereafter govern the territory held separately by the Bosnian Army and the Croat Defense Council. The Federation covered no more than a third of Bosnia during most of the remainder of the war and today controls 51 percent of the territory, as decided at the Dayton peace talks. Serb forces by 1993 had besieged Sarajevo, which was isolated from the main Federation territory except for the UN flights, a road over Mount Igman, and a tunnel under the airport.

I did not get elaborate instructions or any training for my role. Dick had said to me simply, "The Federation is the best thing we've done in Bosnia so far. It ended the fighting between Croats and Bosniaks. You've got to make it function, make it real." He also told me my efforts would be unclassified: no secrets. Off I went, not realizing that I had been asked to take on an enormous responsibility of a sort that would come to dominate American foreign policy challenges for the next two decades. I'd been asked to build a state.

What does that mean? Americans refer to the fifty states, but they rarely use the term "state" in the sense I mean it here. The "state" includes the fifty states, but it also includes the federal government as well as local governments. The state is the set of institutions through which we organize our political lives. In American terms, it is the bureaucracy at all levels, plus the top elected levels of the government and the institutions they run. Its distinguishing characteristic is its monopoly on the legitimate means of force, usually exercised by its police or military forces.[2] We "hail to the chief" because the president is "chief of state." He presides over the state because we have voted for him to do so, giving our consent to his exercising limited power for the common good according to the rules set out in the U.S. Constitution.

There are many debates in America that are essentially discussions of what roles the state should or should not play in our lives. The debate over health care is but one example, as is the debate over whether abortion should be permitted or assault weapons banned. But we all agree that the state should play some role in overcoming conflict in our society. We take our personal disputes into its courts, we expect the local school board to decide what our children can and cannot be taught in school, we follow a policeman's signals when he is directing traffic. Without a state, there would be no one to enforce speed limits or decide the rightful owner of a particular piece of property. The state is the means by which we organize and distribute political power in our society. In the twenty-first century, most of us in Western societies believe it requires for legitimacy the consent of the governed.

What happened in Bosnia, and what happens in many war-torn societies, is that the state collapsed as parts of the society withdrew their consent and tried to establish states other than the one that existed before the war. It had declared independence in 1992 after a referendum that was approved by 90 percent of those voting but boycotted by most Serbs. For all their complexity, the Bosnian wars boil down to this: Why should I live in your state, where I am a minority? Why shouldn't you live in my state, where you are a minority? Substantial parts of Bosnia's Serb and Croat populations did not want to live in a state where they would be a minority. They preferred to live in Serbia or in Croatia, where Bosniaks would be in the minority.

In order to make this happen, what the diplomats term "nationalist" (that is, ethnically loyal) Serbs and Croats withdrew their consent to governance by the Bosnian state, which was one of six "republics" of former Yugoslavia before the war. Their representatives refused to sit in parliament, their police left the force, and their soldiers began to fight not for Sarajevo but for Zagreb and for Belgrade. The fighting aimed to ethnically cleanse territory for a particular ethnic group. Not everyone did these things voluntarily—a good deal of force was threatened and used against those who might have preferred to continue to be governed by the Bosnian state. But enough people withdrew, and enough force was used against the Bosniak population, to leave Sarajevo in control of only about one-third of the territory in central and western Bosnia.

With support from Serbia, the Serbs established a state called Republika Srpska, which still sits on 49 percent of the territory of Bosnia. With support from Croatia, the Croats created Herzeg-Bosna, a state that claimed to govern Croat-majority territory in southern and western Bosnia, as well as Croat enclaves in central Bosnia. Republika Srpska and Herzeg-Bosna tried to remove as many Muslims as possible from their territory. Guns were aimed mainly at civilians, not other soldiers. By the end of the war, the fighting had displaced close to half the population and killed about one hundred thousand.

The state Holbrooke asked me to build combined the Croat "Herzeg-Bosna" and the majority Muslim "Republic of Bosnia and Herzegovina." The Federation needed a parliament, a prime minister, cantonal and municipal governments, a central bank, a finance ministry, a defense ministry, and an interior (internal security, or police) ministry. These are often among the vital pieces that have to be brought together in what is properly called "state-building." That is a term most Americans have never heard, but it is failures in building state institutions that create some of our greatest national security threats—think Somalia, where collapse of the state has created a breeding ground for Islamic extremism, as well as Iraq and Afghanistan, where insurgents have challenged the authority and legitimacy of states established in the aftermath of war, or even Mexico, where the state has been unable to defeat drug traffickers, who control some local governments. Failure to build viable and effective states that can deny haven to international terrorists in Somalia, Afghanistan, and Iraq is costing the United States well over $100 billion per year, tying down American troops and intelligence assets and forcing us to pass up opportunities elsewhere in the world.[3]

Why were we anxious to build the Federation in Bosnia, even while war still raged between the Federation and Serb forces backed by Belgrade? There are really two answers. The one we gave publicly was idealist: we wanted to end ethnic cleansing and preserve multi-ethnic democracy in Bosnia. The second was more realist and not cited in public: we wanted to prevent the emergence in central Bosnia of what we termed "a non-viable, rump Islamic Republic that would act as a platform for Iranian terrorism in Europe." This was a real threat: the Serbs were pushing Muslims into central Bosnia, and in response the Iranians were doing their best to arm and otherwise equip the Bosnian Republic Army, parts of which were increasingly Islamicized. The Federation, which combined Muslims and Croats into a single governing entity, was a way of strengthening resistance to the Serbs while blocking Iranian political ambitions, as the (Catholic) Croats despised Tehran even if they skimmed off a hefty percentage of the Iranian-supplied weapons that got shipped to the Bosnian Army in contravention of the UN arms embargo. The Americans turned a blind eye to the arms supplies.

Bosnia today is still a work in progress, more than fifteen years after the Dayton peace talks brought the fighting to an end but left Republika Srpska and the Federation in an unloving marriage. Fifteen years is a long time for most people, but not in the state-building business. Rarely does serious state-building take less than ten years, and it often takes longer. The marriage may be loveless, but it is not killing anyone either.[4] I hoped for better in Bosnia, but I feared worse, and still do.

Idealism and realism are not necessarily in contradiction. A good deal of what America does in this world has roots in both ideological camps. State-building in the post–Cold War era requires a healthy dose of both. Without a realism that focuses on American interests, we would have to do it everywhere. In fact, we pick and choose, investing taxpayer resources mainly where the investment is feasible and there is a U.S. national interest at stake. Without an idealism that focuses on American values and internationally accepted norms, we might be content to prop up dictators, as we did during the Cold War, when the struggle with the Soviet Union was our dominant concern. The current wave of protests in the Middle East is demonstrating that dictators are a temporary expedient who do not guarantee long-term stability. Across a wide spectrum of the international community—including non-democracies like China and Russia—there is a broad consensus in this early part of the twenty-first century in support of building states that are more or less democratic.[5]

Afghanistan and Iraq

The U.S. military was fabulously successful at making war in both Afghanistan and Iraq. In Afghanistan it was just five weeks from the start of the bombing in October 2001 to the fall of Kabul. Few American ground forces were used, as the Afghan "Northern Alliance" provided most of the soldiering. The Taliban state had collapsed throughout Afghanistan by the end of 2001.[6] In Iraq, an invasion force of fewer than two hundred thousand (counting U.S., U.K., Australian, and Polish forces)—less than half the number used in Desert Storm to liberate Kuwait twelve years earlier—took Baghdad within three weeks, collapsing the Saddam Hussein regime by mid-April 2003.[7] Initial casualties in both conflicts were minimal. An America that was once hesitant about intervening abroad—even about having a standing army—can now field military professionals equipped to invade medium-size countries half a world away and achieve decisive military victory against conventional forces within weeks.

But American military forces in both wars were ill-equipped, ill-trained, and ill-prepared to build a state in either Afghanistan or Iraq.

In Afghanistan, there was at least a plan. Negotiated under UN auspices at Bonn in December 2001, the Agreement on Provisional Arrangements in Afghanistan Pending the Re-Establishment of Permanent Government Institutions created an Afghan Interim Authority, as well as a Supreme Court and a Constitutional Commission.[8] These were the vital first steps in the state-building process, one that would carry Afghanistan several years into the future, with international backing. The U.S. military initially had relatively little to do with this process, in which U.S. diplomats played a strong role. The UN was supposed to lead the international state-building effort, under the experienced Algerian diplomat Lakhdar Brahimi. Intending to avoid the kind of heavy international interventions deployed in Bosnia and Kosovo, Brahimi wanted the UN to adopt a "light footprint," following the lead of the United States, which did not intend to get involved in state-building in Afghanistan.[9]

In Iraq, the Bush administration plan was to "decapitate" the Iraqi state by removing the top layer or two of officials, installing new officials, turning over authority to them quickly, and withdrawing within weeks. This plan evaporated when the Iraqis, encouraged in part by Saddam's "stay-behind" operation, looted the ministries and collapsed the state the Americans were planning to turn things over to.[10] Instead, the Americans found themselves without institutions to decapitate or on which to place new heads.[11] They were compelled—not just by circumstances but also by international law—to occupy Iraq and provide essential services, in accordance with the requirements of the Geneva Conventions.[12]

For this the Americans were thoroughly unprepared. Their prewar planning had emphasized the possibility of humanitarian crisis, so food and other supplies had been pre-positioned. They had also worried about environmental disaster if Saddam set fire to Iraq's oil wells, which he had done during Desert Storm. So the military forces had quickly seized the oil fields and prevented them from being torched. But there was no serious plan for how Iraq would be governed in the absence of its own institutions.

This was not an accident. President Bush had said during the election campaign that "I don't think our troops should be used for nation-building" and added skeptically, ". . . a nation-building corps for America?"[13] Why did the president refer to "nation-building" rather than the term I prefer, "state-building"? The answer is revealing. The building of a nation is rooted in the history, culture, and identity of the people who live in a particular territory. It cannot be done by outsiders. That is the point the president was trying to emphasize. State-building would not have been as readily understood by Americans, but it is also something that *can* be done with help from foreigners. Foreign assistance in constructing the institutions of a state has often been successful.[14] So "nation-building" served the president's point better than "state-building."

State-building should not, however, be understood merely as technical assistance. It has to be based on a political order that all the main components of a society accept: a political compact. Legitimacy with the citizens, or at least with societal elites, is antecedent to functionality, even if at later stages the effective delivery of state services can help to reinforce legitimacy. Facilitating a political process whereby society and elites negotiate the structure and functions of the state thus must precede capacity-building designed to empower the state to fulfill those functions.[15]

It should come as no surprise that the civilian agency preparing for the invasion of Iraq—the Office for Reconstruction and Humanitarian Assistance (ORHA)—intentionally left its third pillar, civil administration, out of its name. It was anathema to President Bush. When I asked how ORHA planned to maintain law and order in Iraq after winning military victory, the head of the unnamed civil administration pillar, Michael Mobbs, replied that the secretary of defense had decided on a "light footprint" for police. Pressed further, Mobbs said that meant a ninety-day assessment mission.

My colleagues and I left Mobbs's office shaking our heads. Ten years of experience—from Somalia through Haiti, Bosnia, and Kosovo—told anyone who was awake that maintaining security after the fall of Saddam would be a problem for the next day, not for three months later. If nothing else, the Americans should have anticipated revenge killings. The ethnic and sectarian divisions in Iraq—the country is thought to be almost 60 percent Shia Arab, 20 percent Sunni Arab, and perhaps 14 percent Kurdish—and Saddam's previous depredations of the southern Shia and the northern Kurds made revenge violence likely. It did not take a fortune-teller to imagine that sectarian and ethnic trouble was brewing. Those who believe Westerners created sectarianism in Iraq are ignoring long experience in conflict societies, which often break down along existing but previously inchoate lines.[16] I am not clairvoyant, but I wrote in the *Los Angeles Times* in October 2002, several months before the war, "Law enforcement has to arrive with the troops, not months later. Post-conflict chaos and revenge lead to protection rackets and organized crime."[17]

Nor was the U.S. military any better prepared for imposing law and order than the civilians. Military planning largely ignored "rear area security," the euphemistic rubric under which the military treats law and order after victory (when the entire country is "rear area"). The American withdrawal was planned to begin in June, and so it did, despite the fact that by then the United States had occupied Iraq and had its hands more than full with law-and-order issues. Only the arrival of a new commander with real experience in previous stabilization operations led to cancellation of these plans for early withdrawal.[18]

The occupation was declared in May 2003 by a civilian, Jerry Bremer, chosen by Secretary of Defense Rumsfeld and sent by President Bush to do what the president as candidate had said we would not want to do: nation-building, or as I would prefer to call it, state-building. Bremer should have been much better equipped and staffed than I was almost ten years earlier in Bosnia. Those of us with experience in Bosnia and Kosovo over the previous decade had tried to offer our best advice in the run-up to war. In quiet, off-the-record meetings, the administration was told it would need a civilian rule-of-law contingent to deploy immediately after the troops, but it decided against this.[19] It was briefed on the experience of vetting former Communist regimes, which suggested that getting rid of human rights abusers and supporters of the previous regime would require repeated culling of civil servants and could not be accomplished in one fell swoop.

Bremer himself, however, had not heard any of that advice. He was chosen only shortly before being deployed and launched quickly into the largest post–Cold War state-building effort the United States has ever attempted. He assembled a team in record time, but it was a team with limited experience, no preparation time, and an already catastrophic situation not only in Baghdad but in a good deal of the rest of Iraq as well. Everything was set up for Bremer and his team to march in the wrong direction.

The initial errors are well known.[20] Bremer disbanded the Iraqi army and prohibited Ba'athists (members of Saddam's political party) above a certain level from serving in the Iraqi state. Why were these mistakes? The Ba'athists after all were bound to be enemies of any new regime, and the army was one the U.S.-led coalition had just defeated. Moreover, lots of Iraqis were delighted that their enemies were discomfited. Kurds in the north had established their own state, Kurdistan, during the Saddam years, under the protection of an American-enforced no-fly zone, and Shia in the south had suffered brutal repression by Saddam after the Americans failed to come to the aid of their rebellion in the aftermath of Desert Storm.

Bremer's decisions were mistakes because they deprived Iraq of the institutions that might have enabled the Iraqis to reconstitute their state, already badly damaged by war, sanctions, and looting, faster than in the event proved possible. Instead, what Bremer did was invest $18.4 billion of U.S. taxpayer money (plus a few billion in Iraqi funds) almost entirely in brick-and-mortar reconstruction of Iraqi infrastructure, which was not only in a parlous state because of the war but also much deteriorated because of lack of investment during Saddam's twenty-four-year rule.

This investment in brick-and-mortar reconstruction was unprecedented and unwise.[21] Nothing even remotely approaching this amount had been spent in Bosnia or Kosovo on a per capita basis. The Americans wanted to repair or replace the massive systems needed to generate electricity, deliver clean water, and provide health and other services to Iraq's population of perhaps 28 million, enabling the American-led coalition to return to its original plan of withdrawing quickly. While the Bush administration was claiming to install democracy in Iraq, and many of its critics excoriate it for wanting Iraq to become instantly a free-market paradise, most of the money was going to support government services that in the United States and many other democracies are not government responsibilities at all.

Virtually no funding was set aside for negotiating and implementing the basic political settlement required as a foundation of the new Iraq or for creating the infrastructure of a legitimate democratic state: elections, free media, political parties, advocacy organizations, women's groups, and the like got the crumbs that fell off the table as major American contractors divvied up a very rich, creamy pie. Bremer and his successors would repeatedly have to shift resources from brick-and-mortar reconstruction to political negotiations and institution building, which were the real challenges in Iraq. It took years, but gradually American assistance focused on what is known in the foreign-aid community as "capacity-building," which meant training the Iraqis to run the institutions of their slowly reconstituted state. As the counterinsurgency campaign associated with "the surge" in U.S. forces (but carried out in large part by Iraqis) started producing results in 2008 and 2009, this capacity-building effort was also bearing fruit. Iraqi soldiers, police, members of parliament, provincial councilors, and bureaucrats were becoming capable of accepting the responsibilities that the Americans were only too glad to pass off to them.[22]

The Iraqi state today is not the world's finest, but it is also not the world's worst. The prime minister has accumulated a great deal of power and has become increasingly authoritarian. Corruption is rife, services are poor, and serious security challenges persist. But there is a presidency, a parliament, a national government and provincial governments, courts, a lively press, and an increasingly vocal civil society. Iraqis across a very broad spectrum of ethnic and sectarian identity as well as political perspectives agree on the constitution adopted in 2006 as the basic political framework. Mostly they want it implemented, not torn up. Many Iraqis are far better off economically than they were under Saddam. This is what success looks like in state-building: fragile, sometimes ugly, but relatively durable, even if unpredictable. Will Nouri al-Maliki be prime minister after the next election? The good news is that it is hard to say. The enterprise in Iraq will be relatively successful if the state holds together and his successor is elected in accordance with the constitution and laws passed in a more or less freely elected parliament.[23]

The situation in Afghanistan was different but not better.[24]

With the Bonn blueprint as a guide to state-building, the first couple of years after the fall of the Taliban regime went relatively smoothly. The Afghans convened a *loya jirga* (grand council of influential leaders) in June 2002 that elected Hamid Karzai president of the Transitional Islamic State of Afghanistan. A second *loya jirga* adopted a new constitution, under which Karzai was again elected president in 2004. By that time, Afghanistan had a parliament, a constitutional court, and a government that resembled on paper most other governments in the early part of the twenty-first century. The international community promised billions in foreign assistance.

There was, however, a giant disconnect between the government in Kabul and the countryside. The political blueprint did not extend into the rural areas where most Afghans live—it said little or nothing about how Afghanistan's provinces would be governed, except that their governors would be appointed by the president. Karzai chose to collaborate with Afghanistan's many warlords rather than trying to impose Kabul's will—something no one had ever succeeded in doing in Afghanistan. But the Americans and other donors had expected Afghanistan to be a centralized state. The Afghan National Development Strategy and many other donor-driven plans implicitly and explicitly assumed a highly centralized and authoritative government that simply did not exist.

The Taliban, who had been excluded from the political settlements decided in Bonn and from the *loya jirgas*, were by necessity decentralized. The war scattered them but did not kill them off. The relatively small deployment of U.S. and NATO troops in the aftermath kept them out of Kabul and many other population centers. Notoriously, even Osama bin Laden escaped at Tora Bora. He was not the only one. Mullah Omar, the paramount Taliban leader, and many of his followers either melted back into village life in rural Afghanistan or crossed the border into Pakistan, where the Federally Administered Tribal Areas as well as North and South Waziristan and other border districts were only nominally under Pakistani government control. Pakistani rule there could be harsh, but it was also sporadic and ambivalent. The Pakistani intelligence service viewed the Taliban as a counterweight to Indian influence inside Afghanistan, which it hoped would provide Islamabad with "strategic depth," a term whose ambiguity makes it no less compelling to Pakistanis. The leaders of a collapsed state found ready refuge in the margins of a weak state.

With the revival of the Taliban in 2004 and 2005 the Americans began to clash again with determined enemies. By then the United States was fighting off an insurgency in Iraq. The coalition presence in the Afghan countryside was too thin to prevent the Taliban from reestablishing itself at the local level, especially in the south. Feeding off the massive opium poppy trade, which neither the Americans nor the Afghan state was in a position to suppress, the Taliban began installing their own institutions to perform state-like functions. They were particularly successful at offering swift and certain justice, through Sharia courts that bore a resemblance to the traditional tribal *jirgas* that continue to decide many issues in rural Afghan communities.[25]

Informal, tribal dispute-settlement mechanisms are not unique to Afghanistan—they exist in many states that look weak from the outside but in fact have strong traditions when viewed from the inside.[26] In South Sudan and Liberia, for example, tribal justice systems are still predominant in the countryside. Why would anyone take a dispute to a group of village elders sitting under a tree rather than to the shiny new courtroom just built by USAID? Let me enumerate the reasons: the village elders don't charge fees, they don't require that you know how to read or write, they decide quickly, their decisions cannot be appealed (and are implemented right away), they cannot normally be bribed, and they try to preserve social relations, usually avoiding a decision on who is right and wrong and preferring to split the difference in a dispute that in a courtroom would lead to a winner and a loser. Informal justice mechanisms sometimes have a legitimacy that courtrooms lack.[27]

It is not easy for the modern state to compete with this kind of traditional system when it comes to disputes within a single community or ethnic group, and likely not wise to try either. But that is precisely what we tried to do in Afghanistan, where an effort was made to install a modern, centralized state in Kabul, which required for its effectiveness many appendages in the provinces and districts of the countryside. Very little attention was paid in the first years after the fall of the Taliban to indigenous mechanisms for local governance or dispute settlement.[28] The most important international program that took seriously village-level organization in Afghanistan was the World Bank's National Solidarity Program, which became notoriously successful by relying on locally elected community leaders to choose, design, and supervise small-scale development projects.[29] Afghanistan's Health Ministry was similarly successful working at the local level.[30]

So in Iraq we failed by investing in bricks and mortar rather than people and capabilities, while in Afghanistan we failed by investing in a centralized state that lacked legitimacy outside Kabul and had little capability of governing in the countryside, where traditional institutions and warlords prevailed. What should we have done?

State-Building Is Art, Not Science

There is no single answer to that question. State-building, for all the universality of the requirement, is still highly contextual, meaning it depends on the local history and culture of the society in which it is done. Programs that work in Iraq may not work in Afghanistan, and what works in Liberia may not work in South Sudan. State-building has to start from what really exists, even if the goal is something different. It made no sense to start in Afghanistan exclusively from the center, when no one had ever managed to govern the country from the center. And it made no sense in Iraq to start with major construction of facilities that the Iraqis would be unable (and in the event unwilling) to operate and maintain. Expertise in state-building starts with expertise in the place where the state is to be built.[31]

This means above all an intimate knowledge of the political and social forces at work within the population. The state needs to be based on a political arrangement that large parts of the society recognize as legitimate and will be willing to defend. The process by which this political arrangement is achieved is important: the more inclusive, the better.[32] But inclusiveness brings with it challenges, especially in a place where people have been at war. At the very least, all those who can spoil the outcome need to be included—we know now it was a mistake to exclude the Taliban in Afghanistan. But including all the spoilers can leave you with a state based on warlords, or one that quickly reverts to violence, or one that excludes women or minorities. "Gender inequality is not likely to produce sustainable results in peace and security," based on careful statistical studies.[33] There is no doubt but that inclusion of women in the postwar state-building processes in Liberia and Rwanda improved the outcome, but quotas for women in the Iraqi and Afghan parliaments have been less effective. Each society has its own requirements.

While there is an amazing variety in the circumstances in which we may be challenged to help build a state, there is a remarkable constancy in the kind of state the international community wants to build. Since the end of the Cold War there have been more or less twenty international interventions that can legitimately be described as "state-building." All aimed pretty much at the same results over the long term, though each began in unique circumstances. It is therefore possible to define what state-building means at the strategic level, even if the tactical steps to be undertaken and their sequence are context-dependent.

Taking our cue from military friends, let's define strategy as ends, ways, and means: the goal I am trying to achieve, the steps I need to take to get there, and the resources (personnel, money, political support, cooperation from others) I'll need along the way.

Each weak state is weak in its own way. Iraq's state collapsed because of invasion and its sequelae. Afghanistan's, never strong, evaporated with the exit of the Taliban. Bosnia's fell apart because of interethnic violence. But when you are trying to build or rebuild a state, the ends you seek are remarkably similar. Since the fall of the Berlin Wall there has been a remarkable consensus on rebuilding states that provide a safe and secure environment, rule of law, stable governance, a sustainable economy, and social well-being.[34] Without significant exception, the internationally mandated efforts since the end of the Cold War have aimed at these "end states." This was not at all the case during the Cold War, when international mandates often called simply for the separation of warring parties, and any number of American, Soviet, and other interventions aimed to install friendly dictatorships that would not in any sense measure up to these post–Cold War end states.

The Bush administration, faced with the real prospect of failure in Iraq, recognized the importance of state-building by 2005, when the Defense Department issued a directive requiring that "stability operations" (the army term for operations after war) be put on a par with offense and defense as a U.S. military function.[35] Shortly thereafter, the White House, reversing the failed approach it took in Iraq, issued an additional directive giving the State Department the lead role in "stabilization and reconstruction," for which it set up a new bureaucratic unit known in diplomatese as S/CRS.[36] Both of these decisions were built on congressional proposals, the most comprehensive of which was the bipartisan Biden-Lugar bill. In 2008 this led to funding for a Civilian Response Corps, the American nation-building corps that candidate Bush had derided only a few years earlier.[37]

These decisions have been partly sustained in the Obama administration, which promised in the first *Quadrennial Defense and Development Review* (issued in late 2010) a major increase in civilian capacity for state-building abroad but removed "stabilization operations" from a determining role in sizing the U.S. armed forces.[38] State-building is now a declared U.S. objective, but one quite properly assigned to civilians and military reservists.

Have we set ourselves an impossible task?[39] I think not, even if we are still significantly far off the mark in Iraq and Afghanistan. Let's go back to a previous case not yet discussed, Kosovo, for some lessons about how to move toward the strategic end states, even in a difficult environment. State-building is difficult, messy, and often less than 100 percent successful, but it need not be a complete failure.

Kosovo

Kosovo emerged from the NATO/Yugoslavia war with no recognizable governing institutions apart from a nominal president and jury-rigged educational and health systems. By 2013, five years after declaring independence, it had functioning state institutions—president, prime and other ministers, parliament, central bank, courts, and municipalities as well as a relatively free press, energetic political parties, and a nascent civil society. All this is far from perfect. Corruption is commonly perceived to be rife. The international community still does not trust Kosovo Albanian judges to try cases that involve disputes between Serbs and Albanians, the Kosovo elections in December 2010 were marred by allegations of ballot-box stuffing, and a portion of the Serb population of Kosovo does not accept the legitimacy of the government, refuses to vote, and is therefore unrepresented in parliament.

How did all this come about? What did the international community do wrong and right?

The international intervention in Kosovo was based on UN Security

Council Resolution 1244, which ended the NATO/Yugoslavia war and set up a UN mission charged with administering what had been a province of Serbia.[40] The mandate was all-encompassing and forceful—it gave the UN the authority to govern the territory as it saw fit and to enforce its decisions, with the assistance of a NATO-led military force known as KFOR. But it also asked the UN to prepare Kosovo for self-governance, with the prospect of an eventual decision on whether it was to remain part of Serbia, become independent, or something in between.

The UN by then had benefited from the experience of Bosnia, where it had participated in, but not led, the post-Dayton international intervention. New York, surprised by the Security Council decision to put the UN in charge after its less than glorious performance a few years earlier in Bosnia, sent the very best—the Brazilian diplomat and UN undersecretary Sergio Vieira de Mello, later killed in Iraq—to set up shop in Pristina, where he faced the immediate problem of Albanian violence against the few Serbs remaining south of the Ibar River. This had become the de facto boundary between the majority Serbian population to its north and the predominantly Albanian population to its south. The UN could not ignore human rights violations occurring on territory it was responsible for governing. Crisis management is never off the agenda in contemporary state-building operations.

But the UN also had a longer-term perspective: Resolution 1244 called on it to build a self-governing state, though without clarity about what the status of that state would be (independent? province of Serbia? confederated republic?). This ambiguity was a major hindrance, but there was nevertheless clarity on a different level: Kosovo should become a free-market democracy at peace with its neighbors. The UN recognized that it could not achieve this alone. The resolution corrected one of the mistakes in Bosnia and instructed the military leadership of KFOR to cooperate closely with the civilian UN leadership. More was needed. The UN mobilized the considerable resources of the international community that lay beyond its direct control. This it did by creating a four-pillar structure: humanitarian relief, civil administration, democratization and institution-building, and reconstruction and economic development. The last two pillars were led by the Organization for Security and Cooperation in Europe (OSCE) and the EU, respectively, under UN auspices.[41]

Nothing like this comprehensive pillar structure had existed in Bosnia, and nothing like it would be created later in Iraq or Afghanistan. But it worked remarkably well. The UN made its share of mistakes—it allowed, for example, the "alternative" health and educational systems the Albanians had run for ten years under Milosevic to be eviscerated when internationals hired away within weeks most of the teachers and administrators as drivers and translators. It tried to use Serbian law in Kosovo, where the Albanian judges refused to apply it. And it was less than fully effective in protecting not only Serbs but also Albanians from revenge killings by the Kosovo Liberation Army.

But on the whole the pillar system and the resources mobilized through it allowed the UN to make good progress toward the end states. It started with virtually dictatorial control over everything and only gradually—in response to Kosovar pressure—transferred responsibilities to the Kosovo institutions it helped to create. Lots of internationals were embedded in those institutions, initially as bosses and later as mentors. The Kosovars were given incentives to create a functioning state, first through a program called "standards before status," which promised a decision on independence if the state could measure up to specified standards, and later through negotiation of a plan for independence that incorporated rules the new state would have to follow, in particular for treatment of Serbs and other minorities.

Today Kosovo is safe and secure even for most Serbs most of the time. Broad international supervision has ended, as its benchmarks have been met. Rule of law is administered reasonably well by both local and—when it comes to interethnic crime—international judges and prosecutors, but organized crime continues to thrive. Governments are formed and fall according to established rules, even if the electoral mechanism is far from perfect. The economy has grown rapidly, albeit not fast enough to reduce very high official rates of unemployment. Food, shelter, water, education, and health services are widely, though not universally, available.

In other words, the UN really did build what is today a functioning, though imperfect, state in Kosovo, one that is now a member of the International Monetary Fund and the World Bank and recognized as sovereign by about one hundred governments. One of its past prime ministers has been tried and acquitted twice in The Hague, its current prime minister is alleged by his enemies to be guilty of heinous crimes right after the 1999 war, and Kosovo struggles to get respect in the European Union, which it wants to join. The EU has been reluctant to allow Kosovars to enter without visas, even though Pristina says it is willing to meet all the technical requirements. But no one doubts that there is a state in Kosovo that will persist, whatever its current troubles, and Belgrade has wisely engaged in a dialogue under EU auspices with that state despite all its imperfections.

I could tell a similar story about East Timor.[42] This one-million-person breakaway from Indonesia came under UN administration in 1999 and gained independence in 2002. It suffered violence in the run-up to its 2007 elections and assassination attempts against its prime minister and president in 2008, but it is today a functioning state endowed with substantial oil assets that fund a transparently and accountably operated national investment fund, though its population remains poor and its institutions are far from fully effective. If South Sudan can somehow manage to steer clear of war with Sudan, from which it seceded in 2011 in accordance with a referendum, and avoid internecine warfare within its own territory, it may follow Kosovo and East Timor in establishing, with less intrusive international tutelage, a viable state capable of delivering minimal services and governing openly and fairly.

A hard look at international interventions since 1989 concludes, "the great majority of postconflict nation-building operations over the past two decades have resulted in improved security, progress in democratization, significant economic growth, advances in human development, and most have done so with a modest commitment of international military manpower and economic assistance."[43]

Is It beyond Our Means? Is It beyond Our Capacity?

The UN's experience in Kosovo tells us that state-building really is possible, even where ethnic differences make it difficult. But is it beyond our means? Kosovo is a small place—fewer than 2 million inhabitants in a territory smaller than Connecticut. East Timor is even smaller. Can it be done in a place like Bosnia (more than twice Kosovo's population) or Iraq (fourteen times Kosovo's population) or Afghanistan (fifteen times Kosovo's population)?

Apart from size, there is a question of duration. International state-building operations tend to last a long time. The NATO mission in Kosovo will last at least fifteen years, perhaps longer. Even when they are successful, such efforts often end in transitions to smaller or lighter operations or other sorts of continued international monitoring.[44] A smaller and less heavily armed NATO "stabilization" mission followed the NATO "implementation" mission in Bosnia. That yielded ten years after the war to a European force, which is still needed there. Promises of quick exits are often unfulfilled.

Size and duration impose costs. Most of them are military.[45] Typically, less than 5 percent of the total U.S. cost of a postwar state-building intervention has been civilian. That is the approximate figure so far in Iraq and Afghanistan, even including the security costs for the civilians involved. There are two reasons for this: we have been using many more troops than civilians, in a ratio of more than ten to one in Afghanistan and in Iraq (at least until the sharp drawdown of troops in 2010); and deployed U.S. troops cost on the order of $1 million each per year in Iraq and Afghanistan, far more than civilians, in a ratio of perhaps three to one. It would be penny wise and pound foolish for the United States not to deploy civilian state-building capacity wherever U.S. troops are engaged in operations if the existence of a state is a prerequisite for withdrawal. Even if the state-building effort can shorten military deployments by only a bit, the savings are likely to be many times greater than what the effort costs.

Money is not the only limit on U.S. state-building capacity. More importantly, it is personnel who are lacking: civilians to staff state-building operations worldwide. The Civilian Response Corps in the State Department in 2011 had roughly 150 U.S. government employees available on twenty-four-hours' notice, and another 800 available within thirty days. But the 2013 State Department budget required cutting those numbers drastically.[46] Wisdom dictates that no more than half deploy at any one time. There are more hundreds on rosters kept by the State Department, USAID, and other government agencies, but these are still very small numbers. Nor are all these people necessarily trained for the purpose, though many will have relevant experience.

The U.S. military is acutely aware of this problem. When I was at the United States Institute of Peace, we briefed Joint Chiefs chairman Mike Mullen and U.S. Army vice chief of staff Pete Chiarelli on a tribal reconciliation conference we had run with support from the U.S. Army's Eighty-Second Airborne. The effort had resulted in an "action plan" that stabilized Mahmoudiya, a community on the southern edge of Baghdad once known as the "triangle of death" because of sectarian violence there.[47] The American commander of the brigade we worked with was unequivocal in saying that our efforts had saved his soldiers' lives. Mullen and Chiarelli were delighted with what we had done but had a tough question: how many more communities can you do it for next year? We imagined two or three, as the effort was labor intensive and tailored to the specific circumstances in each community. They laughed: they needed efforts of this sort in hundreds of communities. How, they asked, can we get you to scale?

The best existing estimate of U.S. civilian requirements is five thousand active-duty government officials plus ten thousand in reserve. These numbers could staff "one large, one medium and four small contingencies." This is far more than the U.S. government currently has available, or plans for. The costs would be substantial, on the order of $2 billion per year. This is a big number. But it is small compared to military costs. If a civilian capability of these dimensions had even a fifty-fifty chance of reducing a deployment like the one in Afghanistan by two weeks, it would be a worthwhile expense, because it would be likely to reduce total U.S. costs. If it could reduce a deployment like the one in Afghanistan by the equivalent number of soldiers, it would also be worthwhile.[48]

Is it likely that civilians could displace soldiers in an operation like the one in Afghanistan? The answer is a resounding yes. We know this because at present we are often using troops to stand in for civilians.

While no one seems ever to have counted the numbers involved, anyone with experience in Iraq or Afghanistan knows that when staffing an important civilian task is difficult—for example, in the initial deployment of Provincial Reconstruction Teams—the U.S. government looks to the Defense Department to fill the gap. Soldiers and marines have also been used extensively as mentors to the defense and interior ministries in both Iraq and Afghanistan. This is inappropriate, since these ministries are supposed to be the agents of civilian control over security forces.[49] We are often using million-dollar soldiers where civilians at less than one-third the cost would not only suffice but also be more appropriate. This is the equivalent of spending your valuable coin collection when recently printed paper dollars you carry in your wallet would suffice. The logic of using civilians where and when possible is compelling. The problem is that we do not have enough of them.

Although this problem is not insoluble, its solution will require a concerted effort over a decade. Money, people, and local knowledge are the vital ingredients for success in state-building wherever it is attempted. But the numbers of people and amounts of money are small compared to military requirements.

5. Who Contributes to This Work?

Jessica Buchanan, for one. She is the thirty-two-year-old American freed by U.S. Navy SEALS from Somali pirates just before President Obama's State of the Union address in January 2012. She and a Danish colleague worked for an NGO, the Danish Refugee Council, on de-mining in central Somalia. The pirates had kidnapped them the previous October. The Danish organization had cleared 1.4 million square meters of Somaliland, a relatively peaceful part of Somalia with its own local governing structures, by the previous spring. Buchanan was an "educational adviser" working closely with the local community to improve mine awareness and prevent injuries to Somalis.[1]

Her rescue attracted more attention to the military operation, performed by the same SEAL unit that killed Osama bin Laden in Pakistan, than to her humanitarian mission. But it is that mission that interests us. Jessica Buchanan is one of about 250,000 people delivering international humanitarian assistance worldwide.[2] If we count "development" assistance, which includes longer-term economic aid and statebuilding, the number might be half a million. Most of these people are host country nationals (for example, Somali), who constitute the majority of the staff of such organizations.

Several hundred U.S.-based NGOs work internationally on humanitarian and development assistance. Dozens of profit-making companies also work in this area, mainly as contractors and subcontractors to USAID. My guesstimate is that something like fifty thousand Americans are involved: de-mining, providing food, water, and shelter, training government employees, setting up health clinics and schools, monitoring respect for human rights, helping communities decide their development priorities, and a bewildering array of other tasks.

Not all of these people are working in fragile or conflict-affected states, where the need for state-building efforts is particularly acute and about half of USAID's money is spent. Fragile and conflict-affected states lag seriously behind even other developing countries—none of them are on track to achieve the UN's Millennium Development Goals by the 2015 "end poverty" deadline. There are perhaps twenty-five thousand Americans involved, working for a few hundred organizations, including the several thousand USAID and State Department staff who set overall policy and supervise the grants and contracts through which funding flows. We are not talking big numbers, but these civilians make vital contributions to American foreign policy and merit a closer look. They are the "tip of spear" in preventing poor, fragile, conflict-affected countries from breeding the wars, terrorism, autocracies, and ungoverned spaces that do harm to Americans and American national security.

They Come from Every Direction

How do people find their way into this international enterprise of helping others prevent conflict and recover from it? Sloan Mann, now busy training other people to do this work, describes his evolution from West Point graduate to aid worker this way:

> The smell of raw sewage filled my nostrils and dust coated my face as I walked the streets of Giliani, Kosovo in 2000. I was carrying a weapon, wearing body armor and a kevlar helmet. I probably looked frightening and surreal to the Kosovars walking the streets. As a U.S. Army Officer deployed to Kosovo as part of KFOR, I was on my way to a United Nations Mission in Kosovo (UNMIK) coordination meeting with the international and non-governmental organizations. I was sweaty and dirty from my walk but the civilians, wearing a mish mash of field clothes and semi-presentable business attire seemed haggard and drained. I learned later of the long hours they put in trying to stand up the Kosovar government, respond to humanitarian crises, and work on a myriad of development programs trying to improve the lives of Kosovars. I was intrigued.

During my brief seven months in Kosovo, I befriended as many international aid workers as I could in an effort to learn where they went to school, the organizations they work for, and the types of positions they held. I was astounded—I had no idea there was an entire world of international development specialists who travel from crisis to crisis. Carrying a gun and wearing a uniform no longer interested me; I wanted to work with local populations directly, help them if I could, and work on intellectually challenging programs in conflict and post-conflict environments. Additionally, as I realized during my time in Bosnia and Herzegovina (my first deployment) and Kosovo, I had a passion for working and connecting with people of all cultures.

So I left the Army and attended Georgetown's Master of Science in Foreign Service Program with a concentration on International Conflict Management. My first post-Army job was a research assistant at the U.S. Institute of Peace. Going from an U.S. Army Captain to a research assistant was quite a shock—both in responsibility and pay—but it immersed me in my chosen field, ideally placed me to continue my steep learning curve, and helped with making critical contacts. In early 2003, just as the U.S. was gearing up to invade Iraq, I caught a break. The U.S. Agency for International Development (USAID) was putting together a human rights focused team—called the Abuse Prevention Unit—and I was lucky enough to get a slot. They needed someone with military field experience to help translate unfamiliar human rights concepts to the military. The APU was charged with increasing the level of awareness, principally of the military but also USAID, Department of State, and NGOs on the importance of integrating/mainstreaming human rights and protection issues into the humanitarian response in Iraq. My one year in Iraq with the APU was the most meaningful and professionally gratifying job I have ever held.

Since 2003, I have worked on humanitarian emergencies and in conflict and post-conflict environments around the world. Not only has it been fulfilling work, it has also kept me constantly professionally challenged. My greatest satisfaction has been the local staff I've mentored and watched grow into exceptionally competent and transformational leaders. This has happened in every country I have worked, and I keep in touch with the all of them. My disappointments are many but topping the list is my frustration with U.S. Government agencies involved in international assistance. Change seems to move at glacial pace when it comes to reforming the way we appropriate money, train practitioners, measure programmatic impact, learn from failed programs, and adapt methodologies to the complex and ever evolving nature of overseas environments.

After two years in Afghanistan as the USAID Development Advisor to the U.S. Special Forces, I resigned in 2008. I wanted to try to impact policy and programming from the outside—the private sector. I co-founded a company, Development Transformations, to focus on training practitioners and designing effective programs in transitional and conflict environments. It was risky to leave the relative security of a Government job but taking calculated risks has been a part of my work and life since graduating from West Point. Sometimes, it takes a bit of risk to have an impact, effect change, or contribute in a meaningful way.

I encourage younger generations eager to enter the field of international development to balance field experience with a healthy dose of time back at headquarters. Taking time off from the field to reflect on experiences helps to solidify lessons learned and often provides fodder for the development of creative programming approaches.[3]

Sloan's frustration is not unusual in the international assistance world. Nor is his enthusiasm for the work and for his "local staff," who are often unusually devoted and talented people running real risks to life and limb to make a difference to their own societies. Thousands of Iraqi "local staff" have had to immigrate to the United States to avoid threats to themselves and their families.

A. Heather Coyne went in the other direction, from a civilian government employee at the White House Office of Management and Budget to U.S. Army captain in Iraq, then back to civilian life at the United States Institute of Peace. After a second army reserve tour in Kabul, she has now joined the United Nations there. This bobbing back and forth is not uncommon among what I term people with "foreign legionnaire's disease." Here she describes her motives for living a difficult but rewarding life:

I wrote my first school paper when I was 7 about the Soviet invasion of

Afghanistan, full of righteous outrage. That outrage sharpened and turned on my own country as I learned in high school and college about the atrocities that we had been at least partially responsible for in Latin America. I felt that issues of genocide, torture, and dictatorship were the most important things we needed to address in the world—surpassing even disease. This is partly because oppression, in all its forms, has such critical effects on such a large number of people, but also because it threatens the things that are the most inspiring about humanity when we get it right: brotherhood, justice, and service. Oppression hurts what is best about us. There are still many serious problems in the U.S. that need dedication and talent, but I felt that if there are still places where the population doesn't enjoy basic human rights or is hungry because their leaders deny them livelihoods, then that must take priority over the fine tuning of our own nation—especially when it is our own policies that often enable tyranny in other countries.

Most people who want to work overseas on governance, development and security reform are similarly driven by the urge to fix things, to improve quality of life. But the most important qualification for such interveners is the ability to overcome their good intentions. Good intentions allow people to ignore their own shortcomings and inefficiencies, in the same way that "national security interests" are sometimes used to trump moral or economic responsibilities. Good intentions are not sufficient to achieve anything positive, even if they are a prerequisite for getting involved, and often do more harm than good. I don't think you have to encourage people to work abroad on governance and development; enough good people will naturally gravitate to the issues. But you do have to encourage them to restrain themselves, to use approaches that don't impose their values and fixes on people who need opportunities to fix things for themselves. . . .

My particular contribution has been in bridging the aspects of our field that often ignore and scorn each other: development and security. I draw from parallel careers in the military and the NGO/IO community, trying to expose each to the constraints faced by the other, and the expertise that both offer. And more importantly than bridging the institutions, I bridge the principles. I try to integrate the best practices from development into our intervention on security issues, using participatory and consultative processes to improve security sector governance.

That bridge was awkward in the making. At the time, my graduate school was divided into either the development and conflict management specialists (the touchy feely types) or the strategic studies specialists (the warmongers) and never the twain did meet. I did a joint concentration in strategic studies and conflict management in order to study both sides of the issues. Since there were few classes on the interrelatedness of security and development, I created a speaker series for my department on unconventional security threats and responses, like peacekeeping, terrorism, drug trafficking, etc. After grad school I was a Presidential Management Fellow at the White House Office of Management and Budget where my portfolio as a program examiner included the military's Special Operations Command and programs to combat terrorism, defense against weapons of mass destruction, and critical infrastructure protection. I developed an interagency process with the National Security Council to make decisions for these programs on a government-wide basis.

While at OMB, I stumbled across my dream job: a liaison between the military and civilians on reconstruction in conflict zones. The only catch was, it was in the Army. I'm a bleeding heart liberal from California—we just don't join the military! But I pursued a commission in the Army Reserve and became a Civil Affairs officer. I left OMB to learn Arabic so that I could do Civil Affairs in the region that I felt had the most important security and governance issues, and after a year and half at the Defense Language Institute, was deployed for the invasion of Iraq in 2003. After serving as the Civil Society Officer for the Baghdad region for more than a year, I transitioned back to civilian life to become USIP's chief of party for Iraq. Although I was working on similar issues in the same place, the approach from the NGO side was a world away from what I'd done with the Army and the Coalition Provisional Authority. I spent several more years with USIP, learning more about those techniques, and then volunteered for a military tour in Afghanistan. There I was the NGO and International Organization Liaison for the NATO Training Mission, responsible for helping civil society to play a role in shaping the reform of the security forces. We made some progress on developing "community" or "democratic" policing, involving civil society organizations in making their police more accountable and responsive to communities. Similar to my transition in Iraq, the UN created a position for me to continue this work as a civilian.

This pattern of establishing a network of efforts through the military and then expanding it on the civilian side is no coincidence. It is based on the overreliance of the U.S. on the military in reconstruction and stability operations—the easiest way to get into the center of what is important is as a military officer. Once there, though, I insist on working on the security-governance/development nexus that the military has neglected, and that work is then seen as relevant to the civilian organizations, who have more expertise to refine and continue it.[4]

People like A. Heather Coyne and Sloan Mann are particularly effective because they can move back and forth between the military and civilian spheres, taking with them knowledge of how things work on the other side. Getting the military and civilians to work in tandem, achieving "unity of effort," is a vital and rare skill.

A. Heather is not alone in emphasizing the need to restrain our own good intentions and take careful account of the environment in which an international intervention takes place. This is the main message from other experienced "practitioners."[5] Context is all-important. Those who intervene may find themselves aiming for the same broad strategic goals wherever they are, but where they start and how they get where they are going will vary, depending on the local context. There is a world of difference between establishing a viable, legitimate state in Bosnia and establishing one in Afghanistan, but recognizing those differences and acting on them has not been our forte. We too often prefer a cookie-cutter approach, transplanting programs successful in one country to another without too much consideration of whether they fit the context. Those involved in an international intervention may know a great deal more about how a mature democracy operates than local people will ever learn, but it is the local people who will have to make things work in their own country. We need to listen to them and respond to their requirements when our own values permit it.[6]

Many people working on state-building do not come to it directly from military experience. Jeremiah Pam, a New York lawyer with experience in finance (who had served earlier in his career as a U.S. Air Force officer), deployed as an official in the U.S. embassies in Iraq and Afghanistan. He describes his decision to join up this way:

> I decided to leave the practice of law in New York and join the Treasury Department to go to Baghdad as Treasury's lead diplomat in 2006 fundamentally because I didn't want to *not* participate in a national endeavor as gravely important as a war. I had some sympathy for but was far from enthusiastic about the specific war. I'd had some relevant experience at the international law firm I'd been working for, where I served as a legal adviser to the Government of Iraq for two years in international negotiations to restructure its debt, so I knew the senior Iraqi finance officials, as well as some of the U.S. officials involved in economic effort. The debt restructuring negotiation itself was actually a successful and fairly well-run U.S. interagency and Coalition effort—and so while I was quite aware through the extensive press coverage and the early critical books that the U.S./Coalition effort in Iraq had been very problematic, my initial personal involvement (based in New York, Washington and business hotels in Amman and Dubai) had been in what was recognized as one of the few bright lights of the effort. Nonetheless, I don't think I volunteered to go out of excessive idealism and naivete. Instead, I figured: (1) that this was too important a national undertaking for people like me to just sit in New York watching, (2) that if I wanted to be able to credibly say that I take international affairs seriously, I had no choice but to put my money where my mouth was, and (3) that while the effort had obviously been seriously troubled during the first few years after 2003, if by 2005 I was reading about the problems in published books, our government too must belatedly have become aware of the problems and taken steps to fix them.[7]

Setting things right is a powerful incentive, but the impulse provides little guidance as to what to do. While writing perceptive analysis of how we should approach complex issues with an eye for simple and incremental solutions, Jeremiah has become pessimistic about our capacity to pursue international state-building, after further difficult assignments to Baghdad, Kabul, and Washington. Postwar transitions like those he has undertaken are enormously challenging and rarely lead to fully satisfying outcomes.[8]

Many Talents Needed

One of the complications is that the role of international experts is not to establish a state or prevent conflict but rather to empower host country nationals to do it. This is not in the first instance a job for specialists. You may know perfectly well how to repair an electrical power plant or build a new one. When I first went into Iraq in 2004, I met some of America's finest engineers working for world-class companies building the most advanced power plants in the world. But the Iraqis did not have the skills required to operate or maintain them or the managerial capacity needed to incorporate them into the grid. Much of the American effort to build power plants was wasted, to the tune of billions.[9]

The people needed may be judges or prison guards. Some may actually go abroad to do that work. A few international judges still sit on some cases in Kosovo courts, and the United States held thousands of Iraqis and Afghans in detention during the past ten years. But the people I am referring to are not usually sent abroad to serve as judges or prison guards; they are sent abroad to help *others* understand the roles of judges and prison guards in the kind of society the local people are trying to build. This requires a much deeper understanding of the local context, good interpersonal relations, and a capacity for mentoring and advising, which is rare.[10]

Training for these roles has been grossly inadequate. Sloan and a colleague described the situation this way in the spring of 2011: "American government civilians taking part in stability operations receive even less training than the military. Most of those deploying to Afghanistan receive only 21 days of preparation, none of which is dedicated to understanding or conducting stability operations. . . . Because of political pressure to get civilians to Afghanistan, there is a limit of thirty days between hiring and deployment, which means little time to train people to effectively conduct stability operations in the complex environments in which they will be working."[11] There is a vicious cycle at work: presidents do not want to do state-building, so the U.S. government does not prepare for it until it is necessary and urgent, which limits the time to train people to do it and reduces effectiveness, reinforcing the next president's unwillingness.

Experience Counts

There are nevertheless thousands of Americans who have gained experience in state-building missions abroad over the past two decades. Many of these have served in what are termed "provincial reconstruction teams" (PRTS) in Iraq and Afghanistan, or with government contractors, both in companies and in NGOs. Relatively few serve as diplomats in embassies. As large as they are, the embassies in Kabul and Baghdad are the tip of the iceberg of the American civilian presence. The same is true in Bosnia, Kosovo, and other places where American intervention has been important. Most of the civilians engaged in state-building, peace-building, development, humanitarian relief, and the like work for private organizations or are hired as contractors by the U.S. government.

The experience has not always been a positive one. Its critics see the effort as ill-conceived, inadequately resourced, and improperly staffed.[12] Others think they were able to accomplish at least part of their mission, especially when isolated in a remote outpost with little interference from what diplomats call "the 5,000-mile screwdriver," the Washington-based officials who try to find the right screw to turn at a gigantic distance.[13] One of the disadvantages of modern communications is the twenty-four-hour ease with which bosses in Washington can call the shots in Kandahar. Not only is it demoralizing to deployed personnel, but it also makes their objective of empowering locals to handle their own problems unachievable. If officials in Washington control the money and want to call the shots, why should anyone in the field take on more than minimal responsibility?

A. Heather Coyne describes the joys and disappointments this way:

> I take great satisfaction when programs intended to open channels for people to defend their own interests get to the point where people see how they can make change for themselves. Whether it is community-police engage-

Who Contributes to This Work?
Who Contributes to This Work?

ment programs in Afghanistan, or inter-sectarian conflict management in Iraq, people radiate joy and pride when they grasp an approach that they can use to improve their own lives. A police officer realizing the gratification that comes from teaching schoolchildren about safety, or a community that learns how to make their police more accountable, or an individual who suddenly sees the value of a negotiating technique . . . there is excitement as they realize that they can be active players in their lives rather than passive victims.

However, witnessing these individual epiphanies are only "temporal" successes for me. The advances that give me more lasting satisfaction are not the localized programs, but the discoveries of techniques and approaches, systems and processes that have meaning in a variety of contexts. Principles that, if applied to take account of the context, can guide attempts to combat atrocities of any kind. The hardest and most frustrating thing to do is to take part in institutionalizing these in a way that they are not lost, as so many lessons are, and that creates a continuing, growing, and systemic capacity to respond to oppression.

The biggest disappointments are opportunities we missed because of our own ignorance or lack of capacity. There are places where, if our interventions had been more sensitive and organized, the local actors would have been able to make change for the better. Instead our lack of understanding of the dynamics, or an overwhelming focus on ourselves, meant that we closed off choices for local leaders or pushed them into destructive patterns. Examples of such failures include entrenching a sectarian basis for leadership in Iraq instead of empowering moderates, forcing a constitutional process there that addressed our needs instead of those of the conflict and training police in Afghanistan to be soldiers instead of service providers.[14]

The use of police to fight insurgents rather than to protect the population is one of the classic, and often repeated, errors of recent international interventions.[15] The problem is that such "lessons learned" do not get applied, either because the experience is lost or because no one wants to admit it might be needed.

Unlike troops, contractors go home after service in conflict zones and are quickly lost in the general population. At the height of the Iraq and Afghanistan wars around 2007, I sat stunned in an audience at the National Defense University when the official in charge of Provincial Reconstruction Teams in Afghanistan said there was no mechanism for transferring lessons learned from Iraq, or vice versa. Even professional diplomats generally get no formal debriefing on their experience after service abroad (they are, however, extensively briefed on U.S. government policy before going on an assignment). Those who have tried to debrief deployed personnel have all too often found it almost impossible to find them. But once you do, it is also impossible to get permission to publish what they tell you, in particular if they want to complain about that 5,000-mile screwdriver.

The Civilian Response Corps was supposed to be the U.S. government's fix for the problem of capturing and applying civilian experience in conflict zones. It has been used in Sudan, Kyrgyzstan, Afghanistan, and elsewhere. They were useful to augment embassy personnel in moments of crisis and to enhance planning capacity—traditional diplomats do little or no planning, which they regard as the refuge of the incompetent. Real pinstripers pride themselves on winging it in a fast-changing world of many words and few big operational challenges. "Sink or swim" is the Foreign Service officer's credo. But the Civilian Response Corps was far too small to give the U.S. government the capacity it needs to meet likely future challenges. Even before sequestration, the State Department was abandoning it.[16]

Isn't It Dangerous?

Walking toward the U.S. Embassy in Baghdad one day in 2004, Sloan and I came within one hundred yards of a rocket that landed on a helipad across the street. Because a rocket travels faster than the speed of sound, you hear the whistle of its flight after it lands and detonates, which makes the experience almost like running a film backwards. We glanced at each other and headed for the concrete "duck and cover" bunkers at the edge of the parking lot. Rockets are often fired in volleys, but running for cover is inadvisable. Another colleague broke a rib when he tripped doing that a few months later.

Much worse can happen. The murder of Ambassador Chris Stevens and three of his colleagues in Benghazi on September 12, 2012, was a sharp reminder of the dangers. Diplomats are not the only civilians at risk. More than 308 international aid workers worldwide suffered 151 major attacks in 2011. Eighty-six were killed. The trend is up, especially kidnapping and road attacks. Afghanistan is particularly dangerous. Violence against aid workers correlates not with the type of government but rather with "the stability and validity of the fundamental institutions of governance, i.e., the underlying strength of the state."[17] That makes work in which the state needs building particularly perilous.

The increased security risks over the past decade raise difficult issues for civilians working in conflict environments. Once upon a time, aid workers regarded themselves as relatively safe, even in conflict zones. In fact, they *were* safe in Bosnia and Kosovo, where NATO forces deployed only after the diplomats negotiated peace agreements. There are even some places where unarmed civilian "peacekeepers" play a useful role as observers.[18] Nothing like these conditions exists in Somalia, Darfur, or Afghanistan. There, aid workers are clearly helping one side in an ongoing conflict. This makes them targets for the other side. Some organizations react by trying to ensure they are distinct from military forces, but this can be difficult in a conflict environment. The Pentagon has agreed to guidelines that require its troops to respect "humanitarian space."[19] Some NGOs also use "shooters" (armed security guards, aka personal security details) to protect civilians in conflict zones. NGO aid workers do not generally carry arms.

Government officials face even more danger than non-officials. Where conflict is ongoing they are "belligerents," even if they are civilians. Half of the people stationed at the American Embassy in Baghdad provide protection and other support to the other half. The ratio of guards to guarded was even higher in PRTs and the District Reconstruction Teams that dealt at an even more local level in Afghanistan. These have been staffed partly with troops, partly with foreign service professionals, and partly with people recruited specifically for the purpose. While I have taken the minimal risk of walking spontaneously a half mile to the American Embassy in Baghdad for dinner, none of my dinner companions had ever taken a walk in the street, even in the Green Zone.

Something for the Less Daring

Working in a war zone during conflict, or even after one, is obviously not for everyone. There are other places and ways the less daring can contribute.

If it is cheaper and better to clean up before war rather than after, it is also safer. Afghanistan, Iraq, Darfur, and other active conflict zones are the exception, not the rule. Most fragile states are either far enough along in recovery that they are relatively safe, at least from large-scale violence, or they have not yet suffered full-fledged warfare. Liberia, Sierra Leone, and Rwanda are postwar countries in which normal assistance missions operate today without close military protection. They rely on good security procedures, the relatively friendly environment, and protection from local security forces.

The Peace Corps operates in many of these more benign environments. It has sent more than 200,000 civilian volunteers to 139 countries over the past fifty years. In 2012 about 9,000 were serving in 76 countries. Thirty-nine percent are in Africa, working mainly on education and health projects. The Peace Corps is of course not alone. USAID today operates in about 80 countries and employs about 2,500 Americans, in addition to 4,500 foreign nationals. The State Department has more than 8,000 American employees overseas. Hundreds of additional Americans are deployed with the UN or UN agencies.

But the bulk of Americans working in fragile states to prevent conflict or rebuild after it are not with the U.S. government, or even the Peace Corps. They are with private organizations: both NGOs and American companies.

NGOs are private nonprofit organizations that work either with grants and contracts from the U.S. government or with privately donated funds. In fragile states, the main players include International Relief and Development, RTI International, Family Health International, CARE, Mercy Corps, International Rescue Committee (IRC), and Worldvision, as well as many others. The private companies that do actual development work (as opposed to providing security and other services) include Chemonics, Abt Associates, Development Alternatives International, Creative Associates International, Tetra Tech, AECOM, Checchi Consulting, MSI, and many others.[20] They are usually contractors and sub-contractors on projects funded by the U.S. government.

There is a third category of important organizations: semi-private, semi-public ones like the National Endowment for Democracy, the International Republican Institute, the National Democratic Institute, the Center for International Private Enterprise, and the United States Institute of Peace. Each has its own peculiarities, but they have these things in common: created by Congress, they work primarily with U.S. government money, but their employees are not U.S. government officials. They are relatively small. Altogether they number around a thousand professional American employees.

One of the obvious ways America might amplify its presence abroad is through national service in less dangerous environments. I am inundated these days with well-educated young people eager to work on international affairs. Many of them would happily go abroad for a few years, especially if their expenses were paid. A bit of relief from student loans would be a big incentive as well. Many of them are spending months and even years working for free as interns in Washington. They could contribute much more if they could sign up for an extended stint overseas, with hope of learning a difficult language and establishing themselves as experienced practitioners. This is what the Church of Latter Day Saints expects of its adherents—Mitt Romney spent his three years of missionary work in France. It is no accident that (in my experience) a disproportionate part of the CIA's operations directorate—where foreign languages are highly valued—is Mormon.

The Corporation for National and Community Service (the umbrella covering Americorps, Senior Corps, and Learn and Serve America) mobilizes more than 1.5 million people each year. This is a small fraction of the 62.8 million adult volunteers who served almost 8.1 billion hours in 2010.[21] Teach for America, which pays relatively low wages to its 9,000 members, is notoriously difficult to enter, and its total costs are significant.[22] Peace Corps likewise is a federal government program whose budget is approaching $400 million per year.

Requiring national service and administering it through the U.S. government would be expensive. It would be far easier and cheaper to provide incentives—partial write-off of student loans, for example—to those who deploy internationally for a year or two with an NGO. Some leading universities already do this for graduates who enter public service. It would be far more effective as a national policy.

The Home Front

If national service is unlikely to find support in a Congress more inclined to cut budgets than increase them and more inclined to rely on private initiative than public, there are still things that need doing on the home front that would enhance the civilian contributions to national security.

The most obvious one is support for those who serve out of uniform. We are all used to the elaborate and much-deserved tributes to our military on many public occasions: not only Memorial Day, Veterans Day, and the Fourth of July but also at football, basketball, and baseball games. While some may complain that these are excessive, I would argue that they are incomplete: we should also be paying tribute to those who serve as civilians. I am pleased to have said as much to White House officials on the eve of President Obama's trip to Fort Bragg in December 2011 to thank American troops for their service in Iraq on the eve of withdrawal. For the first time in my memory of any president, he thanked the soldiers *and civilians* who had sacrificed in Iraq.[23] The numbers are uncertain, but it appears around one hundred aid workers and fifteen hundred contractors (many of them providing security) were killed during the American presence in Iraq between 2003 and 2011. It is not clear how many of them were Americans.

The most important sign of appreciation from the home front would be steady support. This has not been forthcoming. The budgets provided to our foreign affairs agencies are notoriously volatile and unpredictable. Few Americans understand or appreciate what civilians do in war zones, or even know they are there. But when it is explained, they are enormously supportive. Though undoubtedly proud of the troops, Americans are not happy to present only a military face to the world.[24] They want to be seen not only as coercive but as engaged and supportive, in cooperation with others. The civilians who serve abroad—diplomats, aid workers, state-builders, contractors—are the American face much of the rest of the world sees most directly.

Modern communications are, however, changing that. It is now possible for individual citizens to engage abroad for economic and social impact from the comfort of their own computers. I did it for the first time as an experiment in less than five minutes: the website of Kiva, a nonprofit organization with a mission to connect people through lending to alleviate poverty, connected me to worldwide network of microfinance institutions. As a first experiment, I chose to loan $25 to a woman named Mariam in Sikasso, Mali, a country plagued by weak governance and endemic insurgency. Her $800 loan was crowdsourced and fully funded less than twenty-four hours later. Kiva can tell me quite a bit about Mariam:

> For approximately the last ten years, Mariam has bought and sold "pagnes" (traditional printed cloths), bedsheets, shoes, embroidered materials, brooms, etc. She conducts this trade from home and on a mobile basis in the town of Sikasso, where she is much sought after by her customers for the quality of her products. To meet the needs of her ever growing customer base, she decided to join the microfinance institution Soro Yiriwaso five years ago. Following several group loans with an association of women from her area, she is now taking her third personal loan, with which she plans to purchase 10 traditional outfits, 20 pairs of shoes of various quality, 5 embroidered full length outfits and some brooms. She buys her goods locally, and also in Bobo Dioulasso (in Burkina Faso). Accepting cash or credit, she then sells them retail, by going door-to-door, to a customer base composed essentially of women. All her previous loans have been fully repaid.[25]

I got my money back, but nothing more, and Kiva charged me a few dollars for the privilege. But boy did that feel good!

I am not the only one feeling good. Since Kiva was founded in 2005 it has received money from 929,924 Kiva lenders, made $430 million in loans, and gotten 98.98 percent back. To accomplish this, Kiva has 192 "field partners" as well as 450 volunteers in sixty-seven countries.[26] So the new civilian face of America abroad is *your* face and your hard-earned cash, reliably returned to you when it is finished doing some good wherever you want to lend it.

Another example of burgeoning international engagement at a distance is Ushahidi, a nonprofit that develops free open-source software for information collection, visualization, and interactive mapping. Ushahidi ("testimony" in Swahili) originated in mapping reports of violence in Kenya after its 2008 elections. Forty-five thousand people contributed.[27] Since then, Ushahidi's software has been used to map humanitarian needs in Haiti, ensure supply of essential medicines in Kenya and Uganda, document killings in Syria and Libya during their uprisings, and monitor election abuses.[28] It makes this information available as widely as the users want—meaning that I may know as much about what is going on in Sudan if it is mapped on Ushahidi software as someone in Khartoum, which prevents the government from concealing abuses and enables the international community to design appropriate responses.

There are many experiments of this sort. The nonprofit Samasource provides data, research, and archival services performed by women and youth living in poverty via the Internet.[29] Soldiers of Peace aims to mobilize millennial-generation activists worldwide.[30] Twitter, Skype, YouTube, and Facebook have enormously enhanced the capability of "citizen journalists" to report events from crisis zones as well as to receive messages and assistance from abroad. Global Voices aggregates and translates blogs and other citizen journalism from many countries.[31] Thirty years ago, Bashar al-Assad's father, President Hafez al-Assad, killed tens of thousands of people in a crackdown in Homs, without the rest of the world knowing much about it until later. The New York–based Avaaz network, with more than 13 million supporters, played a role in helping the Syrian uprising in 2011 and 2012, providing BGANs (which provide Internet access by satellite with small antennas) that its citizen journalists use to keep the world informed of Bashar al-Assad's attacks on his own population.[32] We would have known little about repression in Syria during the winter of 2011–12 without the videos citizen journalists uploaded to YouTube. Likewise, thousands of citizens have reported bribes to the Indian website "ipaidabribe.com," which uses the data to argue for improved governance and law enforcement.[33] People in Kenya and other countries are quickly setting up their own analogous websites. The citizen perspective adds a vital dimension to understanding what is going on in problem countries.[34]

Modern communications have also enabled a new level of advocacy on international issues in the developed world, especially the United States and Europe. This was apparent in Darfur, where media gained heightened visibility and resources for a conflict that was arguably no worse than what was going on nearby in the Democratic Republic of the Congo at the same time.[35] While there are serious risks of oversimplification, as well as an excessive need for advocacy organizations to demonstrate "success," the focus on Darfur in the developed world unquestionably enabled a level of diplomatic pressure on Khartoum and humanitarian assistance to displaced people and refugees that would otherwise not have been possible. Despite some objections, one clever soul is crowdsourcing support for military intervention to track down rebel leader and war crimes indictee Joseph Kony, the Lord's Resistance Army leader who has in the past recruited child soldiers and wreaked havoc in parts of four countries: Uganda, South Sudan, Central African Republic, and Democratic Republic of the Congo.[36] The *Kony 2012* video reached 50 million people in just a few days in March 2012.[37]

This kind of interconnectedness is more than an Internet curiosity. We really are entering a "new digital age" that will transform relationships, sometimes for the better and sometimes for the worse.[38] Princeton's Anne-Marie Slaughter sees interconnectedness as the source of a new kind of "collaborative" power, neither "hard" nor "soft," with which the United States is unusually well endowed because of its large populations originating in other parts of the world and openness to international communication.[39] Today's technology can mobilize forty-one peaceful "flash" demonstrations in Damascus on a Friday in February 2012, despite the watchful attention of Syria's intelligence agents. It can connect people like Mariam and me, even allowing a virtually instantaneous transfer of resources. It can help me to understand what is going on abroad well enough to adapt my views to a new and different reality, as Bitterlemons.org, a joint Palestinian and Israeli website, did for much of the past decade.[40]

Diplomacy, once the prerogative of states and their representatives, is now wide open to contributions from people in all walks of life.

6. Anticipation Is Cheaper and Better

Recent state-building experience is mostly in postwar countries, which pose far more obvious, thorny, and expensive problems than states that are merely fragile and have not yet suffered all the depredations of armed conflict. What would happen if, instead of waiting until things go to hell in a handbasket, we made a serious effort to anticipate problems and resolve them before conflict, mass murder, state collapse, or some other catastrophe renders the situation difficult to manage? Could states be strengthened in ways that would enable ethnic groups to live peaceably with each other, prevent the harboring of international terrorists, avoid the massive atrocities against civilians that are a hallmark of contemporary wars, and remove autocrats before they do irreparable harm? Could conflicts be resolved in ways that avoid violence? Would we just be wasting our time and effort, or might we find a better and cheaper approach?

In 1996, Michael Lund, one of America's leading prevention experts, suggested that conflict prevention would become more frequent and widely supported, more cost-effective, more advisable, and more politically attractive.[1] That has not happened for the United States, which has deployed its forces in nine wars since the fall of the Berlin Wall: Panama (1989), the Gulf War (1991), Somalia (1992–95), Haiti (1994–95), Bosnia and Herzegovina (1995), Serbia (1999), Afghanistan (2001), Iraq (2003), and Libya (2011). This count does not include no-fly zones, evacuations, embassy protection, targeted counterterrorism operations, drone strikes (which have occurred in Afghanistan, Pakistan, Iraq, Yemen, Libya, and Somalia), preventive deployments, and airlift provided to soldiers of other countries.

Recent American wars have killed relatively few Americans. In Afghanistan, the number who have died in combat was under 1,500 over ten years, a small fraction of the more than 47,000 killed in combat in Vietnam. In Iraq, the number of combat deaths was just over 3,500 over eight years. Five thousand Americans killed in Iraq and Afghanistan is still a large and regrettable number, but it is far smaller than the numbers killed in comparable wars a generation earlier. Wars like those in Bosnia, Serbia, and Libya saw no U.S. combat deaths. The numbers in Panama, Somalia, and Haiti were relatively small.[2] War is never safe, but it has become much safer for American soldiers, sailors, and airmen than at any other time in American history.

Technology has greatly reduced the risks of combat to American troops, who are professionals (not draftees) far better equipped and trained than their recent adversaries. Precision bombing from manned aircraft and remotely piloted drones avoid risk to Americans even as they greatly increase the likelihood of death and destruction to their targets (and whoever happens to be nearby). Robotic warfare also changes public perceptions and sensitivities.[3] There has been far less concern about the "drone war" in Pakistan, which for years was officially a secret but widely reported, than there would have been if manned aircraft were being used. President Obama faces nothing like the criticism aimed at President Nixon forty years earlier for the secret carpet bombing of Cambodia. Obama in October 2011 sent one hundred American troops to help track down Joseph Kony. Americans reacted little. The number was small and they expected few if any casualties.[4]

The net result of hi-tech warfare is to lower the threshold for going to war and reduce attention to preventing it. I know this firsthand. In late 1997, I was an American diplomat without an assignment. I asked to work on Kosovo, at the time a province of Serbia within what was still called Yugoslavia. I had just finished a year working in the intelligence bureau of the State Department, where I had monitored the rise of the Kosovo Liberation Army's violent rebellion against the Yugoslav authorities. I asked for no staff, no title, and no budget. I said I just wanted to see if we could prevent war by diplomatic means. The answer was no, I could not be allowed to work on Kosovo. The reason: I was a senior officer. It would attract too much attention to the issue if I worked on it. Less than a year and half later, the United States led NATO to war against Yugoslavia because of its behavior in Kosovo. No Americans were killed in that conflict, which the Americans fought from the air, but it lasted for seventy-eight days, killed about five hundred civilians, and had cost the United States more than $6 billion by the end of 2002.[5]

On the eve of the Iraq war, my colleagues and I at the United States Institute of Peace sought to brief the National Security Council on a plan to support an indigenous Iraqi rebellion against Saddam Hussein. Our intention was that it be nonviolent, like most of the Arab Spring rebellions that occurred in 2011. We had been successful in 1998 in convincing the U.S. government to support ultimately successful nonviolent protests against Slobodan Milosevic, and we hoped to do likewise in Iraq.[6] We were in touch with courageous Iraqis who claimed to be ready to make it happen. I readily admit it may have been impractical and unrealistic, but it deserved a hearing, if only to ensure that no stone was left unturned, no possibility for avoiding war not considered. The briefing never occurred.

Anticipatory Foreign Policy

There are often better and cheaper ways than war, but they require two things that are in short supply: anticipation and strategic patience. Both are difficult for the U.S. government, which runs on the adrenaline rush of the minute-to-minute Twitter feed, the hourly news broadcast, the daily press briefing, the weekly cycle of Sunday talk shows, and the more or less monthly cycle of presidential popularity polls. The American political environment is not one that lends itself to careful deliberation or waiting for good results, as President Obama discovered when he took a few weeks to reconsider policy in Afghanistan.[7]

The lack of attention and resources devoted in the United States to preventing conflict is not due to its failure to produce cost-effective results elsewhere. Two-thirds of international boundary conflicts (nineteen cases) in the period 1945–2000 were "brought to a settled or nonactive situation, largely through negotiation."[8] Negotiations don't often cost more than $10 million. Wars and their aftermath do not come much cheaper than $10 billion, including the impact on the societies that host them. Ignoring the human costs, this still means a gambler would do well if the odds of success were as little as one in one thousand. Many studies confirm cost-effectiveness of negotiated solutions relative to war.[9] Who would not try the negotiation route?

The answer is, people in a hurry. The many accounts of the American decision to go to war in Iraq, both from people who agree with it and those who disagree, have one thing in common: President George W. Bush concluded early that war was the solution.[10] He did not seriously consider alternatives. He did not want to postpone. He did not want to give the UN nuclear inspectors more time to investigate Iraq's nuclear weapons program. He believed, or at least he says he believed, that time was of the essence to prevent the threat of weapons of mass destruction in the hands of someone who had used them against Iraq's own citizens in the past.[11] Condoleezza Rice, then national security adviser, put it graphically: "we don't want the smoking gun to be a mushroom cloud."[12]

Quite apart from the merits of the particular cases, urgency also underlay President Obama's attitude on Libya. Muammar Qaddafi had threatened to attack the civilian population of Benghazi, and his forces stood within striking distance.[13] Obama had dragged his feet until then, apparently convinced that Defense Secretary Gates was correct to say that the United States did not have vital interests in Libya. But Qaddafi's threat gave new urgency to the situation, encouraged the Arab League to endorse a "no fly" zone, and spurred the Security Council to ask an unidentified group of member states (widely known to be NATO) to lead a response using "all necessary means," diplomatic code for the use of force.[14]

What does it take to prevent presidents, or other national leaders, from getting into a situation where they feel that rushing to use force is the only option?

There are three broad categories of things that can prevent violent conflict. Experts characterize them this way:[15]

1. **Systemic: mitigate global risks.** This is done by building economic, demographic, legal, environmental, trade, and other systems whose good

functioning contributes to maintaining peaceful relations among states and discourages armed conflict.

India's burgeoning business class begged New Delhi not to go to war when conflict with Pakistan threatened in 2001 and 2002.[16] The cost to business would have been too high. Even without war, the confrontation cost billions.[17] Europe's long peace after World War II is generally attributed to NATO and the European Union, as they eliminated military rivalry among their members and created an economic and political space in which Europeans could see the clear benefits of peace. Asia's peace since the Vietnam War is at least in part due to a system of American hegemony, accepted until recently in exchange for other benefits by both China and Japan.[18]

> **2. Structural: mitigate societal risks.** This is done by achieving (before state collapse or mass atrocities) the same end states we discussed in chapter 4 as important to reestablish after a war: a safe and secure environment, rule of law, stable governance, a sustainable economy, and social well-being.

Several key states in Asia (South Korea, Taiwan, Malaysia, Indonesia) embarked on reforms aimed in these directions during the 1980s and 1990s, helping to extend one of the most peaceful periods in Asian history. It was the failure of reforms of this sort that led to the Arab Spring rebellions that broke out in 2011. Or more precisely, the pursuit of economic reforms (in Egypt, Tunisia, Bahrain, and Syria) without corresponding political reforms caused limited distribution of economic benefits to result in unsustainable and exclusionary crony capitalism. The autocrats enriched themselves, their friends, and sometimes their coreligionists without risking opening up the political system. Convincing autocrats to take the risk of inclusive political as well as economic reform before they face revolution, state collapse, or invasion by others is a key element in preventing future risks.[19]

> **3. Operational: halt and reverse escalation of crises.** This is done by facilitating solutions before parties reach the stage of rushing to the use of force, providing incentives for agreement rather than violence, strengthening

those who support peaceful resolution and weakening those who don't, restricting the capacity to wage war, and protecting civilians exposed to threats of violence.

One example of "operational" prevention in recent decades was the American "Christmas warning" to Slobodan Milosevic in 1992 against attacking Kosovo, which was matched with an inverse warning to its Albanian leader, Ibrahim Rugova, against resort to violence.[20] Another example was the UN's one and still only explicitly "preventive" peacekeeping mission to Macedonia (known as UNPREDEP).[21] But such efforts on a less grand scale are common. The UN Human Rights Council, for example, sought in 2011 to deploy observers to Syria, in an effort to prevent the regime from continuing to use force against peaceful demonstrators.[22] The Arab League eventually succeeded where the UN failed, but security conditions deteriorated as the government cracked down and the Arab League observers were unable to stay. Then the UN took over again, only to fail once again. Diplomatic observers deployed to Kosovo in 1998 did not prevent war, but they did clarify the facts of the situation and help to mobilize Western support for the NATO operation against Yugoslavia.[23]

Many well-established diplomatic practices contribute to anticipation and strategic patience. Some would argue that *all* diplomacy in one way or another is aimed at preventing resort to violence. But some preventive features of the modern diplomatic landscape are so new, or so far from our normal experience, that they require further explanation: *the responsibility to protect* civilian populations from mass violence, an innovative principle first explicitly applied in Libya and much in discussion during the Syrian revolution; *conflict prediction* is a longstanding hope that modern statistical approaches are beginning to fulfill.

Responsibility to Protect

The UN Security Council resolution authorizing "all necessary means" to protect civilians in Libya was the first time that the Security Council explicitly acknowledged a commitment the UN General Assembly

Summit had made in 2005 to the "responsibility to protect" (R2P in dip-lomatic parlance). This is today a vital concept in preventing violent repression and the risks to international peace and security that it causes.

The "responsibility to protect" lies in the first instance with the states in which people reside. The UN General Assembly put it this way:

> Each individual State has the responsibility to protect its populations from genocide, war crimes, ethnic cleansing and crimes against humanity. This responsibility entails the *prevention* [my emphasis] of such crimes, includ-ing their incitement, through appropriate and necessary means. We accept that responsibility and will act in accordance with it.

Along with this preventive responsibility for individual states, the Gen-eral Assembly asked that other states (we call them "the international community") should "encourage and help States to exercise this respon-sibility." It added that other action could be taken, *if there is a failure* to protect:

> The international community, through the United Nations, also has the responsibility to use appropriate diplomatic, humanitarian and other peace-ful means . . . to help protect populations from genocide, war crimes, ethnic cleansing and crimes against humanity. In this context, we are prepared to take collective action, in a timely and decisive manner, through the Security Council, in accordance with the Charter, including Chapter VII [which pro-vides for the use of force], on a case-by-case basis and in cooperation with relevant regional organizations as appropriate, should peaceful means be inad-equate and national authorities manifestly fail to protect their populations from genocide, war crimes, ethnic cleansing and crimes against humanity.

Then it returned to the need for prevention:

> We also intend to commit ourselves, as necessary and appropriate, to help-ing States build capacity to protect their populations from genocide, war crimes, ethnic cleansing and crimes against humanity and to assisting those which are under stress *before crises and conflicts break out* [my emphasis].[24]

Too often, "responsibility to protect" is viewed as *only* a means by which a group of states gets to use military force against another state under

Chapter VII of the UN Charter, if authorized by the Security Council. But that is a last resort when the responsibility to protect fails—used explicitly to date only against Muammar Qaddafi in Libya—not the sum total of efforts to protect, which should include "diplomatic, humanitarian and other peaceful means."

Still, the responsibility to protect is a sharp break with the past, when national sovereignty and the principle of non-interference in the internal affairs of another state were regarded as sacrosanct. Its adoption in 2005 stemmed from the experience of the 1990s. That was when the international community failed to intervene in Rwanda, where eight hundred thousand people were murdered,[25] and hesitated to intervene in Bosnia and Kosovo, allowing months and even years of war crimes, mass atrocities, and removal of people from their homes based on ethnicity, a practice generally referred to as "ethnic cleansing." Diplomatic and humanitarian initiatives were frequent and vigorous, but without the backing of force they failed. Benghazi was saved in 2011 because the western Bosnian town of Gorazde was overrun and eight thousand of its male inhabitants slaughtered fifteen years earlier.[26] Likewise, president-elect Alassane Ouattara in Ivory Coast benefited from armed intervention by the UN and France in early 2011 against defeated incumbent Laurent Gbagbo, who precipitated a civil war in order to hold on to his presidency after losing it at the polls.[27]

It is still difficult to mobilize the international community to act on its responsibility to protect, and even when it does the practical problems are significant.[28] Libya was an unusual case in which even the Russians and Chinese, the usual defenders of national sovereignty and the principle of non-interference in the internal affairs of another state, at least momentarily decided it would be a good idea to stop Muammar Qaddafi from killing Libyans. In Syria the Russians have resisted a comparable decision to use force against Bashar al-Assad, who from early in 2011 through the first half of 2013 killed more than eighty thousand of his fellow citizens. Russian resentment of what Moscow regarded as NATO overreach in Libya as well as the Russian naval base on Syria's Mediterranean coast and arms sales to Syria have kept the Russians from abandoning Assad. The Arab League, which deployed international observers but failed to stop the fighting, has not requested armed intervention, as it did in the case of Libya. The responsibility to protect, like many other diplomatic principles, depends for its application on particular circumstances. It is not automatic.

But it is clearly intended to anticipate and prevent. Does it contribute to strategic patience, or does it encourage war? The answer is, neither. A careful look at the historical data demonstrates that neither the frequency of interventions nor their character (more powerful country against less powerful country, for example) has changed as a result of the responsibility to protect.[29] There is, however, evidence that intervention may in the short term increase violence while in the longer term decreasing it, especially if the intervenor is "neutral."[30] What we do not know is whether the responsibility to protect has discouraged some autocrats from mistreating their own populations, which is its primary purpose. It clearly has not prevented President Bashar al-Assad from attacking his own people in Syria. Nor has it prevented President Omar al-Bashir of Sudan from attacking his own people in Darfur and South Kordofan, provinces that have seen remarkable military brutality against civilians. Taking their cue from NATO's Kosovo intervention in 1999, which lacked prior UN Security Council approval, some observers would like R2P to allow under clearly specified conditions for "low-intensity" military action (no-fly zones and humanitarian safe havens) when the Security Council is unable to act.[31]

Predicting Catastrophe

Can we foresee genocide, war crimes, ethnic cleansing, and crimes against humanity and take measures to prevent them? Not, for sure, with 100 percent accuracy, but the techniques for doing so have improved over the last ten years. Political upheaval is not predictable. But once it occurs, the consequent risks are significant. This is a highly technical area of endeavor that has produced various "indices" intended to identify countries most likely to suffer political instability, state fragility and failure, risks to minorities, genocide, and politicide (which targets particular political, as opposed to ethnic, groups).[32] A composite index based on five other indices found in 2009 the following eight countries at the greatest risk: Afghanistan, Myanmar, Democratic Republic of the Congo, Iraq, Pakistan, Sri Lanka, Somalia, and Sudan. Another twenty-five countries follow.[33]

It is instructive that some of America's biggest challenges appear on this list. Afghanistan and Iraq are two countries in which the United States has been a belligerent over most of the past decade. Pakistan, where Osama bin Laden was killed, is believed still to harbor some of our deadliest enemies. America has used drone strikes there more than three hundred times since 2004. American forces and their proxies are also active in Somalia, where extremist groups have tried to take advantage of state failure to establish a harsh version of Islamic rule. This should be no surprise: weak and failing states, though not necessarily the weakest and most failed, present real national security risks, because they are unable to enforce law and order.[34] Early attention to human rights abuses may help to prevent the emergence of serious threats.[35]

What this list is telling us is that things could still get worse in these places before they get better. American military action might even be making things worse if it displaces or weakens local governing capacity and social order required to contain or discourage extremists. So we should be integrating prevention into our strategies for dealing with them. We need not only to win wars in Iraq, Afghanistan, Pakistan, Yemen, and Somalia but also to leave behind viable states that will fulfill the responsibility to protect their own populations.[36]

Let's leave aside those countries in which the United States is already militarily active. What capacity do we have to prevent future problems from arising in a place like Myanmar (formerly called Burma), where a military dictatorship governed for many years and waged counterinsurgency campaigns against armed ethnic rebels, or Sri Lanka, which in 2010 defeated a decades-long ethnic rebellion using military force? What about Sudan, where independence of the South has not ended instability? What tools are we lacking?

The international community for decades maintained sanctions on Myanmar in an effort to get it to stop abusing its own population, respect human rights, recognize the results of elections, and begin to open up to the rest of the world. For a long time, these efforts brought only modest results. Some thought them counterproductive. But a serious reform process has now started, one that has the support of both domestic reformers like Aung San Suu Kyi and major elements of the international community.[37] The wheels of diplomacy grind slow, but the military regime that has governed Myanmar for fifty years seems to be yielding gradually. If diplomacy works in Myanmar, it will save lives, cost little, end armed ethnic rebellions that have plagued parts of the country, and avoid a major international humanitarian effort that might otherwise be required.

The issue is whether Myanmar will be able to undertake political and economic reforms, and end two still-ongoing communal conflicts, without suffering catastrophic collapse of the state or the economy, both of which are unquestionably fragile after years of self-isolation and repression. This is *not* a vital strategic interest of the United States, whose national security would not be threatened even if Myanmar descends into chaos. Myanmar is, however, an opportunity. Washington will try to provide assistance that supports the reform process, gradually relieves Myanmar of sanctions, and weans Myanmar from its dependence on China. The United States will not be alone in this effort. Europe and the UN and its "specialized agencies" will do much of the hard work of encouraging and assisting reform in Myanmar.

The government of Sri Lanka in 2009 won a twenty-six-year war against Tamil Tiger separatists, who sought independence from the majority-Sinhalese (mostly Buddhist) country. The postwar period has so far seen more triumphalism and vindictiveness than accountability and reconciliation. The issue now is whether Sri Lanka's government will move in an authoritarian direction and even refuse to give up harsh military domination of former Tamil Tiger–held areas. International Crisis Group, a nongovernmental (private, nonprofit) conflict-prevention organization, suggests a classic diplomatic approach known as "conditionality": "Partners, especially India, Japan, the U.S. and U.K., European Union (EU) and UN, should send a strong message against increasing authoritarianism, condition aid on transparency and restored civilian administration in north and east and support accountability, including an international inquiry into alleged atrocities by both sides in the war's final stages."[38] Again, American interests in Sri Lanka are not vital—autocracy there would not harm American national security in any direct way, but it could lead to problems in relations between Sri Lanka and India. The United States will do best if it can join with others in conditioning aid to Sri Lanka, a multilateral (as opposed to unilateral) effort to affect its behavior.

More is at stake for the United States in Sudan, which until the negotiated independence of Southern Sudan in 2011 was the largest country in Africa and held large oil reserves of particular interest to China. A Washington special envoy was instrumental in negotiating the 2005 Comprehensive Peace Agreement that ended a decades-long civil war between Sudan's Khartoum-based, Islamist government and the mostly non-Muslim rebels of the Sudan Peoples' Liberation Army (SPLA).[39] This was done without military intervention, which was frequently suggested but never undertaken. The agreement also provided for a referendum on independence that southerners approved overwhelmingly in February 2011.

Independence for the South has not solved all of Sudan's problems, which threaten to spill over its borders and affect a large part of northeastern Africa. UN missions in both Darfur, a region in western Sudan, and in newly independent Southern Sudan are trying hard to prevent further conflict. There is concern as well about Khartoum's military action against ethnic groups that fought with the SPLA during the civil war but live in northern areas along the border with the newly independent South. The International Criminal Court has indicted the president of Sudan for war crimes allegedly committed in Darfur. The United States and the international community have used sanctions to try to affect Khartoum's behavior, with only modest success.

These three examples of possible future conflict illustrate many of the nonmilitary instruments available to affect the behavior of autocrats and limit the risk of mass atrocities, genocide, and state collapse. Sanctions, conditionality, UN missions, aid, criminal indictments, and special envoys are all important tools of modern diplomacy. Do they really work?

Violence Is Declining, for Good Reasons

It is difficult to prove in any given instance that diplomacy, state-building, foreign assistance, peacekeeping, or other civilian peace-building tools have prevented violence, and how much they have prevented. Proving negatives is always problematic, and there will be many claims of responsibility if war does not occur. But there is good statistical evidence of a decline in the duration, intensity, and deadliness of wars since the fall of the Berlin Wall. Andrew Mack writes: "In the post–Cold War world, wars are mostly fought within, not between, states and by small armies mostly equipped with small arms and light weapons. While often characterized by extreme brutality towards civilians, they have killed relatively few people compared to the major wars of the Cold War period."[40] Wars today are still nasty and brutish, but less frequent and shorter, with the obvious recent exceptions of Iraq and Afghanistan.

There are many reasons for this: stronger states (especially in Asia), the end of the free world/Soviet rivalry, more economic prosperity in more parts of the world. Among the reasons for the relative and spreading peace of the 1990s and 2000s are precisely the civilian tools we have been discussing. This "increase in the level of international security activism" includes more UN and non-UN peace operations (including a dramatic increase in the number of UN operations in which the use of force is authorized), as well as dramatic increases in the numbers of UN special representatives doing security-related tasks, multilateral groups with security mandates, multilateral sanctions, and efforts to disarm, demobilize, and reintegrate former combatants. Governments and the UN are acting much more readily and aggressively to try to bring wars to an end and keep them from reigniting. Two observers conclude: "the United Nations' 100,000 deployed peacekeepers have measurably improved the success of peace agreements in civil wars."[41] In the period 1945–1990, 45 percent of 137 international disputes were brought to some level of success (cease-fire, partial settlement, full settlement) by mediation.[42]

In the post–Cold War period, there are striking examples of both success and failure in preventing conflicts. Three countries divided by Cold War politics saw different outcomes: Yemen, Germany, and Korea. After repeated border wars and several failed negotiations, Yemen reunited peacefully in 1990, but it was kept united only by military means several years later, when the South tried to secede. A separatist movement in the South, an insurgency in the North, and al-Qaeda in the hinterland still plague Yemen. Germany is the classic case of peaceful reunification, without any formal international mediation but at high financial cost. Korea is still divided and heavily armed on both sides, but the military incidents between north and south have fallen considerably short of anything that would be considered "war," even though dozens have been killed.[43]

The outcomes were also varied after the breakup of the Soviet Union, which at the time many anticipated would cause widespread and large-scale warfare. Instead, some of the wars, when they occurred, were relatively small: in Azerbaijan, Georgia, and Moldova. International mediation by a regional organization—the Organization for Security and Cooperation in Europe—helped prevent war in Crimea. Tatarstan and Russia avoided war on their own. Russia went to war in Chechnya, twice, at great cost to both Russians and Chechnyans.

What we have is a record of considerable success in preventing conflict, when the effort and required resources can be mobilized in a timely way. The earlier international mediation efforts occur, the better.[44] Relatively little effort, however, is aimed at preventing war before any violence has broken out. This is due in part to the difficulties of predicting where that might happen, but also to the difficulty of mobilizing resources internationally to prevent a hypothetical conflict when there are many already ongoing. No UN member likes to have its internal conflicts brought up in the General Assembly or the Security Council as a potential threat to international peace and security. Many have a friend or two among the five permanent members ready to block any serious action to prevent brewing conflict—witness Syria's successful effort to get Russia and China to block even a relatively mild denunciation of its violence against peaceful demonstrators in 2011 and 2012.

If systematic prevention efforts are what the current international system still needs, the burden will fall mainly to individual states, often those that carry greater political, military, and economic weight. The United States is first among its peers in all these respects, and will remain so for several decades more. Anticipation is cheaper and better, but our current civilian foreign policy institutions are not configured to deliver the goods. They are reactive, not proactive, and hamstrung in many different ways. In the next chapters we will consider in detail what is lacking and how we can begin to supply the institutions needed.

7. Five Missing Pieces

If an anticipatory foreign policy is cheaper and better in ensuring national security, what are the capabilities that might make it possible?

There are far too many ingredients to discuss them all: humanitarian, intelligence, diplomatic, economic, political, and military means all need to be brought to bear. Much of this capacity already exists and works well once mobilized. Humanitarian and military organizations work with amazing speed when Myanmar floods, a tsunami strikes the Indian Ocean, or an earthquake shatters Kashmir. Diplomats and spies work every day to detect problems and shore up weak states. There is a vast literature on what works and does not work in promoting economic development, with small-scale, community-based projects as well as policies that promote trade and investment winning the day, at least for now.[1] The international mechanisms for organizing elections are amazingly well oiled, as the successful Libyan election of July 2012 demonstrated.[2]

These capabilities have grown organically, the way the weeds in your garden grow, guided only by their own requirements and without much attention to the broader strategic end states outlined in chapter 4. There are bare patches in our international garden, and others where the jumble is so intense that it needs sorting out, pruning, and replanting. We'll discuss some of the jumble and the bare patches in this chapter and consider in chapter 10 how the U.S. government garden would need to be reconfigured to fix the problems.

There are many weak or missing capabilities, but five specific areas important to preventing future threats to American national security are badly configured at present: mobilizing early action, supporting democracy, reforming security forces, countering violent extremism, and promoting citizen-to-citizen outreach between Americans and non-Americans. These activities all lie at the margins of traditional foreign policy thinking and practice. It is not surprising they have been ignored. But unless we strengthen them, we will not be able to operate in a preventive mode that is cheaper and better than what we have been doing. As always, military capabilities shape the environment in which each of these activities is pursued, but none of them are primarily (or properly) military responsibilities. All require civilian capabilities that are starkly inadequate or hopelessly confused in our current institutions.

Mobilizing Early Action

An anticipatory foreign policy would require that we have the capability to look forward at least a few years. Statistical and other techniques for anticipating problems have improved in recent decades, and various watch lists of countries at risk have proliferated. Classified versions circulate in secret within the U.S. government, so as not to upset foreign governments. Also confidential are the conflict assessments U.S. government agencies undertake. They have become more frequent in recent years, using standardized frameworks.[3] Government people know that prevention is cheaper than cure.

It is not easy to mobilize preventive action, but Congress has taken an important step by authorizing a Global Security Contingency Fund that could in principle make substantial resources available.[4] Otherwise, existing U.S. government mechanisms for turning early warning into early action have barely budged. A Council on Foreign Relations review found that "The United States has considerable influence and resources at its disposal to carry out various forms of preventive action. What it lacks are effective organizational arrangements to make the most of this latent capacity and help overcome some of the more common hindrances to preventive action."[5] These can be provided, the council report suggests, by rearranging government agencies and programs without major new expenditure of resources.[6]

Under administrations both Democratic and Republican, the U.S. government remains preoccupied with immediate crises. Its leadership rarely looks forward more than six months to anticipate problems, and it quite rightly focuses on areas where U.S. interests are clearly and immediately at risk. The many watch lists and intelligence reports fall quietly on the desks of people too pressed to pay much attention to them. Some high-priority issues—like the disposition of nuclear weapons in the Soviet Union at the end of the Cold War—get prompt and effective treatment. Others, like the rebellion in Chechnya, are left to other powers to handle, or bungle, at great human cost.[7]

Sometimes real threats to the United States like al-Qaeda are left to grow far too long.[8] By the time an issue attracts much attention, it is often too late for preventive action. The aftermath of genocide like the one in Rwanda has lasted two decades, with the *genocidaires* and their adversaries still causing death and destruction in important parts of the Democratic Republic of the Congo even today. The Lord's Resistance Army, which the United States ignored for more than a decade, is now the subject of an international manhunt, assisted by U.S. troops.

The most recent effort to institutionalize prevention in the U.S. government comes in the form of an Atrocities Prevention Board.[9] This is intended to ensure that events with the potential to cause mass atrocities get the early attention required to mobilize an effective response.[10] What is still missing are established "trip wires" to trigger action. Without them, an autocrat like Bashar al-Assad can kill more than eighty thousand of his own citizens without precipitating an international response. The board risks becoming an atrocities detection board, which would be no better than the many interagency policy committees of the National Security Council. Its creation does, however, reflect a change of focus.[11] "Responsibility to protect" is having a real impact on how governments think about their responsibilities, and even how the United States conceives its role in the world.

Supporting Democracy

Democracy promotion is well established as a U.S. foreign policy objective. "Promote democracy and human rights abroad" is the formulation in Barack Obama's 2010 *National Security Strategy,* which adds, "Political systems that protect universal rights are ultimately more stable, successful, and secure."[12] This is arguably as strong as President George W. Bush's prior formula, in 2002 and 2006: "Expand the circle of development by opening societies and building the infrastructure of democracy."[13] The roots of this democratic commitment run deep, at least as deep as Woodrow Wilson's 1917 speech seeking a declaration of war against Germany so that the world might be "made safe for democracy." Wilson claimed, "A steadfast concert for peace can never be maintained except by a partnership of democratic nations."[14] But its origins lie in the American Revolution, which proclaimed the universal principle that "all men are created equal." If you accept that (and think it covers women as well), you are condemned to favoring democracy. We were thinking of ourselves as "conquering people into liberty" (whether they agreed or not) as early as 1775.[15]

There is ample empirical evidence in favor of what later generations have labeled "democratic peace theory."[16] Established democracies rarely, if ever, go to war against each other, though they do go to war against non-democracies. Newly born, not-yet-consolidated democracies are also prone to conflict. These academic caveats are often overlooked in the political world, where the conviction that making the world more democratic will over the long term reduce conflict and benefit the United States is dominant among both Democrats and Republicans, with minorities in both parties doubting that it can or should be done. In fact, the world has become both more democratic and more peaceful since the end of the Cold War.[17]

But even if agreed in principle, there is often controversy about specific cases, since short-term U.S. interests are not always well served in elections. The anti-Israel Islamist group Hamas came to power in the Palestinian Authority in 2006 in an election, then kicked its competitors out of Gaza. Democracy promotion is also fraught with difficulty. Does it require a minimal level of economic development? Can it be exported? Is it consistent with traditional values in non-Western countries? Does it need to be generated locally? To what extent does local culture need to adapt to what the West considers democratic norms like a free press, gender equality, and freedom of religion? What role do elections play, and under what circumstances can they be regarded as democratic? What electoral systems are most appropriate? Should American embassies be involved, or should democracy support be done through NGOS?

The Bush administration's effort to associate democracy promotion with the war in Iraq generated strong criticism, as did America's effort to export democracy after 9/11 while undertaking counterterrorism measures at home and abroad that appeared profoundly contradictory.[18] President Obama minimized the "d" word in his Cairo speech reaching out to Muslims in June 2009, though his presentation was imbued with references to democratic principles.[19]

There is nevertheless a clear post–Cold War record of nonviolent pro-democracy movements succeeding and benefiting the United States.[20] The fall of the Berlin Wall, the reunification of Germany, the dissolution of the Soviet Union, and the democratization of Eastern Europe brought the United States enormous benefits, removing its Cold War rival from the map, gaining it new and supportive allies, resolving the German question peacefully (and within NATO), and extending the democratic space called the European Union five hundred miles eastward. While there have been ups and downs, on the whole the United States has also benefited from more or less successful (and more or less nonviolent) revolutions in Serbia (2000), Georgia (2003), Ukraine (2004), and Lebanon (2005).

The "Arab Spring" (or "awakening," the term experts prefer) that started in January and February of 2011 is the most important wave of democratization since the liberation of Eastern Europe at the end of the Cold War. While its manifestations in Tunisia, Egypt, Libya, Bahrain, Yemen, and Syria have each been distinct, they share this: they took Washington by surprise and owed little to its democracy support programs.[21] Despite many years of pressing for reform and providing democracy assistance in a number of the countries involved, neither American officials nor scholars anticipated the uprisings. Nor did the autocrats in charge. No one did.

The first official American reactions were surprise and hesitation rather than enthusiasm. The Obama administration shifted its stance within weeks, helped to convince Egypt's Hosni Mubarak to step down in favor of a military-guided transition, and supported the NATO effort that assisted Libyans to remove Muammar Qaddafi by force. But it remains wary of the impact of regime change in Bahrain, which hosts the U.S. Fifth Fleet, and Yemen, where it failed to back the street demonstrators and opted instead to support a gradualist Gulf Cooperation Council transition plan. Yemen, after all, does battle against al-Qaeda in the Arabian Peninsula, an organization that has attempted to attack the American homeland several times.

There are good reasons for the U.S. government to hesitate. The Arab uprisings grew from demands for dignity and may offer a general "counter-jihad" narrative that provides an alternative to violent Islamic extremism.[22] But illiberal Islamist political forces, repressed for decades but themselves unprepared to defend civil liberties, have emerged as strong players in Egypt.[23] Relatively moderate Islamists won a plurality in Tunisia's constituent assembly, which is struggling to write its new constitution. Resentment of past American support for Arab autocracies and for Israel is palpable among many Arab awakening protesters. New Arab democracies will need to be much more sensitive to domestic political opinion, which is strongly pro-Palestine and anti-Israel. The transition from Arab autocracies to Arab democracies is likely to raise many difficulties that will need careful diplomatic and political management as well as economic and humanitarian assistance.[24] Relationships with the United States are fraught, so even assistance becomes problematic.[25]

It is hard to be upbeat about the effectiveness of American government support to democracy abroad, even if there are notable successes.[26] Knowledgeable commentators are not.[27] Neither the Obama administration nor its predecessors have straightened out the "democracy bureaucracy," which democracy advocates describe as "politicized, unwieldy, misunderstood, uncoordinated, and characterized by scant strategic thinking and a cumbersome management system."[28] Embassies and diplomatic instruments have roles to play, but they have to play them with skill and finesse.[29] One of the critical issues is targeting assistance to non-state actors, a task that is often not suitable for the U.S. government. It has to remain on good terms with many autocrats, until they fall. Even non-official entities run into difficulty, as the Egyptian government raids on National Democratic Institute and International Republican Institute offices in Cairo in December 2011 illustrate.[30] Democracy may be in our foreign policy interest, but how best to make it happen is not obvious. And the relationship of politically focused assistance to the broader development assistance enterprise is also fraught.[31]

Reforming Security Forces

One of the main complaints in virtually all the popular rebellions of the past two decades is the behavior of the state's forces responsible for internal security. In democratic societies, the police pledge to "serve and protect" the population, though of course there may be instances of abuse. In autocratic societies, the police, non-uniformed internal security services, and even the army serve and protect those who hold power, not the population or the country. Changing the mind-set of security services from protection of rulers to protection of the ruled is vital to postwar reconstruction wherever it has been undertaken in recent decades.[32]

Can it be done preventively? Certainly not in the absence of overall movement toward a truly more democratic regime. Autocrats need protection for good reason: they lack the legitimacy with the population that comes from free and fair elections in an open society. There is really no point in equipping and training their police forces as if they exist for any reason other than enabling people without democratic legitimacy to stay in power. The United States made the mistake of equipping and training security forces in Latin American autocracies for many years, leading to abuses that caused the Congress to end funding for USAID participation in police training.[33]

But once a society has made a clear decision in favor of democracy, including not only free and fair elections but also protection of human rights, transforming its police and other internal security services becomes an important goal. This is not merely, or even primarily, a matter of providing better guns and body armor, or even of training the police to be kinder and gentler to the population, though all of that may be needed. It also requires institutionalization of standards for how the internal security forces behave under civilian oversight, usually exercised by defense and interior ministries and ultimately by parliament and the courts.

The Centre for Democratic Control of Armed Forces (DCAF) is the leading international organization for this kind of "security sector reform." It is a Swiss-led foundation supported by sixty-one countries, including the United States. Its remit is a broad one:

Parliamentary oversight

Police and border management

Defense reform

Intelligence governance

Privatization of security

Gender and security

Human rights and the rule of law

Civil society capacity-building

DCAF is, however, a relatively modest organization, spending about $50 million per year worldwide. Its capacity is therefore limited, even if its mandate is broad.[34]

There is no counterpart organization in the United States, where these functions, and the capability to train others to fulfill them, are spread widely around the federal and state governments, with many gaps and overlaps. The Justice Department is certainly the lead "human rights and rule of law" organization, but it has direct control only over the U.S. Marshals and the Federal Bureau of Investigation, neither of which is a community-based police force. The federal government in fact has no direct control over most American police forces, which belong to the states and local communities. Guarding American borders is a function that belongs to the Department of Homeland Security. The Defense Department oversees America's armed forces, but the United States lacks a national civilian institution to oversee its many police forces. Almost all other countries call those institutions "interior" ministries. Germany has nineteen of them, one at the federal level and eighteen at the "state" level.

This complex institutional morass constrains what the United States can do for security sector reform, and how it does it, abroad. The U.S. military has made training of the Iraqi and Afghan armies an important objective in recent years, but there is no comparable institution to train police, which is done mainly through contractors. Without appropriate training, experience, and background, they have often performed badly.[35] Defense and interior ministries—vital to civilian oversight of military and police forces—have been staffed by a mixture of contractors and military officers, few of whom have ever worked in an interior ministry. The performance of contractors in these roles has also fallen far short of the ideal.[36]

Defense and interior are among the most difficult of all public-sector institutions to build. This is because they have to make a lot of decisions whose results are difficult to measure.[37] This creates uncertainties about performance, reduces the likelihood of improving it, and increases the difficulty of giving instructions to those who are supposed to carry out the tasks. But without civilian control of police and armed forces, there is little hope that a democratic system can be established or maintained.

Countering Violent Extremism

Even with the best police and military forces, countering violent extremism is not only a matter of bullets.[38] The U.S. government has done surprisingly little to apply what is known about effective counter-efforts, even after 9/11. The State Department coordinator for counterterrorism, Daniel Benjamin, claimed on March 10, 2010, at a Senate hearing on countering radicalization that "there is a broad understanding . . . about the strategic nature of this endeavor, and I think there is, really, broad understanding, across the executive branch, of the importance of this work and just how vital it is for our success against the terrorist threat." He went on to cite $100,000 allocations to ambassadors for this work in fiscal year 2011, totaling $15 million worldwide, which is less than the cost of a few drone strikes. In a clear breach with normal practice when testifying as an administration witness, Benjamin added: "We are resource-constrained in this area, and we would really appreciate any support."[39] Administration witnesses are supposed to support the president's proposed budget, not declare it grossly inadequate, even if it is.

Independent experts are no more enthusiastic about government programs in this area: "despite the sharp rise in terrorist plots and cases of homegrown radicalization, specific policies and programs aimed squarely at countering the radical narrative remain few and far between."[40] Scott Atran, professor of anthropology and psychology at the University of Michigan and John Jay College of Criminal Justice, says succinctly of countering violent extremism: "There is no program out there for that, that I see."[41]

This is despite the existence of careful research and well-documented successes. Community-based remedies requiring more soft power than hard are known to be effective.[42] Terrorist groups are rarely defeated by military means, which are the principal means the U.S. government is using against them not only in Iraq and Afghanistan but also in Yemen, Somalia, and elsewhere. They far more often join a political process or find defeat at the hands of law enforcement authorities.[43] "War on terror" is therefore not merely a misnomer but also a mistaken policy prescription, because it encourages the exclusive use of military instruments that are not as effective as other approaches. On the harder end of the spectrum, policing and intelligence are the primary tools required to meet terrorist threats, in addition to military force. But the softer end is also effective, especially in preventing radicalization in the first place, as the Saudis have demonstrated.[44]

The role of religion, and especially Islam, in generating terrorist threats is often exaggerated. Most extremists in Iraqi and Afghan prisons, U.S. Marine Corps general Douglas Stone found, had no religious education and could not even read the Koran. This left them susceptible to extremist manipulation. That susceptibility had more to do with ignorance than with religion. Stone advocates literacy programs that enable potential recruits to read the Koran for themselves.[45] In Iraq, some prisoners refused release until they had completed literacy training.

Some would go as far as to claim that religion is more part of the solution than part of the problem: "Equally as notable as Islamic militancy but less noted are Muslims' 1) widespread condemnation of terrorism and other violent acts; 2) promotion of interfaith dialogue; 3) education of Muslim youth and reeducation of extremist Muslims; and 4) promotion of peaceful conflict resolution."[46] Islam, not the secular West, is the best antidote to extremism.[47] Mainstream Muslim voices "who are competing with extremists and offering an alternative vision for society" need support and encouragement. This is far more effective than traditional U.S. public diplomacy, which seeks to improve the image of the United States.[48] Neil J. Kressel puts it this way: "only Muslims can delegitimize and root out Muslim extremists in a lasting way. The struggle must come from within and, despite the West's vast resources, good intentions, and occasionally important support, this must, ultimately, be a battle waged by Muslims for the heart of their culture."[49] Mobilization of Islam to deal with its own internal problem is, however, nontrivial. Only in September 2011, a decade after 9/11, did the United States and Turkey lead the launch of the Global Counterterrorism Forum focused on rule of law, which in turn has spawned an International Center for Countering Violent Extremism in the United Arab Emirates.[50]

The U.S. government has particular difficulties engaging religious communities directly. Except when defending religious freedom, diplomats are often leery of dealing with religion at all, due to separation of church and state. In much of the Muslim world, U.S. government officials do not engage with mosques, and many think it undesirable or even prohibited. But engagement is precisely what is needed to counter extremism. As Maajid Nawaz, the director of the Quilliam Foundation, Britain's "first counter-extremism think tank," puts it: "This approach . . . involves networking amongst normal non-Islamist local Muslims who are working in their communities to make better neighborhoods for all. Governments cannot win arguments in communities; only civil society can achieve this. Governments can, however, empower civil society to make the necessary arguments."[51] He goes on to cite positive examples, but these derive exclusively from the European context. While government funding may be necessary, gaining the ability to work in Muslim communities in the Arab world will not be exclusively a government responsibility.

The fact is that American security now depends as much on nongovernmental as governmental threats and responses. "Civil society," the nongovernmental organizations that deal with social and political issues outside the formal structures of government, is vital not only to countering violent extremism but also to economic development, empowerment of women, conflict prevention, and postwar stabilization and reconstruction.[52] But the means we have for engaging our own civil society in international affairs, and interacting with civil society in other countries, are underutilized.

Promoting Citizen and Cultural Diplomacy

Engaging with citizens, whether at home or abroad, is not generally one of the stronger points of diplomats and other government officials, even if some do it extraordinarily well. Anyone who has witnessed an American ambassador boring an audience with a written text of elaborate talking points knows what I mean. A plurality of State Department officials score, in a commonly taken personality survey, as introverted, intuitive (meaning they like to interpret and add meaning to information), and thinking (rather than feeling).[53] Diplomats live in a rarefied world of instructions and reporting, tightly controlled and hierarchical communications, not free exchange and unbridled debate. Even if they claim to be speaking in "personal capacity," they are cautious about what they say in public and how they say it. "Words have consequences," Dick Holbrooke often said.

So too do relationships. That is the idea behind citizen diplomacy, "the concept that the individual has the right, even the responsibility, to help shape U.S. foreign relations, 'one handshake at a time.' Citizen diplomats can be students, teachers, athletes, artists, business people, humanitarians, adventurers or tourists. They are motivated by a responsibility to engage with the rest of the world in a meaningful, mutually beneficial dialogue."[54] Thirty million Americans travel abroad each year. That is a relatively small percentage of the total population, since Americans travel internationally less than citizens of many other countries. Not every trip involves engagement in meaningful and mutually beneficial dialogue, but it is still a lot of potential citizen diplomats.

Writing more than sixty years ago in the aftermath of World War II and impressed with citizen participation at the founding conference of the United Nations in San Francisco, one critic of the State Department's preference at the time for consulting only in narrow circles of well-connected expertise said: "If, as is commonly believed today, it is men rather than states that are the ultimate foundations of good will, then every possible means must be explored to enable men to plan and participate in the expression of international good will. We shall continue to require the skills of Talleyrands and Franklins. But to be effective in maintaining peace, they must now speak the minds of citizen diplomats, of great masses of people, rather than of dynasties, political parties, or ruling groups."[55] That is a tall order, but NGOs have grown up to help individual citizens speak their minds and participate. The U.S. Center for Citizen Diplomacy lists close to fourteen hundred such private-sector organizations, with a wide array of interests: business, development, health environment, poverty, human rights, religion, education, food, finance, culture, youth. The value of Americans' volunteer work abroad amounted to $3 billion in 2007.[56] The Center has set itself a goal of doubling the number of Americans involved in citizen diplomacy by 2020. This will not be easy and will require a concerted effort to train a leadership cadre for internationally active NGOs.

The best and brightest of American diplomats stay in close touch with the NGOs that work on the issues they deal with. Many major diplomatic conferences today include a parallel nongovernmental segment. Citizen support or opposition can make or break any diplomatic effort. American diplomats regard the Fulbright exchange program (active with over 150 countries) as well as the International Visitor Program, which brought 5,256 embassy-selected foreigners to the United States in 2010, as among their most important diplomatic tools.[57] Fulbright is a mostly government-funded program that relies a good deal on private partnerships and even attracts one-quarter of its funding from abroad. This kind of public/private partnership is a formula that works well and might well be applied to other citizen diplomacy initiatives. Fulbright had been increasing in recent years, but it leveled off at $238 million in 2011. An additional $12 million was requested for fiscal year

2013.[58] Evaluations of Fulbright and other exchange programs have demonstrated their effectiveness in improving both American understanding of the world and foreign understanding of the United States.[59]

Another important program is one that connects foreign countries with American states. Starting in the 1990s, the National Guard has built partnerships between its state contingents and foreign countries.[60] The Macedonian army, for example, partners with the Vermont National Guard, with which it has done combat duty in Afghanistan. The nascent Kosovo security force partners with the Iowa National Guard, Serbia with Ohio. These partnerships often expand well beyond the military sphere to politics, business, investment, universities, and municipal administration. The State Department has also initiated a program for engagement between subnational governing structures and launched the International Diaspora Engagement Alliance, focused on "entrepreneurship, volunteerism, philanthropy, social innovation, and diplomacy."[61] Cities are also playing increasing roles internationally.[62]

That does not mean, however, that we are doing enough to promote exchanges. "Cultural diplomacy," the rubric under which official exchanges are conducted, may rightfully be the "first resort of kings," but it is too often an afterthought in democratic America.[63] We are lagging in sending our own citizens abroad and preparing them to deal with the rest of the world. There are more than twice as many foreign students studying in the United States as there are Americans studying abroad. Foreign-language study in primary and secondary schools is at an all-time low and is concentrated in Spanish, an obviously necessary but not sufficient requirement. Few are learning the hard languages that will be important in the future: "All you need to know about the study of foreign languages in the United States is that many more middle and high school students are studying the dead language spoken by Caesar and Nero than such critically important tongues as Chinese, Arabic, Hindi, Farsi, Japanese, Russian and Urdu combined."[64] Teaching of foreign languages in American elementary and middle schools is declining.[65] Teaching of Arabic and Chinese—the hard languages arguably most relevant to today's foreign policy requirements—is increasing rapidly, but from a tiny base. America's relatively high rates of immigration and large diaspora populations from virtually every country on earth provide some capabilities that would otherwise be lacking.

More generally, America's citizen-based connectedness is vital to maintaining its power in the twenty-first century, when networks as well as hierarchies will be an important source of power.[66] Communications technology—e-mail, Twitter, Skype, cell phones, the Internet, and who knows what in the future—is making it far easier and cheaper to maintain citizen-to-citizen relationships over long distances and times. Mariam in Mali may not be a personal friend, but we have communicated well enough for her to tell me what she does for a living and for me to invest a small amount of money in her efforts. Formal government-to-government communications will remain important, but they no longer dominate the world of international affairs as much as they once did. The web of relationships that enables Americans to understand the world better and promote prosperity abroad will help protect American national security in the future, just because it extends far beyond the traditional *aide-memoire* that diplomats carry to their counterparts in foreign ministries all over the world every day.

Conclusions

What do these missing pieces of anticipatory foreign policy have in common? They all go beyond the normal, traditional tools of diplomacy and international statecraft. Most of them require people from beyond the normal circle of diplomats: police officers, judges, businesspeople, corrections officers, democracy and human rights activists, clerics, language teachers, ordinary citizens.

Nor do they all need to be in the State Department, which has to adapt to a world in which most communication detours around diplomats rather than going through them. In chapter 10 we'll have a look at how these missing pieces fit into the institutional puzzle of how America might conduct a more anticipatory foreign policy. But first we need to look at two other important areas of diplomacy: energy security and burden-sharing.

8. The Energy Conundrum

Unlike the five national security issues discussed in the previous chapter, energy is a traditional American national security concern that somehow never makes it into presidential documents on national security. It has stymied at least seven presidents. President Nixon called for energy independence four decades ago. Since then, the United States has quintupled its oil imports, increasing the need to protect oil-producing countries and oil-shipping routes. This meager result is not for lack of trying: the U.S. economy has become less dependent on energy to produce a given quantity of goods and services, oil's share in total energy use has declined, and total oil consumption even dipped during the recession in 2007–9. We are much more energy efficient than in the 1970s, when oil supply disruptions devastated the American economy, but our total oil use is greater because the economy is larger.

The incremental costs of oil-related military operations are about $83 billion per year, to which have to be added intelligence, diplomatic, and other costs.[1] The total would likely be around $100 billion. Military means have been used many times to try to ensure that oil continues to flow from the Middle East. But they cannot fix the problem. To the contrary, every time a president uses the U.S. Navy to protect oil tankers or stare down Iranian gunboats, nervous traders bid up the price of oil up in the short term, even if the military action is successful. Higher oil prices deprive U.S. consumers of funds and hurt American economic growth. We use our military instruments to compensate for the lack of civilian ones, but at great cost.

Oil is a fungible commodity traded in a global market. There are variations in prices based on delivery dates, contract terms, and qualities of crude (oil that comes out of the ground) and product (the stuff that comes from a refinery, like the gasoline you buy to fill the tank or the heating oil to fuel your furnace). The price of crude oil and refined oil products before taxes is essentially the same regardless of where they were produced. Oil arbitrage is highly developed. If an oil trader has an opportunity to make a bit more money selling into a different market, he'll do it. A barrel of oil may change ownership dozens of times during its voyage from wellhead to your gas tank, so the price to consumers (without taxes or subsidies) is essentially the same worldwide, with any small differences reflecting quality, transport costs, delivery dates, and other relatively small factors.

On most days, this system works without much variation in price. We pay whatever the world price happens to be, a bit more or a bit less than yesterday. But if supply is disrupted anywhere in the world—or even threatened with disruption—prices *everywhere* move upward, sometimes very quickly. On an ordinary day in January 2012, the price of a particular "benchmark" crude oil (Brent) was hovering somewhere around $100 per barrel. It was up a bit in the previous week because of Iranian threats to close the Strait of Hormuz, the narrow exit from the Gulf between Iran and Oman (twenty-one miles wide, only six of which are navigable). Twenty percent of the world's oil production (40 percent of its seaborne traded oil) passes through this vital strait. If the Iranians try to close it, stopping tankers or refusing them passage, the price could soar overnight all over the world, as the U.S. and allied navies force the Iranians to stand down. Prices will increase for a while even if the military effort is 100 percent effective. No one knows how expensive it could get, but in 2010 it reached about $140 per barrel and as recently as 2007 it was $40 per barrel. A price of $200 or more is not inconceivable.

This price volatility happens with many commodities. It matters more for oil because it is crucial for transportation, an important input to many industries, and because gasoline and heating oil are important consumer products. Production costs throughout the economy rise when oil prices rise. In addition, consumer buying power falls quickly if they have to spend $4 per gallon of gasoline rather than $3. So oil prices have an important effect on economies all over the world, raising production prices for many goods and services and reducing the amount of money in consumers' wallets. The oil supply disruptions of the 1970s precipitated two deep recessions. High oil prices in 2010 contributed to slowing recovery from recession. Continued dependence on oil exposes the United States to the risk of future oil supply disruptions, associated price increases, and the costly effect they can have on the economy.

American oil dependency also affects the role we play in the world, making us befriend and defend regimes that we might otherwise rather keep at arm's length, and enriching adversaries. Saudi Arabia, Kuwait, and other Gulf countries would be far less important to the United States if they were not major oil exporters. Many oil-producing countries collect amounts far over and above the costs of production and transport. As the costs of delivering some oil to market are only a few dollars per barrel, and the market price is closer to $100, we are talking about a lot of what is termed "rent" (payments over and above what would be required to get producers to bring their oil to market, including a normal profit) that flows from the wallets of American consumers to the investment funds of oil producers. The member states of the Organization of Petroleum Exporting Countries earned more than $1 trillion from oil exports in 2011. Of that amount, more than $400 billion came from the United States.

Venezuela, Russia, and Iran gain most of their foreign currency earnings from oil exports. Each would pose fewer problems in a world that did not enrich them with oil at close to $100 per barrel. Oil exports produce 94 percent of Venezuela's export earnings.[2] Oil and gas represent two-thirds of all Russian exports by value (and a third of general government revenue).[3] Oil exports provided half of Iran's government revenues until recently, while crude oil and its derivatives account for nearly 80 percent of its total exports.[4] When Tehran is short of cash, all it needs to do is threaten to close the Strait of Hormuz to get oil consumers to pour millions more into its coffers through sharply higher oil prices.

Oil is an enormous burden on American foreign policy. Barack Obama found his intention of "pivoting" to Asia in 2012 frustrated as the possibility of war with Iran and other Middle East contingencies keep his administration focused on the Gulf, the Levant, and North Africa.[5] America's support for the Arab awakenings of 2011–12 stopped at the Gulf because the more or less absolute monarchies there are major suppliers of oil to the world market. Revolution in Saudi Arabia, the United Arab Emirates (UAE), Kuwait, or Qatar would cause serious disruption of the world oil market.[6] Bahrain, where the Sunni monarchy has repressed a largely Shia rebellion, is important to the United States mainly because it hosts the Fifth Fleet, which protects the Gulf's oil production and exports. Washington has hesitated to criticize Iraq's prime minister, Nouri al-Maliki, who is re-concentrating power in ways that could eventually imperil the imperfect democracy the Americans left there, because he has dramatically increased oil production. This is particularly important when sanctions on Iran are sharply curtailing its sales into the global market and Iran's threats to close the Strait of Hormuz are putting upward pressure on prices.[7]

Prices rise in the United States when a supply disruption threatens even if we import no oil at all from Iran, because prices are determined in a global market. It would be true even if President Nixon's wishes for energy independence had been fulfilled. Countries like Norway, which produces more oil than it consumes, may benefit from higher oil prices because the money goes into their own companies' coffers, but they still suffer the increased production costs and decreased consumer spending that also affect the United States. Like it or not, we are tied into a global oil market that amplifies the importance of events occurring far from our shores. Oil shocks are felt worldwide.

What can we do to protect our producers, consumers, and the economy in general from hikes in global oil prices and supply disruptions? How can we reduce the flow of revenue to oil-producing countries that are hostile to the United States? How can we make sure oil supplies are more reliable? Basically there are three options: first, conserve energy, reduce dependence on oil, and get more from more reliable sources; second, make sure we have adequate stocks of oil and other emergency measures in place that can be used in case they are needed; and third, make foreign sources of oil more reliable. All of these are civilian efforts that reduce the need for military action, which may be necessary in a crisis but only if other efforts fail.

Energy from More Reliable Sources

America today produces more than half of its own oil supplies.[8] After many years of decline, domestic production is now increasing, due to advanced technologies like hydraulic fracturing (fracking) and horizontal drilling, which in the past five years have enabled oil and gas recovery from deposits that previously could not be exploited economically. The International Energy Agency (IEA) predicts that increasing American oil production will make it the world's largest producer by around 2020 and, combined with greater energy efficiency, a net oil exporter around 2030.[9] Shale oil has generated a boom of production and employment, especially in North Dakota.[10] The United States in 2011 surprisingly became a net exporter of refined oil products, though it remains for now a large net importer of crude oil.[11] At the same time, increased domestic natural gas production has caused a sharp decline in its price relative to oil. Natural gas is now the fuel of choice for new electricity generation capacity, beating out both coal and nuclear as well as oil. Increasing American oil and gas production could continue for decades, providing significant relief to the global oil market, where economic growth in China and other emerging economies has been driving a sharp increase in demand.

America currently imports the other half of its total oil supplies. About 18 percent of it passes through the Strait of Hormuz, which makes it less than completely reliable.[12] More than two-thirds of U.S. oil imports come from Canada, Saudi Arabia, Mexico, Venezuela, and Nigeria. Of these sources, Canada is secure, but the others are not. Saudi Arabia has participated in past Arab embargoes against the United States. The aging leadership there faces an uncertain succession to next-generation leadership as well as unrest in Shia-majority areas, which happen to coincide in part with oil-producing areas. Labor unrest sometimes disrupts Mexican production, which is declining in any event, and drug cartels are challenging government authority in parts of the country. Venezuelan production decreased under Hugo Chávez, who was no friend of the United States. His exit from the scene left Venezuela politically divided and economically challenged. Local gang violence often disrupts production in the Niger Delta, and Nigeria is also facing growing conflict between Muslims and Christians.

Fortunately, there are good prospects for increasing oil imports to the United States from relatively secure sources in the Western Hemisphere.[13] Canada is increasing its production from vast oil sands in Alberta. The proposed Keystone pipeline could carry it directly to U.S. refineries on the Gulf Coast, provided environmental issues are resolved.[14] Brazil is increasing offshore production from huge deposits off its southern coast.[15] These more reliable sources do not insulate the United States from increases in oil prices, but they do decrease supply from the Middle East, reduce upward pressure on global oil prices, limit the flow of funding to adversaries, and decrease the call on the U.S. Navy to defend insecure sea lanes.

Recognizing the need to reduce oil dependency, successive U.S. administrations have tried to promote conservation and subsidize alternatives. The government requires that automobile manufacturers meet Corporate Average Fuel Economy standards, which will rise to 54.5 miles per gallon in 2025, up from 35.5 miles per gallon in 2016. The federal government also subsidizes domestic oil and gas, coal, nuclear, and renewable energy sources by about $37 billion per year.[16] There are additional costs associated with ensuring against an oil supply disruption, along with the actual costs to the economy if oil supply is disrupted. Overall costs to the U.S. government of energy vulnerability, including military and non-military costs, are well over $100 billion per year and amount to over $20 per barrel of imported oil.

The United States could in theory increase the portion of its oil supplies that come from domestic sources by trying to recover these costs as an oil import fee, which would make oil consumers pay the military and civilian costs associated with imported oil and oil products, giving domestic producers a fiscal advantage over foreign production. But America long ago "bound" its tariff on oil products under the General Agreement on Tariffs and Trade, which means its trading partners could levy tariffs on American products to compensate for any decrease in their exports to the United States due to an increase in the "bound" tariff. Oil is such a large portion of our trade—it accounted for about 18 percent of American imports by value in 2011—that compensation would lead to sharply increased tariffs on U.S. exports of many kinds and devastate the world's trading system. It would also wreak havoc with America's relations with oil-producing countries. America could raise its tariff on crude oil without being required to provide compensation, but that would encourage imports of oil products and undermine the domestic refining industry.[17]

Another possibility is to raise the excise tax on gasoline or other oil products, regardless of their origins. This would not disrupt America's trade relations. It was last done in 1993. The Bowles-Simpson National Commission on Fiscal Responsibility and Reform recommended in 2010 a 15-cent-per-gallon increase in gasoline tax to fund the Transportation Trust Fund, but there is little sign of political support for the idea.[18] Full funding of the Transportation Trust Fund and the costs of securing energy supplies would require a much larger increase, on the order of $1 per gallon, which would face major political opposition.

It is difficult to think about raising federal gasoline taxes while a fragile economic recovery is in progress. The price of gasoline and other oil products is not the third rail of American politics. It is the train itself. The current federal gasoline tax, which is smaller than most state gasoline taxes, brings in about $25 billion per year, or significantly less than the amount the federal government spends on road transportation, and much less than it spends on protecting international shipment of oil. But no president wants to be standing on the tracks when prices go up, no matter what the cause. Increasing gasoline taxes would be politically and economically risky, even if it would reduce energy dependence, pay for at least a portion of the costs associated with importing oil, and limit the flow of money to America's adversaries.

Oil Stocks
When preventive measures fail, oil supplies are disrupted, and the price soars, there is little that can be done other than to restrain demand with emergency measures and draw stocks, which enter the market and soften

the price spike that might otherwise occur. The United States has accumulated a Strategic Petroleum Reserve of more than 700 million barrels, enough to replace roughly sixty days of imports. Just as important: we have convinced allies in Japan and Europe also to accumulate stocks, and to use them in a coordinated way early in a supply disruption.

This was not easy. I know, because I was responsible for convincing our allies to build stocks and commit to their coordinated, early use in the 1980s, when the policy was put in place. At the time, there was little threat from supply disruptions or increased oil prices. Prices fell to their lowest levels in a decade in the mid-1980s and did not recover until after 1990. But we knew from the experience of the 1970s how devastating an oil supply disruption could be, and we knew that the long-term trend of oil prices would be up. The Europeans and Japanese had relatively low oil stocks, far less than sixty days of imports, which they intended to use only as a last resort. So we set out in the Paris-based IEA, established in the aftermath of the 1970s oil crises, to make sure that we could protect the American economy from an oil supply disruption. This required a coordinated effort with other oil-consuming countries. If the burden were to be shared fairly, Europeans and Japanese needed to acquire more stocks and change their approach to using them.

This is a classic diplomatic challenge: getting other people to do what you want them to do.[19] Even when it is demonstrably in their own best interest, it can be difficult and accomplished only with time, effort, and persuasive argument. First we needed to explain clearly why the United States had accumulated large government-held stocks (over and above those that were commercially held) and why we thought it best to use them early rather than as a last resort. This we did by careful analysis of the oil supply disruptions of the 1970s, which demonstrated that the damage done to the world economy was not due to physical shortage of oil but rather to the sharp run-up in prices. The idea, still prevalent in the 1980s, that we could solve the problem by "allocating" oil to priority users at pre-crisis prices and insulate them from price increases was false. It made the price run-up even worse, because those denied oil would bid up prices even further if they could afford it. What we needed was not rationing or physical allocation but market intervention by the most direct and powerful means available: replacing lost supply by drawing on government-held strategic stocks.

Having established the virtues of early stock draw, we then had to point out that it would be difficult to convince the President of the United States to do it without participation by our allies—otherwise, it would look as if they were free riders. If they wanted a voice in deciding when stocks would be drawn, they would have to contribute. What we needed was oil stock burden sharing, a multibillion-dollar affair. Only gradually did this idea take hold. Encouraged by simulation exercises in which the United States drew from its Strategic Petroleum Reserves, reducing the American call for oil on the world market, the Germans and Japanese eventually came around to the idea of government-initiated early stock draw, which would make more oil in the world market available to them at more moderate prices. Others followed.[20]

The United States has used the Strategic Petroleum Reserve three times in response to supply disruptions: at the beginning of Desert Storm in January 1991 in cooperation with Gulf War allies, in September 2005 after Hurricane Katrina, and in June 2011 in coordination with IEA partners to offset the supply disruption caused by unrest in Libya and other Arab countries as well as the NATO intervention.[21] It works. It is no longer controversial—to the contrary, it has become so easy to do that it is arguable its use in the third instance was inappropriate. There was no major supply disruption from Libya, which exported only about 1.2 million barrels per day, about 2 percent of global supply. The United States was importing little of that amount. But global oil prices were climbing, threatening the world's economic recovery.

President Obama decided to draw stocks, in cooperation with our IEA partners. His concern was not the volume of supply but the impact of higher prices on the U.S. economy. Every barrel other countries draw from their stocks or save due to demand restraint in a crisis is a barrel that—like our own draw from the Strategic Petroleum Reserve—lowers pressure on world oil prices and improves the situation for the United States, which can be bolder in pursuing vital national security objectives because it knows it has the civilian instrument of coordinated early stock draw at its disposal. "All for one, one for all" is a diplomatic slogan with many applications, as we will discuss in chapter 9.

Making Foreign Sources More Reliable

With a growing economy and rising standards of living, we can expect to continue to import oil for the next decade, and possibly longer. Even if we become energy independent, the risk of a supply disruption to the American economy will remain. When world prices go up, ours do too. We can try to shift to more reliable oil sources, and we can prepare for an oil supply disruption by building stocks and coordinating stock draw and other emergency measures. We can also make foreign sources of oil more reliable.

Oil adds an important global dimension to concerns about governance in other countries. Gang violence has wracked the Niger Delta for many years, sometimes causing producers there to close down as much as 800,000 barrels per day in production.[22] That is too little to trigger a stock draw from the IEA, but it is a lot of oil leaving the market, enough to bump up global oil prices. The price increase affects all users, not just those that import from Nigeria (which, as it happens, we do).

For the United States, this means worrying about oil production and whatever may hinder it all over the world. Governance in almost all oil-producing countries is problematic. Oil has perverse effects on both politics and economics. Oil production and export raises the value of a producing country's currency, making its other industries less competitive in world markets and leaving its population idle. This phenomenon is known as "Dutch disease," because it afflicted the Netherlands after it started to export natural gas in the 1960s. Oil also provides governments with a flow of revenue over which there is little oversight. Most oil-exporting states have little or no need to levy taxes, which interrupts one of the key mechanisms of accountability in any society. Taxpayers demand to know where and how their tax money is spent, but in *rentier* states that live off oil revenues there may be little or no mechanism for deciding where and how oil money that flows directly to the state is spent. Corruption in oil-producing states is rife.

Nigeria is again a classic case. It has little to show for the hundreds of billions of dollars in oil it has exported in the past fifty years. Oil accounts for 98 percent of its exports and 83 percent of its government revenue. Its currency is overvalued, and other exports are therefore minimal. Oil money flows directly to the central government, where it is spent with little accountability and rarely trickles down to communities in which oil is produced. This is the underlying reason for the gang violence. Youth in the Niger Delta fight for control of oil-producing areas, where they steal oil or establish protection rackets. Local authorities have limited means with which to establish law and order or provide alternative livelihoods. Helping Nigeria overcome these problems has not, however, been a foreign policy priority for the United States. We have few civilian instruments that can be used in an oil-producing country like Nigeria, which is not a proper target of foreign assistance intended for poor countries.

There are solutions to governance problems in oil-producing states. The two biggest success stories are Norway and East Timor (Timor l'Este).[23] Both are small countries that have chosen—Norway on its own and East Timor at the behest of the UN in the transition to independence—to invest their oil income outside their own borders in a way that is fully transparent to their citizens. Norway spends only the investment income, making it an endowed country. East Timor, whose population is dirt poor, spends some of the oil revenue, but in a way that is transparent to its own citizens and to the international community.

These are the exceptions, not the rule. Not only Nigeria but also Saudi Arabia, the UAE, Qatar, Bahrain, and other major Gulf oil producers have little or no transparency about how their oil revenue is spent. At times they make little distinction between personal income and state revenue. They buy off any signs of citizen protest with substantial distributions of money and doses of repression. The risk to oil monarchies in the Gulf comes less from the prospect of *citizen* unrest and more from their substantial numbers of *non-citizens*, compounded in the cases of Saudi Arabia and Bahrain by populations of marginalized Shia and youth. Thirty-eight percent of the Gulf Cooperation

Council (GCC)'s population were foreigners in 2006.[24] About one-third of these are Arabs. They are regarded as more of a security threat than Asians, whose percentage has been increasing in recent years.

Political and economic reform in the Arab world was already a major issue for academics and think tankers before the Arab Spring of 2011.[25] It will remain a major challenge in the next several decades. So far, the revolutions of 2011 have left the GCC countries and other Arab monarchies virtually unscathed. Kuwait had already begun a reform process that brought women into the political sphere and has begun tentatively to empower the parliament. Morocco's monarchy is trying to stay ahead of the curve with modest constitutional reforms and the promise of free, fair, and competitive elections. Algeria is trying to do likewise, albeit more hesitantly. But the other monarchies, oil producing and not, are moving only slowly to reform.[26]

The lack of reform matters most of all for Saudi Arabia. It is the world's second-largest oil-producing country, after Russia. At least one Saudi expert urges that we do nothing about the situation there and elsewhere in the Middle East.[27] But in practice we are already doing a good deal by providing a vast supply of arms to Riyadh and to other GCC countries, in the hope that this will protect them from enemies foreign and domestic and help ensure that Gulf oil continues to flow to world markets.[28] So once again the military instrument has trumped civilian ones in dealing with energy security.

There are civilian measures that could vastly improve the reliability of supplies from the Gulf and reduce U.S. military burdens significantly, but we have done little or nothing diplomatically to pursue these options. It does not make sense for virtually all Gulf oil to be shipped through the Strait of Hormuz. Iraqi oil could be sent by pipeline north to Turkey, a far more secure and economical route to European markets. The UAE in July 2012 opened a major pipeline (2.4 million barrels per day) to carry some of its production around the strait.[29] Far more could be done to make Gulf oil exports less vulnerable.[30] The UAE could double its new pipeline or build a pipeline through Iraq to Turkey or Syria, once the war there is over. Saudi Arabia could double or triple the volume handled by its pipeline to the Red Sea.[31]

There has been little sign of serious American diplomacy aimed at convincing Gulf oil producers that they need to ensure their exports can reach world markets more reliably by circumnavigating the Strait of Hormuz. Instead, we pump arms and military assistance into Gulf states and burden the U.S. Navy with the task and expense of protecting Gulf oil supplies. This $100-billion-per-year military burden could be significantly reduced with a much smaller investment by oil producers in pipelines and a miniscule investment in more active pipeline diplomacy. The Iranians are unlikely to be as slow as we are: they are planning to build a new export terminal on the Gulf of Oman that would eliminate their need to use the Strait of Hormuz, enabling them to undertake a much more aggressive stance on closing it.[32]

American dependence on Middle East oil is declining. The United States should expect other powers to pick up more of the burden. Protection of the sea lanes from Somali pirates off the Horn of Africa is already primarily the responsibility of European powers, who lead a multinational effort there.[33] China, which participates in the Gulf of Aden, is importing ever larger quantities from the Middle East. It needs to increase its oil stocks, which are remarkably low (about twenty days of imports). The United States will not want to subcontract protection of the Strait of Hormuz to the Chinese, for fear of boosting China's influence in the Middle East and providing it with a strong incentive to accelerate its already rapid naval buildup. But it is reasonable to think China will want to play a stronger role elsewhere. Negotiating that kind of burden-sharing could significantly decrease American military expenditures and make resources available for stronger civilian efforts.

It is often said that the United States does this or that—makes war in Iraq, coddles the Saudis—because of oil. These allegations are sometimes true. But in my experience we think too little about oil, not too much. Why did we fail to do anything about encouraging Iraq to export oil by pipeline to Turkey during the years we had influence there? Instead, we focused on exports through the Gulf, which gave Iran increased leverage over Iraq.

Oil is a vital commodity, even for our post-industrial society. Oil dependency strengthens our adversaries and limits our options. It would be wise to think about it more deeply and take more serious measures to limit demand and ensure its supply. The military measures we take—deploying the U.S. Navy to keep the Strait of Hormuz open—are too often counterproductive, lifting the price of oil rather than reducing it. What we need is broader focus on both domestic measures that can reduce demand for foreign oil—shifting more of our transportation requirements to electricity and natural gas is one obvious example—and international efforts to ensure that our imports come from reliable sources via reliable routes. This would require less saber rattling and more vigorous diplomacy.

9. Sharing the Burdens

Anyone faced with difficult challenges will look around for others willing to share the burden of meeting them. States are no different. We have seen how well this works in responding to oil supply disruptions, where the "all for one, one for all" philosophy behind early stock draw aims to eliminate what could otherwise be a mad scramble to secure oil supplies that would drive up prices and hurt everyone. Most countries are unable to secure even their vital interests on their own. Of the European powers, only Britain and France maintain even a pretense of capacity for independent military action. The others look to cooperation within the EU and NATO to supplement clearly inadequate national capabilities.

The United States is different. No American president wants to rely on others to meet top-priority national security requirements. If superpower status means anything today, it is the capacity to act unilaterally worldwide to protect vital national interests. But that does not mean we always *have* to act alone. There are occasions when other countries will be ready and willing, for their own reasons, to pitch in to share burdens that they would not dare take on themselves. The American mantra is "multilaterally when we can, unilaterally when we must."[1] Sometimes presidents are seen as leaning more to unilateral action (like George W. Bush) or more to multilateral action (like Barack Obama). But in reality what often happens is that presidents decide unilaterally but quickly look around for others to help. George H. W. Bush was so successful during the Gulf War that the entire enterprise cost the United States about $7 billion, less than the *monthly* cost of the Iraq war to the United States a decade later.[2]

During the lead-up to the Gulf War of 1990, the CIA station chief in Rome came to my office with a small suitcase and plopped it on my desk. "That's for you," he said. "What's in it?" I wondered. He opened it with a grin to show me $5 million in newly minted, still-wrapped-in-plastic 100,000-lire notes. The ambassador and I had pestered the Italians so much about a promise they had made—to pay $5 million for "ro-ro's" (roll-on, roll-off ships that carry tanks and other heavy equipment to a war zone)—that they felt obliged to ask their military intelligence service to ante up until the parliament could approve the payment. That is a material way of sharing burdens, one that caused hilarity in Washington when we reported in a cable that the Italians had paid up with cash in a suitcase.

The United States has had remarkable success in getting others to help with military tasks. In Iraq at least forty countries deployed troops during the eight years of U.S. presence there. In Afghanistan the number over ten years was even greater: at least forty-seven participated in the NATO-led International Security Assistance Force. Many countries do it because they believe in the mission. Others do it because they think it will buy them some credit with the United States, which will sometimes pay for the costs involved. Some do it just to be seen as doing it, which brings prestige with their own populations and sometimes with the neighbors. Sharing military burdens is more the rule than the exception.

The circumstances of each war or peace operation are different. When it is prepared to lead an intervention, the United States will often turn first to NATO, its premier multilateral alliance, for military burden-sharing. NATO has followed Senator Richard Lugar's advice from twenty years ago to go "out of area" (otherwise, he said, they would be "out of business").[3] The alliance is now active far beyond the borders of Western Europe, which it defended during the Cold War. My instructions from the early 1990s to tell our Italian allies that Yugoslavia was "out of area" and therefore no concern of NATO are long forgotten. Now committed to protecting the security of the alliance from threats wherever they may arise, NATO has proven extraordinarily flexible and able to incorporate what diplomats call "variable geometry" operations among "coalitions of the willing," groups of countries that join together for a particular operation.[4] But NATO runs on consensus, which was not available for the Iraq war due to French and German opposition. Instead the United States cobbled together an ad hoc coalition outside NATO. Consensus, though not universal participation, was achieved for Afghanistan and Libya, where non-NATO members also participated in NATO-led operations.

Civilian burden-sharing is a path less taken. It rarely comes in a suitcase of cash. Instead, it comes in donor coordination meetings, ad hoc groupings of "friends" and in multilateral institutions that states create to share responsibilities. Today there are three main organizations to turn to for significant expeditionary civilian capabilities: the United Nations, the European Union, and the Organization for Security and Cooperation in Europe. Other regional organizations, such as the African Union and the Organization of American States, sometimes step in as well. The UN and the EU have global mandates, though the EU is principally concerned with its "neighborhood, " including the entire Mediterranean. OSCE operates mainly in the countries of "Europe," broadly defined. This includes a vast expanse: Russia as well as the former Soviet states of Central Asia and the Caucasus. NATO might also contribute to civilian burden-sharing, as it has a substantial civilian staff, but European preference for the EU has largely blocked use of the alliance for this purpose. This is unfortunate, especially when it comes to activities in which Turkey should participate.

The United Nations

The UN distinguishes between two types of missions that may be helpful to the United States in achieving its national security objectives: UN peacekeeping operations involving deployed police or military forces, mainly for postwar situations, and what are termed UN "political" missions, which are primarily civilian.[5] But all UN operations are fundamentally political and civilian-led, even if manned by substantial numbers of troops. They are significantly cheaper than U.S.-only operations, and the United States pays a bit over 27 percent of the total.[6] The UN would not have been able to lead in either Iraq or Afghanistan, where

war-fighting rather than peace-building has been the primary requirement, but it has contributed civilian capabilities in those situations and
handled some more permissive situations well.

When American politicians denounce the UN and threaten to stop
paying U.S. dues or peacekeeping contributions, they are in effect advocating that we stop doing things the cheaper and easier way. They may
imagine a new organization that would do America's bidding more
readily or more cheaply, but the creation of one would be a major diplomatic initiative with little likelihood of success. Other countries are
not going to be interested in giving the United States more control over
what a new organization does than it already has over the UN, whose
rules the United States wrote at a moment of American predominance
toward the end of World War II. Any new organization that draws on
Chinese, Brazilian, or Indian resources will have to give them more say,
not less, than they got in 1945.

Others may imagine that the world could do without missions of
the sort the UN undertakes. All UN operations are approved in, and
report back to, the UN Security Council, where the United States could
block them with a veto if it thought they were unwise. But blocking
new UN missions— or disbanding old ones that some claim have been
around too long—would create risks to peace and security in fragile
parts of the world. Involved as a peace-builder in about half the wars
ended since 1988, the UN is our often-chosen instrument for preventing postwar situations from returning to violent conflict, something
that happens all too often.[7] If it does, burden and expense will all too
frequently fall to the United States. Better to spend a relatively small
amount on a UN operation than risk the consequences if Liberia or Sierra
Leone goes back to war, even if they are not at the top of America's
priorities.

The UN could certainly be more effective and efficient, in particular if it merged the two separate departments that currently run its not
very distinct political and peacekeeping operations, which are all fundamentally political.[8] UN operations could also be more carefully super-
vised: several have been plagued with misbehavior by their troops,
including involvement in prostitution and trafficking of women and

children.[9] But without the UN, either U.S. costs would rise dramatically or a lot of things we think worth doing would go undone. Or both.

In 2012 there were twenty-three UN political missions, without peace-keeping forces, spread around the world in conflict-affected states looking for political solutions that would avoid war or a return to war.[10] Some of these are in places the United States would not consider top priority in terms of threats to American national security. The UN presence in places like Nepal, Sierra Leone, and Burundi helps to ensure that postwar situations there do not get out of hand, thus avoiding American engagement. American officials also appreciate UN help in higher-priority efforts. In Afghanistan the UN helps facilitate negotiations with the Taliban, which have so far proved unproductive. In Iraq it has done extensive fact-finding on Arab/Kurdish and other potentially explosive issues. Then there are other places where UN civilians operate but U.S. officials are severely restricted: that was true until recently in Myanmar. It still is the case in Somalia and Western Sahara.

The UN at the end of 2010 also had fifteen "peacekeeping" missions around the world, mainly in postwar situations in Africa. Total troops deployed exceeded 80,000, in addition to 5,500 non-local civilians and over 14,000 police as well as 2,300 UN volunteers.[11] By December 2011 the total for troops and police was over 98,000 and not likely to decrease.[12] The soldiers come mainly from the Third World: Pakistan, Bangladesh, India, Egypt, Nigeria, Rwanda, and Ghana were the biggest "troop contributors" in 2010. The United States rarely contributes troops to UN operations. Nor does the EU, except in instances of particular European interest like Lebanon and Cyprus. Cyprus is a favorite example of an interminable UN peacekeeping mission, one Americans regard as a failure because the UN Security Council authorized it fifty years ago. But Europeans regard it as a success because no war has recurred during that half century. Absent a negotiated solution to the decades-long division of the island, no U.S. administration has been willing to hit the kill switch at the Security Council, for fear of the consequences both within Cyprus and in relations with our allies Greece and Turkey.

The UN missions in Lebanon and Sudan are two of the easier ones to justify. In Lebanon the UN helped reestablish a modicum of stability in the aftermath of the 2006 Israel/Hezbollah war. In Sudan the UN is trying to prevent instability within the south as well as renewal of the war between Khartoum in the north and the newly independent South Sudan. Failure of either of these missions could lead to wars that damage American interests, albeit not vital ones that threaten the American homeland. Hezbollah presents a growing threat to Israel that the UN helps to monitor. South Sudan's independence is the result of a Bush-era diplomatic initiative that ended a decades-long conflict that endangered the country's substantial Christian population. Its reversion to war would undermine a major U.S. accomplishment.

The European Union

The European Union is preoccupied with its own financial difficulties, including the euro crisis, and it lacks anything like U.S. military capabilities.[13] But the EU has substantial civilian capabilities to encourage political and economic reform beyond its immediate borders. Within the European continent, the EU's process for bringing in new members (known as "enlargement") and the European Neighborhood Policy can be driving forces behind reforms that lead to peace and stability.[14] For conflicts outside the European neighborhood, the Europeans have established a common security and defense policy (CSDP) that is supposed to guide planning and operations of the EU's civilian and military missions for international crisis management. Since 2003, the EU has conducted thirty-three missions, sixteen of which were on-going as of January 2013.[15] There are four primary areas of European civilian action in crisis management: police, rule of law, civilian administration, and civil protection.[16]

The Europeans are particularly strong in policing capacities, having sent six police missions into crisis zones between 2007 and 2012. EU police missions are staffed by the EU Police Force, which is a reserve force of up to more than 5,500—including a 1,400-member rapid reaction force that can leave on thirty days' notice. Unlike the United States, which lacks a national police force and therefore relies on expensive contractors, the EU Police Force draws its personnel from a variety of European national police forces, including the European Gendarmerie

Force and the Italian Carabinieri.[17] It is intended to cover a range of conflict prevention and crisis management operations—including providing security, advice. and mentoring—in international missions. There are ongoing EU police missions in Bosnia-Herzegovina, Palestine, Afghanistan, and Democratic Republic of the Congo.[18]

The EU has one crucial experience that the United States lacks: running interior ministries. These are the non-uniformed organizations that elsewhere set the strategic direction for police and other internal security forces, hire and pay their uniformed and other cadres, and are ultimately responsible for their behavior. While courageous and committed Americans have mentored the interior ministries in Iraq and Afghanistan, none of them has had a career in an interior ministry, since the United States does not use them at any level of government. The U.S. Interior Department is responsible mainly for administering federal lands, conservation, and Native Americans; it does not provide strategic direction to police, except the U.S. Park Police. The EU, by contrast, has prepared twenty-one interior ministries to meet EU standards since its founding.

While EU-led police missions have the training and expertise necessary for the job, they have not always had the numbers.[19] The European Union Police Mission in Afghanistan had difficulties recruiting people. The European Gendarmerie Force (EGF) may solve this problem.[20] As a partnership between France, Italy, the Netherlands, Portugal, Spain, Romania, Lithuania, Poland, and Turkey, the EGF knows how to operate in a multinational environment. The EGF can deploy up to eight hundred gendarmes within thirty days and reach twenty-three hundred with reinforcements. It can provide rapid civil security in crisis situations (either alone or under military command), can offer expert training, and is capable and willing to perform under the most difficult circumstances—particularly useful when the EU has trouble recruiting police for dangerous environments.

The European Union can also offer experienced rule of law specialists to peace-building operations. As of June 2008, EU member states had committed 631 officers—prosecutors, judges, and prison officers—to rule-of-law crisis management operations. These missions aim to strengthen the rule of law and promote human rights through properly functioning judicial and penitentiary systems.[21] The EU's largest civilian mission under the CSDP for some years was its rule-of-law effort in Kosovo. Its Iraq mission was also important.[22]

EU monitoring missions—recognized by the European Council in December 2004 as a civilian CSDP priority area—serve as a tool for conflict prevention, management, and resolution and aim to deter conflict through physical presence. An EU border-assistance mission monitored operations at the border crossing point in Rafah in support of Israel and the Palestinian Authority's "Agreement on Movement and Access." The concluded Aceh Monitoring Mission oversaw the successful implementation of the August 2005 peace agreement between the government of Indonesia and the Free Aceh movement.[23]

The EU has a growing interest in security sector reform (SSR). It has incorporated aspects of SSR into its accession and development policies. But it was not until 2005 and 2006 that the EU presented a single policy framework for SSR in the form of three key documents, defining a holistic approach that takes into account the entire security sector. The framework remains a work in progress.[24] The EU is making an effort to fix the flaws that hamper the planning and design and lessen the impact of SSR missions and to ensure that all missions on the ground reflect the framework's holistic approach.[25] In the meantime, the EU continued to provide SSR assistance to weak and failed states, including in the Democratic Republic of the Congo—where activities include providing technical and logistical support to military institutions—and one in Guinea Bissau that closed in 2010—where the mission was helping implement the country's national security strategy.[26]

The Organization for Security and Cooperation in Europe

OSCE is the direct descendant of the 1975 Helsinki "final act," an agreement on democratic principles that is generally credited with helping to generate the pressures that ended Communism in Eastern Europe and the Soviet Union, leading eventually to its breakup. It is the main institution concerned with creating a Europe "whole, free and democratic," a goal of all American presidents since the end of the Cold War.

With fifty-six members spread over North America, Europe, and Asia, OSCE has fourteen "political" missions helping with the transition to democracy in the Balkans, Caucasus, and Central Asia. These are places the United States would rather not have to worry too much about. The OSCE is a relatively cheap and easy way to share the burdens. This is clearest perhaps in Bosnia and Kosovo, once subject to major U.S.-led NATO military interventions but now well below the threshold of daily concern at high levels in Washington.[27]

The OSCE has been particularly effective in three areas: human rights (especially election observation), free media, and protection of the many minorities that dot what we used to call Eastern Europe. Macedonia has an Albanian-language university in Tetovo, Tajikistan hosts a staff college for border guards, and years of effort have gone into resolving conflicts between Azerbaijan and Armenia (over Nagorno-Karabakh) and in Moldova because of the OSCE, which spends well under $200 million per year, a pittance by military standards. The United States pays just 14 percent.[28] While these places may all seem obscure and even unimportant to people in Des Moines, conflicts in Europe have repeatedly required deployment of American troops and civilians over the past century. Even a small war where no U.S. deployment is involved— the one between Russia and Georgia in 2008, for example—causes the United States to move naval and air assets and to ante up for reconstruction after the fact. The United States and Georgia would have been far better off had the OSCE and UN monitors been successful in preventing that conflict, which unfortunately they were not.

More Effective Burden-Sharing
There is of course a good deal of interaction between deployed American and European civilians in many contexts: Afghanistan, Palestine, and the Balkans come immediately to mind. There are also more-or-less ad hoc coordinating mechanisms in many situations, and sometimes much more: USAID provided virtually all of the personnel for the EU-led economic pillar in Kosovo for the first year after it was created, U.S. customs officers deployed into a European customs mission in Bosnia after the war there, and Europeans participated in the Coali-

tion Provisional Authority that administered occupied Iraq in 2003–4. There is also a good deal of interchange and communication between the State Department and its counterparts in Europe, not only in the EU but also in the UK, the Netherlands, Germany, and elsewhere.

Missing is a common strategic framework for civilian/military state-building missions. This hamstrung the effort in Afghanistan, where European militaries were deployed as part of a UN-approved and NATO-led peacekeeping mission (limited initially to Kabul at U.S. insistence) while the Americans were still fighting a counterterrorism war (later morphed into counterinsurgency). A "lead country" formula for civilian efforts, which gave responsibility for the courts to Italy and the police to Germany, for example, failed miserably. The resources committed initially in Afghanistan were ludicrously inadequate.[29] Had there been a common strategic framework, with a clear definition of what the international community was trying to achieve, the inadequacy of the resources would have been obvious.

The best-organized effort in the past two decades was in Kosovo, where a "pillar" structure focused on humanitarian assistance (later police and justice) and civilian administration (both UN-led), democratization and institution-building (OSCE-led), and reconstruction and the economy (EU-led). While far from perfect, this structure gave all concerned a clear sense of strategic direction. The many national governments and NGOs active in Kosovo knew whom to consult when considering assistance and how their distinct activities fit into a broader framework. But Kosovo is the exception, not the rule. Civilian efforts do not generally have even this kind of organizational clarity.

This is on the one hand understandable—neither the United States nor the EU has formally adopted a strategic framework—and on the other hand completely incomprehensible: how do we expect to be able to work together effectively for common purposes without defining what the desired end states are? Unity of command—clearly desirable in many instances—is usually unachievable: the United States will not generally put its troops or civilians under any command other than its own, and Europeans are often unwilling to put their civilians under a military commander. Unity of purpose—which entails working toward the same ends, even if there is no single "commander"—is the best we are going to get, but we have not been good about spelling out what that means.

Proposals for a strategic framework are not lacking. This is where the end states discussed in chapter 4 come into play. If you look at international interventions (unilateral and multilateral UN and non-UN) since the end of the Cold War, they do in fact share—virtually without exception—those five end states, either explicitly or implicitly:

Safe and secure environment

Rule of law

Stable governance

Sustainable economy

Social well-being

The only one of these on which there is much debate is stable governance, which some of us would prefer to define as "stable democracy" and others like to label "good governance." Whichever it is, the point is the same: these five end states are common to international interventions after the fall of the Berlin Wall. It is time we started organizing ourselves along these lines if we ever expect to reach these end states.

This is particularly important because more than governments are involved. While the United States and the EU have been focusing lately on "whole of government" approaches, in many operations the bulk of the work is actually done by non-government people, be they contractors, NGOs, or international organizations—not to mention the host government, local NGOs, and host-country citizens. Commonality of purpose among these various actors requires some sort of strategic framework.[30]

The definition of end states may need to be adjusted for particular contingencies, but having a starting-point framework agreed upon by Europeans and Americans would enable a good deal of cooperation in the assessment and planning phases of an operation that is not in fact being done today. Each participant or potential participant would know to expect that there will be a group, led by someone (be it the UN, an NGO, a lead nation, or the local ministry of social affairs), dedicated to "social well-being," for example, that would deal with access to and delivery of basic needs services, access to and delivery of basic education, right of return and resettlement, and social reconstruction issues. The leadership and priorities might shift over the course of a contingency, but the focus on end states would remain.

This process will not be easy or smooth. The United States has a hard enough time creating and supporting its own interagency operations—largely due to competition, different cultures, and lack of political will making the development of a transatlantic "whole of government" approach seem daunting, especially given that Europeans have "a distinctive European approach to foreign and security policy" that may at times seem at odds with an American approach.[31] Still, the United Nations went some distance in this direction when it developed its *Peacekeeping Principles and Guidelines*—often known as the Capstone Doctrine. But much of that document is occupied with issues unique to UN operations, which have their own constraints. The U.S. Army's Stabilization Doctrine explicitly recognizes the overarching importance of the five end states outlined above.[32] The G7+, a group of nineteen of the world's most fragile and conflict-affected countries, has adopted a similar set of "peacebuilding and statebuilding" goals:

Legitimate Politics: Foster inclusive political settlements and conflict resolution

Security: Establish and strengthen people's security

Justice: Address injustices and increase people's access to justice

Economic Foundations: Generate employment and improve livelihoods

Revenues & Services: Manage revenue and build capacity for accountable and fair service delivery[33]

The notable lack of attention to social well-being, including reconciliation, in this framework should not detract from the significance of agreement among aid recipients. The particular chosen framework is far less important than settling on one that can be used in, and adapted to, different national circumstances.

Without a common strategic framework, the international community will continue to reinvent the organization of each intervention from scratch for each contingency, often spending a year or two figuring out how it will be organized and missing some of the best opportunities in the meanwhile. The High Representative in Bosnia for years did not publish an organizational diagram because of internal quarrels about how to organize the operation. The difficulties of the current intervention in Afghanistan derive in large part from a failure to define objectives clearly or to find agreement on them among the many different actors involved, including the host government. As U.S. troops withdrew from Iraq, lack of clarity about end states was a major issue—how can you hand off to the host government if it does not share your objectives?

There is no excuse for this: a simple and straightforward framework eventually adopted by the OSCE, the EU, NATO, and the UN would go a long way to overcoming bureaucratic obstacles, jump-starting international interventions, and ensuring that we are all aiming for the same broad objectives. It would help to legitimize an intervention by providing a clear vision of the mission's purpose. It would facilitate civilian/military cooperation—for the first time, military officers would know where to look in a civilian operation for particular functions. It would also become apparent within such a preestablished framework where capacities are lacking and need to be enhanced, whereas today we largely organize international intervention by assembling those who are willing, without regard to requirements, and therefore lack a clear sense of the gaps. We can and should do better.

Better would entail establishing, at least between Europeans and Americans if not in the UN context, an agreed starting-point framework, one that might be adapted for a particular contingency. In Syria, for example, we are faced with an uncertain and likely chaotic situation once Bashar al-Assad falls from power. If all concerned can agree in advance that a safe and secure environment, rule of law, stable governance, economic sustainability, and social well-being are the end states outside powers as well as Syrians seek, we can begin to think about and organize the post-Assad effort even without being certain how he will fall.[34]

The end-state framework may need to be adjusted to Syria's particular circumstances. If the Syrians decide that they prefer to define their economic end state as "Employment and improved livelihoods," the adjustment can readily be made—but at least they will know that they need an economic end state. Or they might seek "representative governance," even if it is not entirely stable. The postwar stabilization and reconstruction effort would then be organized according to end state, with a clear lead for each one. Leadership might from the first be in the hands of the host government authorities—as it was in Libya and Egypt— or an external peacekeeping force might, for example, start the process and turn over leadership to the Syrians once a semblance of centralized control has been established over the various security forces. Whoever leads, others would know whom to follow.

This approach may seem simple—even obvious—but in fact it is not used. The more usual process is a chaotic one in which all parties decide for themselves what they think needs to be done and pursue it without any clear leadership or organizational structure. A strong personality like Zalmay Khalilzad, who led efforts in both Afghanistan and Iraq for the Bush administration, may be able to ensure more unified effort than usual. But it should not depend on personalities. Burden-sharing is good, but it is better when everyone knows what the burdens are and who is available to lift them.

10. Reorganizing for Hard Times

"Do you know why the State Department is called the State Department?" This is a question I ask new acquaintances, including those who work there. My non-scientific poll suggests 98 percent of Americans do not know; 95 percent of State Department officials don't know either.

The answer is important to understanding the problems we face. America is the world's last remaining superpower, having won the Cold War. But it lacks the civilian institutional capacity to deal with the post–Cold War world within the means at its disposal. What is wrong with the State Department and the U.S. Agency for International Development, which should be among the government's primary tools to deal with current national security challenges?

The State Department's Shortcomings

State is one of the original four departments of the U.S. government, which at the time of George Washington were known as War, Treasury, the Attorney General, and State.[1] The State Department was *the* department of *the* state. It handled state functions other than war, finance, and justice. These included the minting of coins, the taking of the census, and official sealing of government documents. That is why the Great Seal of the United States, still pictured on the dollar bills in your wallet, is kept in the State Department. Visit it in the display room near the cafeteria next time you manage to get past security.

The Department of State was prestigious. Five of its first ten secretaries became president. As the federal government acquired responsibilities, or those within State grew to significant dimensions or political importance, Congress created new institutions to take care of them.

During my career, State lost international responsibilities like negotiation of trade agreements (now the responsibility of the U.S. trade representative), international monetary policy (Treasury is in charge), commerce (the Commerce Department), and international energy policy (shared between State and Energy). State had already lost intelligence (1947), propaganda (1953, since folded back in, arguably because it was viewed as less important after the Cold War), and agriculture (1954). The State Department today does diplomatic and consular work because those are the functions left to it after more than two hundred years of other institutions taking over its domestic and some international functions.[2]

If you understand "foreign policy" to mean mainly political relations with other states, it was relatively unimportant even within the State Department until about 1900. Promoting trade and the welfare of Americans traveling abroad occupied most of the far-flung and independently operated *consular* staff, which was distinct from the fewer diplomats. That changed in the aftermath of World War I. Today's professional Foreign Service, which includes both diplomatic and consular functions, dates from 1924.[3]

It was not until World War II and its Cold War aftermath that State's diplomatic apparatus grew to significant dimensions, but its growth was no more than proportional to the growth of the federal government as a whole, leaving it to this day one of the smallest cabinet departments. It has been more than 150 years since a secretary of state went on to occupy the White House.[4] The job ended Colin Powell's distinguished career of government service, as it did Warren Christopher's and many of their predecessors'. Today it is hard to picture a secretary of state having a future political career, much less becoming president, after serving in Foggy Bottom, though Hillary Clinton may an exception to the rule.

At home, the State Department is a weak player in a bureaucracy where size of budget and number of personnel count. State has little domestic constituency. It spends few of its limited resources outside Foggy Bottom. There are no big State Department bases in Kansas (or anyplace else within the United States) and relatively few contractors providing domestic employment and economic benefit. Most Americans are unaware of what it does until they lose a passport in Vladivostok, are robbed in Naples, or get arrested in Mexico. Even then, they use State's consular, not its diplomatic, services, though the distinction would be lost on most people. Only when an ambassador and three of his colleagues are murdered in Benghazi do ordinary citizens become aware of the people who are representing them abroad, conducting international operations on behalf of the United States, and helping to define how American national interests are best pursued internationally.

State is also surprisingly weak abroad. While the ambassadors, their deputies, and a handful of political, economic, consular, and public affairs staff belong to the State Department, at many embassies more than 50 percent, and sometimes 90 percent, of the staff belong to other U.S. government agencies or exist to service other government agencies. Some of them have military, intelligence, or foreign assistance functions closely linked to foreign policy issues, but most come from agencies that station people abroad in order to fulfill their domestic missions: the Drug Enforcement Agency has hundreds of agents stationed overseas, the FBI has dozens, and even Social Security, Agriculture, Commerce, NASA, and Energy have overseas staff.

When I was the deputy to the ambassador in Rome, I calculated how many people we needed to conduct the essential diplomatic and consular business of the U.S. government in Italy, an important country many of whose sovereign functions have been transferred to the European Union in Brussels. The total was many fewer than 10 percent of the eight-hundred-person staff, including necessary support personnel. Thirty-six different agencies of the U.S. government operated in Italy at the time: the Justice Department had dozens of people there (immigration, criminal division, FBI), not to mention the agencies I'm not supposed to mention. The Secret Service, fearing that the ambassador would force them out of cushy Rome, deposited $15 million in counterfeit bills seized by the Carabinieri on his desk one morning, as evidence that they had important work to do. The ambassador was tickled, but I was unimpressed: the main source of counterfeit bills in Italy was the Bekaa Valley in Lebanon, hundreds of miles to the east. The

Secret Service used Rome as a reward for those who had served on presidential protection details or other stressful jobs. It did not want its people stationed in Beirut, an embassy terrorists have attacked with deadly consequences several times.

Senator Kerry, later to be named secretary of state by President Obama, visited one summer and threatened to cut State's budget because he thought we were overstaffed. I agreed but pointed out that fewer than 10 percent of the personnel were performing State functions. The rest came from other agencies or were State personnel there to support other agencies. Cutting the embassy budget would only indirectly affect most of the staff, which got support (for which their agencies pay) but no salaries from State. You could reduce some embassy budgets to zero and still find hundreds of non-State personnel clamoring for State Department services. An embassy is a mini-U.S. government, with many of the problems associated with getting something done in Washington.[5]

In order to ensure coherence at an embassy with many domestic agencies represented, the American ambassador is endowed with what is called "chief of mission" authority.[6] This means she is the nominal boss of all U.S. government personnel stationed in the "host" country (that was Italy in my case). Deployed military personnel are the exception. They remain under a military command that interacts with the ambassador, usually through a general or admiral, but does not report to her. In theory, chief-of-mission authority empowers the ambassador to remove embassy personnel from any agency, to instruct them what to do, and to prevent them from doing things she doesn't want done. This authority enables the ambassador to require better integration and unity of effort. It is a good thing in principle. It has even been proposed as a model for interagency integration on the home front.[7]

In practice, it does not always work well. While most people stationed in an overseas mission treasure the ambassador's time and attention, lining up to salute when she makes a request, there are exceptions. Controlling non-State agencies explicitly using chief-of-mission authority is difficult, because State lacks clout in Washington. My ambassador in Rome, Michigan lumber distributor Peter Secchia, felt he had a mandate from President George H. W. Bush to cut staff and set out to reduce embassy personnel by 10 percent. His first efforts to send people home using chief-of-mission authority failed because State could not get other agencies to concur. Secchia also thought his authority extended to attending meetings when the treasury secretary visited Italy. He lost that fight too. The domestic agencies consistently best State and block an ambassador's moves when they want.[8]

Instead, in Rome we decided to work cooperatively with other agencies to reduce staff. We appealed over the heads of those stationed in our plum post, asking their bosses in Washington whether they really needed so many people in expensive Rome now that the Cold War was over and the Soviet Union no longer a threat. Many thought not and were prepared to reduce their presence abroad. The CIA—oops, that's one I'm not supposed to mention—gave me a gold medal for my successful appeals to remove excess staff from its station, thus making them available for higher-priority work elsewhere. The medal sits on a dusty shelf at home—it's not the kind of thing you want to display to everyone. But it reminds me of how important it is not to confuse authority on paper with effective exercise of leadership.

Few ambassadors set out to shrink staffs. Embassy Rome was back up to eight hundred not long after I left. Reginald Bartholomew, the professional Foreign Service officer who succeeded Secchia, was a veteran of more than thirty years. In bureaucracy, people and money are power. In most capitals, chiefs of mission exert their authority to *gain* non-State staff and budget, which creates an obligation to provide support to the other agencies at post, a reason for further staff *increases*. A former ambassador at a remote Pacific Ocean post recently boasted how he had more than doubled the embassy staff during his tenure, though for the life of me I could not figure out what America's interests in the host country were. He was sure he had done the right thing. He had certainly done what was expected of him.

Most important of the ambassador's many responsibilities is security. In exchange for nominal chief-of-mission authority, domestic agencies deployed abroad demand the same level of security and other services as that provided to the ambassador and her State Department contingent. This is why we left behind in Baghdad after the military withdrawal a leviathan embassy, where twenty-foot-high walls topped with machine-gun emplacements protected a staff of six thousand, more than 50 percent of whom provide support and only a few dozen of whom were there to do diplomatic and consular work. State, the agency that has lost functions for more than 220 years, gets a lingering taste of its former glory as the department of *the* state by housing, feeding, and protecting other agencies of the U.S. government abroad.

Preoccupied with providing services to other agencies and saddled with leviathan embassies, our diplomatic establishment has too often ignored the issues discussed here: state-building and conflict prevention may be essential to protecting American national security, but they are not what most of our diplomats are doing. For those not servicing other agencies, the primary function is the traditional one of communicating with the host government and reporting. You may have read the admirable results in Wikileaks, which has published many thousands of U.S. diplomatic cables. More are available for the asking, at the George Washington University National Security Archives or directly from the State Department.[9] I have a declassified stack two feet high in my office from the time of the Bosnian war that you can read anytime you like.

Our diplomats are paragons when it comes to delivering messages as well as understanding and narrating what is going on in other societies. Those are vital functions, arguably the most important, even if they no longer have a monopoly over them.[10] But that is not all we need them to be doing in today's world. The State Department cannot be only "our government's efficient arm for dealing with the world in situations short of war."[11] We also need it to anticipate problems and take measures to head them off. When the effort fails to prevent conflict, State also has to be prepared to help clean up in the aftermath, helping to restore functioning states to countries that otherwise may present serious national security threats to the United States.

The State Department is not alone in failing to meet these requirements: it has a partner in USAID, the agency that provides assistance abroad.

What about USAID?

The history of USAID is as complicated as the State Department's, but shorter and can be reduced to a few words: the idea that foreign aid to reduce poverty and enlarge markets abroad could redound to America's benefit originated in the Marshall Plan, which revived West European economies after World War II and gave America the prosperous allies and markets it needed to compete with and face down the Soviet Union during the Cold War.[12] The institution that provides U.S. government aid abroad has been called by different names and has alternately been inside the State Department or outside. Today USAID is an autonomous agency, but without cabinet status and no clearer relationship to the State Department than throughout much of its history.

USAID is an economic development organization.[13] It has a twofold purpose of furthering America's interests while improving lives in the developing world. Unlike State, which has managed in recent years to gain significant personnel, USAID was until recently hollowed out, losing after the Cold War a significant portion of its staff and coming to rely extensively on contractors—both profit and nonprofit—to do the lion's share of the projects it funds.[14] Moreover, the Millennium Challenge Corporation (MCC) and the Defense Department have captured substantial amounts of foreign assistance funding that might otherwise have gone to USAID. Together, MCC and Defense now have foreign assistance budgets equivalent to that of USAID, which amounts to no more than one-half of one percent of the federal budget.[15] While candidates for president may announce with fervor and conviction that they intend to solve America's fiscal problems by starting foreign aid from zero each year, offering cash only in exchange for benefits to the United States, USAID is already so strapped that the amount of money to be saved is tiny compared to America's deficit.

This has happened not for lack of trying on the part of USAID, which has scrambled to adjust to changing requirements, even if much remains to be done to improve aid effectiveness and save money.[16] It has doubled and redoubled its efforts on democracy and governance, established an office for conflict management and mitigation, and issued a "development response to violent extremism and insurgency."[17] All to little avail. Though it has in the past few years gained additional staff, USAID remains a stepchild in a U.S. government that is increasingly focused on threats to national security and less concerned with poverty alleviation and economic development abroad. There is little confidence in a Congress that doubts the government's ability to create jobs and alleviate poverty at home that USAID can do it overseas.

State and USAID Together: Greater Than the Sum of the Parts?

The shortcomings of State and USAID are no secret and have generated a lot of discussion in recent years. A congressionally mandated commission concluded in 2007: "Our foreign assistance system is broken. We ignore this reality at our peril. . . . [N]ot one person appeared before this Commission to defend the status quo. . . . The world has changed and U.S. assistance programs have not kept pace. . . . An integrated approach to our government's development assistance is needed."[18] It hasn't happened. The integrated approach is nowhere to be seen. The Foreign Assistance Act has not been rewritten, the international affairs functions of the United States have not been reorganized in any of the ways the commission contemplated, substantial new resources have not become available, and no national security budget combining Defense and State has been created (though they have been lumped together for some deficit reduction purposes).

Hillary Clinton made a valiant stab at mapping out reform of both State and USAID in her 2010 Quadrennial Diplomacy and Development Review (QDDR), *Leading through Civilian Power*.[19] This was an attempt to emulate the Defense Department's Quadrennial Defense Review, which is supposed to shape the Pentagon's budget requests around a clear set of objectives. The State and USAID version has many of the essential ingredients of an effort to make sense of the civilian instruments for projecting power. It commits the United States to elevate civilian power as an equal pillar of U.S. foreign policy, along with the military. It aims to cut back excessive reporting requirements, focus development on top priorities (sustainable economic growth, food security, global health, climate change, democracy and governance, and humanitarian assistance), improve prevention and response to crises, and enhance capability for justice and security sector reform.

But as the QDDR itself admits, "Execution is everything."[20]

It isn't really happening. The QDDR failed to connect resources to policy. While State created a Conflict and Stabilization Operations (CSO) Bureau toward the end of 2011, the 2012 budget crunch put a damper on anything that required additional funding.[21] The administration requested additional funding for fiscal year 2013, but sequestration intervened. The Civilian Response Corps and other important instruments needed to implement the QDDR have been reduced, not increased.[22]

New Institutions and Objectives Are Needed

Failure to implement the QDDR is not the only problem. While right about many things, Secretary Clinton proposed adjustments to a system that is profoundly broken. New wine should not be put into old bottles, "else the bottles break, and the wine runneth out, and the bottles perish: but they put new wine into new bottles, and both are preserved."[23] State and USAID were not designed for today's problems and will not be able to meet today's challenges. We need to break with their origins in the eighteenth century and in the Cold War and rid ourselves of a legacy that is more encumbering than ennobling.[24]

America's primary foreign policy challenge today is to protect its national security within the means it has available. The circumstances in which this challenge is arising are so radically different, even from the first decade of this century, that we need to rethink the institutions we bring to bear on the problem from the ground up. America is a young country, but it is an old governing system—few can claim to be older. It is not going to be easy to break the mental habits of 224 years and reimagine our foreign policy apparatus.[25] It is much easier to suggest increased staff and hiring flexibility, without reforming the institutions in which they work.[26]

We should try, at least as a thought experiment. What if we established new institutions to meet current needs? What would our civilian foreign policy instruments look like if they were invented today to meet today's and tomorrow's problems? What if we were to commit to dissolving the State Department and USAID three years from now? We could then spend those three years building new institutions to replace these two venerable but broken ones, drawing on experience but ignoring State's burdensome legacy of commitments to house and protect other U.S. government agencies as well as USAID's traditional economic development focus. I cannot predict precisely what the new institutions would look like, but I am convinced that they would look different from those we have today, which have far more to do with victory in World War II, the Cold War, and the more equivocal outcomes in Iraq and Afghanistan than with today's requirements. There is no reason why the bottles should have the same shape, and no reason why there should be two. One or three might do better.

First things first: objectives. The overall purpose should be protection of America's national security. The current State Department mission statement reads this way: "Shape and sustain a peaceful, prosperous, just, and democratic world and foster conditions for stability and progress for the benefit of the American people and people everywhere."[27] While I share much of the sentiment, it would be far better policy to put the security and welfare of the American people first, especially if you want their support and funding in a period of budget tightness. Something like the following would be more in keeping with the need for an anticipatory foreign policy committed to protecting national security: "Protect the United States and its citizens from foreign threats to their security, welfare and other interests by preventing them from arising and blocking them when they do." This is definitively not the State Department's self-concept today. Protecting national security is not even listed among the ten things State thinks you as a citizen should know about it.[28]

Some may find my formulation excessively defensive and lacking in vision, or what the experts like to call "grand strategy."[29] Their paradigm is "containment" of the Soviet Union, a strategy of countering Soviet pressure wherever it appeared on the globe that in retrospect we see as having shaped for forty years our military, intelligence, economic, diplomatic, propaganda, and other approaches to a single, powerful adversary capable of destroying the United States in a matter of minutes.[30] But the efficacy of containment was not so clear at the time (its inventor even forswore it). Had it continued in its purest form the Soviet Union might not have collapsed.[31]

The odds-on favorite for a grand strategy these days among foreign policy realists is known as "offshore balancing." This is the notion that America should seek "to maintain benevolent hegemony in the Western Hemisphere and . . . maintain a balance of power among the strong states of Eurasia and the oil-rich Persian Gulf."[32] It is an idea premised on military power, in particular a strong navy. There is a good deal to be said in its favor as a military strategy, but it would do little or nothing to prevent the nonmilitary risks we face or meet the demand for civilian fixes. It amounts to continued reliance on military (mainly naval) power to carry the entire burden, with civilian instruments neglected. Nor will a more explicitly military strategy of "ensuring access" to the maritime environment (including the seabed), outer space, and cyberspace do anything to fix many of the problems with failed and fragile states we've discussed here.[33] Neither offshore balancing nor ensuring access will protect American national security interests in the next decade or two, even if they are reasonable approaches to achieving some military objectives.

Another approach would like to be known as "restoration": "an American foreign policy based on restoring this country's strength and replenishing its economic, human and physical resources."[34] It is not as pretty a word, but this amounts to retrenchment. Under this strategy, America would be far more selective about commitments abroad, and hesitant to use military force: "the United States would carry out foreign policy based less on the optimistic view of what America might accomplish if everything were to break its way, and more on a realistic view of how to position ourselves in case things do not. One might call it a less discretionary, less upbeat (at least in terms of its assumptions) approach to the world. Above all, there would be less resort to military force." It would also entail more reliance on diplomatic and other civilian capacities, emphasizing anticipation and prevention. As is all too evident in the Obama administration's failure to respond effectively with either military or diplomatic means to the burgeoning crisis in Syria, we do not today have the means to make it work. Those who think we should retrench need to consider how to fill that gap in capabilities.

Grand Strategy Is Less Important Than Flexibility and Agility

Grand strategy is not, however, what the "frugal superpower" really needs. Today's world does not present the kind of single challenge to vital American interests that the Soviet Union posed.[35] Instead it presents many different problems, often shifting in importance and even in where they pop up on the globe. Offshore balancing in this situation is a formula for constant redeployment of an already exhausted navy. One day it is pirates off Somalia, next week it is Iran threatening shipping in the Gulf of Hormuz or a North Korean missile launch into the Pacific Ocean. On 9/11 it was a foreign-based terrorist organization, but today it might be homegrown terrorists. Looming at a distance of decades is the possibility of Chinese naval challenge, but there are few other conventional military challenges on the horizon.[36]

If a single overwhelming threat emerges, we may want a grand strategy, but in the meanwhile we should start from what the American people want from their foreign policy, which is not a grand strategy but a profound commitment to protecting them from foreign threats, no matter what their origin, and pursuing other American interests. These include not only the traditional threats from other states but also, as enumerated in the QDDR:

Violent extremists

Proliferation of nuclear materials (especially to extremists)

Economic shocks

Irreversible climate change

Cyberattacks

Transnational crime

Infectious diseases

This is an extraordinary array of diverse challenges, requiring many different capabilities and responses. The situation gets even more complex if we look at the global landscape in which these challenges will arise, again as described in the QDDR:

Newly emerging powers (Brazil, China, India, Indonesia, Mexico, Nigeria, Russia, South Africa, and Turkey)

Large and rapidly growing youth populations in the Middle East and North Africa yearning for "dignity"

Diffusion of power to non-state actors (NGOs, multinational corporations, criminal networks, terrorist groups, rebel movements)

Weak states

Recurrent conflicts

Natural disasters

Cheaper, faster, and easier communications and transportation

Our future institutions are going to need to be far more agile and flexible than those we have today.[37] They will also need instruments in addition to the U.S. military to meet the challenges.

The Shape of Future Institutions: New Model Embassies

The starting point for thinking about our new, more flexible and agile foreign policy institutions should be a blank slate, starting not with the State Department itself but with redesign of our overseas presence to meet national security requirements in the twenty-first century. Imagine Rome without those thirty-six agencies of the U.S. government. Imagine Baghdad without its six-thousand-person leviathan. Imagine no consulates in any city where the capital is less than a three-hour flight away. Imagine no marine embassy guards, who at most embassies are more decorative than functional. Embassy security is properly the responsibility of the host government, most of which bend over backwards to make sure the Americans are not attacked. The marines' primary purpose is to ensure that classified material is protected, not to protect the embassy or its staff, which they do only in a crisis in which the host government fails to fulfill its responsibility.

Then imagine diplomats not only willing but determined to take advantage of technology that enables them to report securely from most places on earth with nothing but a laptop and a cell phone, or maybe a satellite phone or Internet connection. Imagine officials strongly committed to protecting American national security and willing to take reasonable risks to do so. Imagine only the most essential U.S. government personnel stationed abroad, with others traveling to visit as needed and using all the technological means at their disposal to avoid it. Our diplomacy would be expeditionary and anticipatory rather than static and reportorial.

In more than 90 percent of foreign capitals, this imaginary world would require American embassies with far smaller staffs than exist today. I would imagine no more than fifty Americans in most capitals, enabling dramatic reductions from present levels. Copenhagen today has 59 Americans, plus 30 locally hired.[38] Bosnia has 97, plus 11 locally hired.[39] Kuala Lumpur has 107, plus 13 locally hired.[40] Shaving 10 percent off an embassy like Rome only scratches the surface of what can and should be done. Especially in Europe, where twenty-eight countries have delegated large areas of national sovereignty to the European Union in Brussels, there is simply no need for a large official American presence in most capitals. A very few embassies—the American mission to the EU in Brussels is one, Moscow another—would need more than the fifty, but exceptions to that limit should be made on a case-by-case basis, after a thorough examination of the national security interests involved. London, Paris, Berlin, and Rome would need to justify staffing more than fifty Americans.

What about those other agencies that are today housed in American embassies? Some would continue to be accommodated within the fifty Americans: CIA station chiefs and defense attachés for sure, plus the occasional representative of other parts of the U.S. government. Giving all but a few ambassadors a ceiling of fifty would ensure that only the top priorities get staff in the embassy. Any other staff that domestic agencies think they need could also be sent abroad. There is no need to block them from establishing their own offices outside the embassies. They would still be obligated to observe chief-of-mission authority but would not get services (security, housing, administrative support) from the embassy. Precious few will take the trouble.

The State Department and USAID in Washington could also be dramatically downsized if they were not supporting so many people overseas. There is more than one domestic American employee for every one stationed abroad.[41] Cutting those stationed abroad by two-thirds would allow a more or less proportional cut in Washington.

It does not follow that our new institutions will necessarily be smaller than the existing ones, though cutting the presence abroad will ensure that they are cheaper. Agility and flexibility will require that we have a substantial number of people who can be assigned temporarily at home or abroad, depending on specific contingencies. Embassy Baghdad would no longer need six thousand, but it would still need hundreds if not thousands—given the requirement for people to train Iraqi security forces—rather than fifty.

The Shape of Future Institutions: More Private Sector, Less Public Sector

We discussed in the previous chapter five missing pieces that will need to be strengthened in the future. What does the need to provide for these capabilities tell us about our future foreign policy institutions?

Those five missing pieces fall into two categories:

1. Things that the U.S. government needs to do: mobilizing early preventive action and reforming security and justice sectors.

2. Things that need government financing but are better done primarily through private-sector organizations: supporting democracy, countering violent extremism, and promoting citizen-to-citizen outreach between Americans and non-Americans.

The first category is one that would readily fit into a foreign office: this would be a new government institution that replaces both the State Department and USAID. It would operate the embassies, much as foreign offices in many other countries do without an excessive presence of other agencies. It would provide consular and other citizens' services. It would also program and supervise foreign assistance, which would be tightly tied to protecting American national security by building friendly, capable, democratic states that can become markets for American goods and partners in dealing with the rest of the world.[42]

The Special Inspector General for Iraq Reconstruction has proposed a different solution. He would take contingency operations out of the State Department and USAID and house them in a separate United States Office of Contingency Operations.[43] This proposition has the virtue of providing a dedicated bureaucracy that would respond to international emergencies the way the Federal Emergency Management Agency responds to domestic ones, but it would not put appropriate emphasis on prevention or ensure integration with foreign or defense policy. There is little likelihood that the administration or Congress, shy of post-conflict reconstruction operations after the costly experiences in Iraq and Afghanistan, will want to create an institution whose reason for existence is something they would like to avoid.

How much money and staff is needed over and above the fixed embassies to provide an agile, anticipatory, and responsive capability? One rough estimate is five thousand active-duty government civilians and ten thousand civilian reserves to perform a wide range of complex operations (wider than that discussed here).[44] This is broadly consistent with the increased demand for such contingency operations over the past two decades.[45] Costs for such a civilian capacity would be several billion dollars per year, an amount easily less than what could be saved from the radical downsizing of American embassies and the State Department proposed here, or paid for from reduced military operations required to protect sea lanes in the Middle East.

The second category requires a more innovative approach. It is not always wise for an embassy whose responsibility it is to maintain good relations with an autocratic host government also to hand out assistance to those protesting that government for human rights abuses or failure to hold free and fair elections. Nor is it wise for embassies to engage with extremists in the hopes of persuading them to give it up. Supporting democracy, countering violent extremism through engagement with Muslim communities, and promoting citizen-to-citizen outreach are functions best performed outside of government, even if it involves using government funding provided because the efforts serve the national interest.

We already have organizations that do this work, mostly using U.S. government funds. There is an International Republican Institute and a National Democratic Institute. There is a National Endowment for Democracy and a United States Institute of Peace. There are NGOs like the American Bar Association's Rule of Law Initiative, many of them working with U.S. government funding. They need to be unchained from the increasingly intrusive management that the State Department and USAID have subjected them to in recent years. Their funding needs to be redoubled. The activities that go under the headings "democracy," "peace," "security sector reform," "rule of law," "countering violent extremism," and "citizen diplomacy" are vital components of a foreign policy that protects American national security, but they should be conducted at arms' length from bureaucratic structures that inhibit their initiative and limit their ingenuity.[46]

The Bottom Line

A diplomat, or an ordinary citizen, who wants to get the best deal for America today will recognize that State and USAID are broken and cannot be fixed. He would recognize that citizen-to-citizen connections are increasingly important in a world where communications costs are declining sharply even as the ease and speed of communications increase. He would see our enormous embassies in Baghdad and Kabul as monstrosities. He would acknowledge that diplomats who regard their primary (or even exclusive) role as carrying messages back and forth are outmoded.

The precise shape and structure of successor institutions to the State Department and USAID is difficult to predict. But it is clear enough that they fall into two categories:

1. A new, more flexible and agile foreign office that combines the reshaped functions of State and USAID but lives within their current budget and staff constraints.

2. An amplified array of nongovernmental institutions operating with at least some U.S. government funding that provide political and economic reform capacity to support peaceful transitions in autocratic countries, before they become basket cases.

War has come close to overwhelming America's military capacities in the last twenty years. It has demanded far more of our civilian foreign policy institutions than they have been able to deliver. In the next twenty, we'll need to be far more selective and anticipatory in our commitments abroad. Protecting national security will require revamped, consolidated, and upgraded civilian institutions that can anticipate and prevent problems, reducing the call on our capable but overworked troops.

Notes

1. We Are All Diplomats

1. "America Is Broke," YouTube video, 3:04, from a speech televised by CSPAN on December 10, 2011, posted by "JohnBoehner," December 10, 2011, accessed December 11, 2012, http://www.youtube.com/watch?v=v-oj4hfcGxU.

2. Michael Dobbs and John M. Goshko, "Albright's Personal Odyssey Shaped Foreign Policy Beliefs," *Washington Post*, December 6, 1996, accessed February 8, 2010, http://www.washingtonpost.com/wpsrv/politics/govt/admin/stories/albright120696.html.

3. Vali Nasr, *The Dispensable Nation: American Foreign Policy in Retreat* (New York: Doubleday, 2013).

4. Dana H. Allin and Erik Jones, *Weary Policeman: American Power in an Age of Austerity* (London: International Institute for Strategic Studies, 2012).

5. Charles A. Kupchan, *The End of the American Era* (New York: Knopf, 2002). See also Robert Kagan, *The World America Made* (New York: Knopf, 2012).

6. Philip Rucker, "Mitt Romney Calls for New 'American Century' with Muscular Foreign Policy," *Washington Post*, October 7, 2011, accessed February 8, 2012, http://www.washingtonpost.com/politics/mitt-romney-calls-for-new-american-century-with-muscular-foreign-policy/2011/10/07/gIQABi4wSL_story.html.

7. Jim O'Neill, *The Growth Map: Economic Opportunity in the BRICs and Beyond* (New York: Portfolio/Penguin, 2011).

8. "How to Get a Date: The Year When the Chinese Economy Will Truly Eclipse the US Is in Sight," *The Economist*, December 31, 2011, accessed February 8, 2012, http://www.economist.com/node/21542155; and "Charting China's Economy: 10 Years Under Hu," China Realtime Report, accessed December 26, 2012, http://blogs.wsj.com/chinarealtime/2012/11/16/charting-chinas-economy-10-years-under-hu-jintao/?mod=WSJBlog&buffer_share=d2fe3&utm_source=buffer.

9. See, for example, "Muddy Waters," *New York Times*, April 24, 2012, accessed April 30, 2012, http://www.nytimes.com/2012/04/25/opinion/the-philippines-china-and-the-us-meet-at-sea.html?_r=1.

10. Thomas G. Mahnken, *Competitive Strategies for the 21st Century: Theory, History and Practice* (Stanford CA: Stanford University Press, 2012).

11. Nina Hachigian, *Managing Insecurities across the Pacific* (Washington DC: Center for American Progress, 2012), 5, accessed February 8, 2012, http://www .americanprogress.org/issues/2012/02/pdf/china_paranoia.pdf.

12. Office of the Secretary of Defense, "Military and Security Developments Involving the People's Republic of China 2012," Annual Report to Congress, May 2012, accessed December 26, 2012, http://www.defense.gov/pubs/pdfs/2012 _CMPR_Final.pdf; and Patrick Cronin, ed., "Cooperation from Strength: The United States, China and the South China Sea," Center for a New American Security, January 2012, accessed December 26, 2012, http://www.cnas.org/files/ documents/publications/CNAS_CooperationFromStrength_Cronin_1.pdf.

13. William J. Burns, "The United States and Russia in a New Era: One Year after 'Reset,'" April 14, 2010, transcript and video, 46:08, U.S. Department of State, accessed February 8, 2012, http://www.state.gov/p/us/rm/2010/140179.htm.

14. "Turkey Is First among Rising Powers, Says New LSE Report," London School of Economics, June 7, 2011, accessed February 9, 2012, http://www2.lse.ac .uk/newsAndMedia/news/archives/2011/06/turkey.aspx.

15. Scott Snyder, "South Korea's Emerging Global Security Role," *World Politics Review*, Council on Foreign Relations, March 23, 2010, accessed February 9, 2012, http://www.cfr.org/international-peace-and-security/south-koreas-emerging -global-security-role/p21717; Jacob Zuma, "*The Cairo Review* Interview: South Africa's Clout," interview by Scott Macleod, *Cairo Review of Global Affairs*, American University in Cairo, May 26, 2011, accessed February 9, 2012, http:// www.aucegypt.edu/gapp/cairoreview/pages/articleDetails.aspx?aid=73.

16. O'Neill, *The Growth Map*.

17. Clyde V. Prestowitz Jr., *Trading Places: How We Allowed Japan to Take the Lead* (New York: Basic Books, 1988); Brink Lindsey and Aaron Lukas, *Revisiting the "Revisionists": The Rise and Fall of the Japanese Economic Model* (Washington DC: Cato Institute, July 31, 1998), accessed February 10, 2012, http://www.cato.org/publications/ trade-policy-analysis/revisiting-revisionists-rise-fall-japanese-economic-model.

18. Ian Bremmer, *Every Nation for Itself: Winners and Losers in a G-Zero World* (New York: Portfolio/Penguin, 2012).

19. Kagan, *The World America Made*; Charles Kupchan, *No One's World: The West, the Rising Rest and the Coming Global Turn* (New York: Oxford University Press, 2012); and Bremmer, *Every Nation for Itself*.

20. "Financing Peacekeeping," United Nations, accessed April 30, 2012, http:// www.un.org/en/peacekeeping/operations/financing.shtml.

21. Clearly they date from a time when French was the principal diplomatic language: a *demarche* is a formal call by a diplomat on a government official, an *aide memoire* is an informal written note conveying the intended substance of a demarche, and a *note verbale* is a formal, official communication from one government to another.

22. Anne-Marie Slaughter, "A New Theory for the Foreign Policy Frontier:

Collaborative Power," *Atlantic*, November 30, 2011, accessed April 10, 2012, http://www.theatlantic.com/international/archive/2011/11/a-new-theory-for-the-foreign-policy-frontier-collaborative-power/249260/.

23. Joseph S. Nye Jr., *The Future of Power* (New York: PublicAffairs, 2011).

24. Barack H. Obama, "The President's Speech in Cairo: A New Beginning," June 4, 2009, transcript and video 54:57, Office of the Press Secretary, The White House, accessed February 1, 2012, http://www.whitehouse.gov/the-press-office/remarks-president-cairo-university-6-04-09.

25. Stephen Glain, *State vs. Defense: The Battle to Define America's Empire* (New York: Crown, 2011); and David Rohde, "The U.S.'s Anemic Civilian Outreach Abroad," *Atlantic*, May 4, 2013, accessed May 20, 2013, http://www.theatlantic.com/international/archive/2013/05/the-uss-anemic-civilian-outreach-abroad/275547.

26. Fen Osler Hampson and I. William Zartman, *The Global Power of Talk: Negotiating America's Interests* (Boulder: Paradigm, 2012).

27. David Smock and Daniel Serwer, eds., *Facilitating Dialogue: USIP's Work in Conflict Zones* (Washington DC: United States Institute of Peace Press, 2012).

28. Kofi Annan and Nader Mousavizadeh, *Interventions: A Life in War and Peace* (New York: Penguin, 2012); and Lakhdar Brahimi and Salman Ahmed, "In Pursuit of Sustainable Peace: The Seven Deadly Sins of Mediation," New York University Center on International Cooperation, May 2008, accessed December 30, 2012, http://www.cic.nyu.edu/peacekeeping/docs/archive/2008/brahimi_7sins.pdf.

29. Richard N. Gardner, *Mission Italy: On the Front Line of the Cold War* (Lanham MD: Rowman and Littlefield, 2005), 43–44.

30. See, for example, Craig Cohen, "Measuring Progress in Stabilization and Reconstruction," Stabilization and Reconstruction Series, No. 1, March 2006, accessed December 31, 2012, http://www.usip.org/files/resources/srs1.pdf.

31. *Guiding Principles for Stabilization and Reconstruction* (Washington DC: United States Institute of Peace Press, 2009).

32. Frank Jacobs and Parag Khanna, "The New World," *New York Times*, accessed October 29, 2012, http://www.nytimes.com/interactive/2012/09/23/opinion/sunday/the-new-world.html.

33. Diane Cardwell, "Despite the Delay, the 100-Watt Bulb Is on Its Way Out," *New York Times*, December 17, 2011, B1.

34. James Dobbins, Dalia Dassa Kaye, Alireza Nader, and Frederic Wehrey, "How to Defuse Iran's Nuclear Threat: Bolster Diplomacy, Israeli Security, and Iranian Citizens," *RAND Review* 36, no. 1 (2012), accessed May 17, 2012, http://www.rand.org/publications/randreview/issues/2012/spring/iran.html.

35. Tom Mahnken, "Heresy Over Defense," *Shadow Government* (blog), *Foreign Policy*, October 13, 2011, accessed February 9, 2012, http://shadow.foreignpolicy.com/posts/2011/10/13/heresy_over_defense.

36. Phil Stewart, "U.S. Won't Cut Carrier Fleet to Fix Budget, Panetta Says,"

Reuters, January 21, 2012, accessed February 15, 2012, http://www.reuters.com/
article/2012/01/22/us-usa-defense-idUSTRE80L00R20120122.

37. The figure of $1 million has been used to justify budget requests. The actual
number may be lower or higher, depending on what you count. Mary Louise Kelly,
"Calculating the Cost of the War in Afghanistan," *All Things Considered*, transcript,
NPR, October 29, 2009, accessed March 5, 2012, http://www.npr.org/templates/story/
story.php?storyId=114294746; Congressional Research Service, *The Cost of Iraq,
Afghanistan, and Other Global War on Terror Operations since 9/11* (CRS Report RL33110,
March 29, 2011), by Amy Belasco, accessed March 5, 2012, http://www.fas.org/sgp/
crs/natsec/rl33110.pdf; Larry Shaughnessy, "One Soldier, One Year: $850,000 and
Rising," *Security Clearance* (blog), CNN, February 28, 2012, accessed March 5, 2012,
http://security.blogs.cnn.com/2012/02/28/one-soldier-one-year-850000-and-rising/.

2. War Shapes the Nation

1. Phil Plait, "Death by Meteorite," *Discover,* October 13, 2008, accessed May 1,
2013, http://blogs.discovermagazine.com/badastronomy/2008/10/13/death-by
-meteorite. If that comparison doesn't suit, try these: "You're More Likely to Die
from Brain-Eating Parasites, Alcoholism, Obesity, Medical Errors, Risky Sexual
Behavior or Just about Anything OTHER THAN Terrorism," *Washingtonsblog*, April
28, 2013, accessed May 1, 2013, http://www.washingtonsblog.com/2013/04/
statistics-you-are-not-going-to-be-killed-by-terrorists.html.

2. U.S Department of State, Bureau of Consular Affairs, Office of the Coordinator for Counterterrorism, *Terrorism Deaths, Injuries, Kidnappings of Private U.S.
Citizens, 2011* (Washington DC, 2012), accessed May 1, 2013, http://www.state.gov/
j/ct/rls/crt/2011/195556.htm.

3. Charles Kurzman, *Muslim American Terrorism in the Decade since 9/11 Report
no. 3* (Durham NC: Triangle Center on Terrorism and Homeland Security, 2012),
accessed February 23, 2012, http://sanford.duke.edu/centers/tcths/documents/
Kurzman_Muslim-American_Terrorism_in_the_Decade_Since_9_11.pdf.

4. Jeffrey M. Jones, "Americans Most Confident in Military, Least in Congress," *Politics* (blog), June 23, 2011, accessed February 11, 2012, http://www.gallup
.com/poll/148163/Americans-Confident-Military-Least-Congress.aspx.

5. David C. King and John Della Volpe, "Attitudes and the Formation of
Attitudes toward the U.S. Military" (presentation, Harvard Kennedy School,
Cambridge MA, July 9, 2008), accessed March 5, 2012, http://www.hks.harvard
.edu/fs/dking/King%20&%20Della%20Volpe_JWT_USMC.pdf.

6. Shanea Watkins and James Sherk, *Who Serves in the U.S. Military? The
Demographics of Enlisted Troops and Officers* (Washington DC: The Heritage
Foundation, 2008), accessed February 6, 2012, http://www.heritage.org/research/
reports/2008/08/who-serves-in-the-us-military-the-demographics-of-enlisted
-troops-and-officers.

7. Gallup, "Confidence in Institutions," June 7–10, 2012, accessed December 31, 2012, http://www.gallup.com/poll/1597/confidence-institutions.aspx.

8. Jeremi Suri fleshes out this idea in *Liberty's Surest Guardian: American Nation-Building from the Founders to Obama* (New York: Free Press, 2011).

9. Joshua Goldstein, "Think Again: War, World Peace Could Be Closer Than You Think," *Foreign Policy*, no. 188 (September/October 2011): 53–56, accessed October 18, 2012, http://www.foreignpolicy.com/articles/2011/08/15/think_again_war.

10. Rachel Maddow, *Drift: The Unmooring of American Military Power* (New York: Crown, 2012).

11. John Ferling, *The First of Men: A Life of George Washington* (New York: Oxford University Press, 2010), 44.

12. Eliot A. Cohen, *Conquered into Liberty: Two Centuries of Battles along the Great Warpath That Made the American Way of War* (New York: Free Press, 2011).

13. George Washington, "Farewell Address," *Miller Center Presidential Speech Archive of the University of Virginia* (September 19, 1796), accessed February 6, 2012, http://millercenter.org/president/speeches/detail/3462.

14. Jon Meacham, *American Lion: Andrew Jackson in the White House* (New York: Random House, 2008).

15. The delay in America's expansionist efforts—from the end of the Civil War until the 1890s—is the subject of Fareed Zakaria's *From Wealth to Power: The Unusual Origins of America's World Role* (Princeton: Princeton University Press, 1998).

16. Zakaria, *From Wealth to Power*; Warren Zimmermann, *First Great Triumph: How Five Americans Made Their Country a World Power* (New York: Farrar, Straus and Giroux, 2002).

17. Caspar W. Weinberger, "The Uses of Military Power" (speech, Washington DC, November 28, 1984), *Frontline*, Public Broadcasting Service, accessed March 6, 2012, http://www.pbs.org/wgbh/pages/frontline/shows/military/force/weinberger.html.

18. Colin L. Powell, "U.S. Forces: Challenges Ahead," *Foreign Affairs* 71, no. 5 (1992): 32–45. Rachel Maddow believes the important constraint on American war-making was the need to call up the reserves, which had become a necessity after the Vietnam War in accordance with the Abrams Doctrine (aka the Total Force Policy). Maddow, *Drift*, 20–22.

19. Powell discusses the decision to stick with the exit strategy from Iraq in his memoir. Colin Powell, *Every War Must End* (New York: Columbia Classics, 2005), 526–27.

20. Charles Krauthammer, "The Unipolar Moment," in "America and the World 1990," special issue, *Foreign Affairs* 70, no. 1 (1990): 23–33.

21. Andrew Bacevich, *Washington Rules: America's Path to Permanent War* (New York: Henry Holt, 2010), 14.

22. P. W. Singer, *Wired for War: The Robotics Revolution and Conflict in the 21st Century* (New York: Penguin, 2009).

23. Michael R. Gordon and Bernard E. Trainor, *The Endgame: The Inside Story of the Struggle for Iraq, from George W. Bush to Barack Obama* (New York: Pantheon Books, 2012).

24. Nathan Hodge, "U.S. Help to Upgrade Iraqi Air Force Will Take Time," *Wall Street Journal*, December 14, 2011, accessed March 6, 2012, http://online.wsj .com/article/SB10001424052970204336104577096670191102742.html.

25. "Enduring Strategic Partnership Agreement between the United States of America and the Islamic Republic of Afghanistan," May 2, 2012, T.I.A.S. 12-704, accessed May 5, 2012, http://www.whitehouse.gov/sites/default/files/2012.06.01u.s .-afghanistanspasignedtext.pdf.

26. "The Year of the Drone," Counterterrorism Strategy Initiative, The New America Foundation, updated July 24, 2012, accessed May 7, 2012, http:// counterterrorism.newamerica.net/drones.

27. Thom Shanker, "Warning against Wars Like Iraq and Afghanistan," *New York Times*, February 25, 2011, accessed February 6, 2012, http://www.nytimes.com/ 2011/02/26/world/26gates.html?_r=2.

28. Charles A. Kupchan, "Libya's Strains on NATO," interview by Bernard Gwertzman, Council on Foreign Relations, April 4, 2011, accessed February 3, 2012, http://www.cfr.org/libya/libyas-strains-nato/p24582.

29. Barack Obama, "Remarks by the President on the Middle East and North Africa," May 19, 2011, transcript and video, 49:49, The White House, Office of the Press Secretary, accessed February 3, 20120, http://www.whitehouse.gov/the-press -office/2011/05/19/remarks-president-middle-east-and-north-africa.

30. Roger Cliff, Mark Burles, Michael S. Chase, Derek Easton, and Kevin L. Pollpeter, *Entering the Dragon's Lair: Chinese Antiaccess Strategies and Their Implications for the United States* (Santa Monica CA: RAND, 2007), accessed May 5, 2012, http://www.rand.org/pubs/monographs/MG524.html; Ashley Tellis, *Punching the U.S. Military's "Soft Ribs": China's Antisatellite Weapon Test in Strategic Perspective* (Washington DC: Carnegie Endowment for International Peace, June 2007), accessed May 5, 2012, http://carnegieendowment.org/2007/06/19/ punching-u.s.-military-s-soft-ribs-china-s-antisatellite-weapon-test-in-strategic- perspective/3eua.

31. Charles A. Kupchan, *The End of the American Era* (New York: Knopf, 2002). The situation remains more or less as it was then, despite the recession and subse- quent slow recovery; Ian Bremmer, "Five Myths about America's Decline," *Washing- ton Post*, May 3, 2012, accessed May 5, 2012, http://www.washingtonpost.com/ opinions/five-myths-about-americas-decline/2012/05/03/gIQAvlnvzT_story.html.

32. Edward Luce, *Time to Start Thinking: America in the Age of Descent* (New York: Atlantic Monthly Press, 2012); Roya Wolverson and Christopher Alessi, "Confronting U.S.-China Economic Imbalances," Council on Foreign Relations, November 2, 2011, accessed March 19, 2012, http://www.cfr.org/china/confronting -us-china-economic-imbalances/p20758.

33. "Fiscal Facts: The Great Debt Shift," Pew Charitable Trusts, April 2011, accessed February 6, 2012, http://www.pewtrusts.org/news_room_detail.aspx ?id=85899359317.

34. Dana Priest and William Arkin, "Top Secret America: A Hidden World, Growing beyond Control," *Washington Post*, July 19, 2010, accessed February 7, 2012, http://projects.washingtonpost.com/top-secret-america/articles/a-hidden -world-growing-beyond-control/; see also Dana Priest and William Arkin, *Top Secret America: The Rise of the New American Security State* (New York: Little, Brown, 2011).

35. Priest and Arkin, "Top Secret America."

36. Greg Miller, "Budget 2012: CIA/Intelligence Agencies," *Washington Post*, February 14, 2011, accessed February 7, 2012, http://voices.washingtonpost.com/ 44/2011/02/budget-2012-ciaintelligence-ag.html.

37. Daniel Wirls, *International Security: The Politics of Defense from Reagan to Obama* (Baltimore: Johns Hopkins University Press, 2010), 129. See also Dylan Matthews, "Defense Spending in the U.S. in Four Charts," *Wonkblog* (blog), *Washington Post*, August 28, 2012, accessed October 29, 2012, http://www .washingtonpost.com/blogs/ezra-klein/wp/2012/08/28/defense-spending-in-the -u-s-in-four-charts/.

38. Linda J. Bilmes and Joseph E. Stiglitz, "The Iraq War Will Cost Us $3 Trillion, and Much More," *Washington Post*, March 9, 2008, accessed March 6, 2012. http://www.washingtonpost.com/wp-dyn/content/article/2008/03/07/ AR2008030702846.html; Linda J. Bilmes and Joseph E. Stiglitz, *The Three Trillion Dollar War: The True Cost of the Iraq Conflict* (New York: Norton, 2008); these numbers are broadly consistent with Brown University's "Costs of War" project, accessed May 3, 2013, http://costsofwar.org.

39. Anna Simons, "Twenty-First Century Cultures of War: Advantage Them," Foreign Policy Research Institute, April 2013, accessed May 18, 2013, https://www .fpri.org/docs/Simons_21st_Century_Cultures_of_War.pdf. See also Christoph Zürcher, Carrie Manning, Kristie D. Evenson, Rachel Hayman, Sarah Riese, and Nora Roehner, *Costly Democracy: Peacebuilding and Democratization after War* (Stanford: Stanford University Press, 2013).

40. Veronique de Rugy and Jakina R. Debnam, "Does Government Spending Stimulate Economies?" *Mercatus on Policy* 77 (2010), accessed February 7, 2012, http://mercatus.org/publication/does-government-spending-stimulate-economies.

41. Daniel W. Drezner, "Military Primacy Doesn't Pay (Nearly As Much As You Think)," *International Security* 38, no. 1 (2013): 52–79. Drezner looks at whether military hegemony attracts private investment or public resources from countries that live under the hegemon's "security umbrella." He also considers the return to the hegemon from "public goods" like an open global economic order, financial liquidity, and stability. He finds the returns from the specifically military component of hegemony overstated: "Overreliance on military preponderance is badly

misguided. . . . It is not that military power is useless; it is that the law of diminishing marginal returns has kicked in" (79).

42. Congressional Research Service, *Osama bin Laden's Death: Implications and Considerations* (CRS Report R41809, May 5, 2011), by John Rollins, accessed May 5, 2012, http://www.fas.org/sgp/crs/terror/R41809.pdf; Sam Stein, "From 9/11 to Osama Bin Laden's Death, Congress Spent $1.28 Trillion in War on Terror," *Huffington Post*, July 2, 2011, accessed May 5, 2012, http://www.huffingtonpost .com/2011/05/02/osama-bin-laden-dead-war-on-terror-costs_n_856390.html.

43. Richard N. Haass, *War of Necessity, War of Choice* (New York: Simon and Schuster, 2009).

3. More Than a Military Mission

1. U.S. Constitution preamble, accessed February 2, 2012, http://www.archives .gov/exhibits/charters/constitution_transcript.html.

2. George W. Bush, *National Security Strategy*, September 2002, accessed February 7, 2012, http://georgewbush-whitehouse.archives.gov/nsc/nss/2002/.

3. Barack Obama, *National Security Strategy*, May 2010, accessed February 7, 2012, http://www.whitehouse.gov/sites/default/files/rss_viewer/national_security _strategy.pdf.

4. George W. Bush, *National Security Strategy*, March 2006, accessed February 7, 2012, http://georgewbush-whitehouse.archives.gov/nsc/nss/2006/.

5. George W. Bush, "Graduation Speech at West Point," transcript and video 47:19, White House Archives, accessed February 2, 2012, http://georgewbush -whitehouse.archives.gov/news/releases/2002/06/print/20020601-3.html; Bush, *National Security Strategy*, March 2006.

6. Bush, *National Security Strategy*, September 2002.

7. James Locher and Christopher Holshek, *America's First Quarter Millennium: Envisioning a Transformed National Security System in 2026* (Washington DC: National Defense University, November 9, 2011), accessed February 7, 2012, www .pnsr.org/data/images/pnsr_americas_first_quarter_millennium.pdf.

8. *Preventive Priorities Survey: 2012* (Washington DC: Council on Foreign Relations, 2012), accessed February 7, 2012, www.cfr.org/content/publications/ attachments/CPA_Preventive_Priorities_Survey_2012.pdf. Europeans, not surprisingly, come to even more civilian conclusions: Gabor Ikoldy, "The Next Steps for NATO," *Carnegie Europe*, June 5, 2012, accessed June 7, 2012, http:// carnegieeurope.eu/publications/?fa=48318&lang=en.

9. Project for a United and Strong America, "Setting Priorities for American Leadership: A New National Security Strategy for the United States," March 2013, accessed May 18, 2013, http://www.nationalsecuritystrategy.org/pdf/pusa-report -march-2013.pdf.

10. Robert D. Lamb and Sadeeka Hameed, "U.S. Policy Responses to Potential Transition: A New Dataset of Political Conflicts, Protests, and Coups," Center for Strategic and International Studies, March 2013, viii.

11. But it is relevant to note that Wikileaks has not had access to the limited distribution diplomatic cables that constitute the most sensitive, and often most valuable, ones. See Daniel Serwer, "A Diplomat's Guide to Wikileaks," *Wired,* October 7, 2011, accessed November 27, 2012, http://www.wired.com/threatlevel/2011/10/diplomat-guide-wikileaks/.

12. *Structures of Peace: Identifying What Leads to Peaceful Societies* (Washington DC: Institute for Economics and Peace, April 4, 2011), accessed May 5, 2012, http://www.visionofhumanity.org/wpcontent/uploads/2011/10/Structures-of-Peace.pdf; see also Micah Zenko and Michael Cohen, "Clear and Present Safety: The United States Is More Secure Than Washington Thinks," *Foreign Affairs* 91, no. 2 (2012), accessed May 5, 2012, http://www.foreignaffairs.com/articles/137279/micah-zenko-and-michael-a-cohen/clear-and-present-safety.

13. Gordon Adams, *Buying National Security: How America Plans and Pays for Its Global Role and Safety at Home* (New York: Routledge, 2009), 253.

14. For one example of the difference a unified national security budget might make, see the Task Force on a Unified National Security Budget, "Rebalancing Our National Security: The Benefits of Implementing a Unified Security Budget," Center for American Progress, October 2012, accessed December 26, 2012, http://www.americanprogress.org/wp-content/uploads/2012/10/UnifiedSecurityBudget.pdf.

15. James R. Locher and Christopher Holshek, *The Role of the Reserve in National Security Transformation* (Washington DC: Reserve Officer's Association of the United States, January 2011), accessed February 2, 2012, http://www.roa.org/site/DocServer/Natl_Security_Transformation_Report_DEF.pdf?docID=32183.

16. Catherine Dale, "National Security Professionals and Interagency Reform: Proposals, Recent Experience, and Issues for Congress," Congressional Research Service RL34565, September 26, 2011, accessed May 21, 2013, http://www.fas.org/sgp/crs/natsec/RL34565.pdf.

17. Nina Serafino, Catherine Dale, and Pat Towell, "Building Civilian Interagency Capacity for Missions Abroad: Key Proposals and Issues for Congress," Congressional Research Service R42133, February 9, 2012, accessed May 21, 2013, http://www.fas.org/sgp/crs/row/R42133.pdf.

18. "Historical Tables," U.S. Office of Management and Budget, accessed August 1, 2012, http://www.whitehouse.gov/omb/budget/Historicals/.

19. Anthony H. Cordesman, Robert Hammond, and Jordan D'Amato, *The Macroeconomics of U.S. Defense Spending* (Washington DC: Center for Strategic and International Studies, November 9, 2010), accessed March 5, 2012, csis.org/files/publication/101108_FY11_macro_defense.pdf.

20. Anna Mulrine, "Budget Cuts Force Pentagon to Redefine Priorities: What Can't We Afford to Cut?" *Christian Science Monitor,* May 20, 2011, accessed March

5, 2012, http://www.csmonitor.com/USA/Military/2011/0520/Budget-cuts-force
-Pentagon-to-redefine-priorities-What-can-t-we-afford-to.cut.

21. Douglas MacGregor, "A Radical Plan for Cutting the Defense Budget and
Reconfiguring the U.S. Military," *Foreign Policy*, April 26, 2011, accessed March 5,
2012, http://www.foreignpolicy.com/articles/2011/04/26/a_radical_plan_for
_cutting_the_defense_budget_and_reconfiguring_the_us_military.

22. Substantial, but far less radical cuts, are looking more likely. Gordon Adams,
"Budget Agreement Reached!" *Foreign Policy,* November 27, 2012, accessed
December 26, 2012, http://www.foreignpolicy.com/articles/2012/11/27/budget
_agreement_reached#.ULVhHYkhmwo.twitter.

23. John D. Banusiewicz, "Secretary Urges Careful Thought in Spending
Reductions," *American Forces Press Service*, U.S. Department of Defense, May 19,
2011, accessed March 5, 2012, http://www.defense.gov/news/newsarticle.aspx
?id=64010.

24. Gordon Adams, "Unfinished Business: Ten Huge Challenges Bob Gates
Leaves Behind," *Foreign Policy,* June 3, 2011, accessed March 5, 2012, http://www
.foreignpolicy.com/articles/2011/06/03/unfinished_business?page=full.

25. Office of the Secretary of Defense, *Quadrennial Defense Review Report*
(Washington DC: United States Department of Defense, February 2010), accessed
February 23, 2012, www.defense.gov/qdr/images/QDR_as_of_12Feb10_1000.pdf.

26. Elaine Wilson, "Gates Unveils Strategy to Cut Cost and Boost Efficiency,"
American Forces Press Service, U.S. Department of Defense, September 14, 2012,
accessed June 30, 2012, http://www.defense.gov/news/newsarticle.aspx?id=60854.

27. Donna Miles, "Lynn: U.S. Must Prepare for Future Warfare Trends,"
American Forces Press Service, Department of Defense, June 8, 2011, accessed
February 23, 2012, http://www.defense.gov/news/newsarticle.aspx?id=64242.

28. Patrick Stewart, *Weak Links: Fragile States, Global Threats, and International
Security* (New York: Oxford University Press, 2011).

29. Peter Kennet, "What Is the Foreign Service?" *TheDipNotes* (blog), February
6, 2010, accessed February 23, 2012, http://thedipnotes.com/about_the_foreign
_service/.

30. "USAID Primer: What We Do and How We Do It," United States Agency for
International Development, January 2006, accessed February 23, 2012, www.usaid
.gov/about_usaid/PDACG100.pdf.

31. "Foreign Assistance and the U.S. Budget," Center for Global Development,
2010, accessed February 23, 2012, http://www.cgdev.org/section/initiatives/_active/
assistance/budget.

32. Ben Connable and Martin Libicki, *How Insurgencies End* (Santa Monica CA:
RAND Press, 2010), 154.

33. Some argue they should not do it at all: Bing West, *The Wrong War: Grit,
Strategy and the Way Out of Afghanistan* (New York: Random House, 2011).

34. *Hearing to Receive Testimony on the Situation in Afghanistan, Before the Senate*

Committee on Armed Services, 11th Cong., 1st sess. (2011), 13, accessed March 5, 2012, http://armed-services.senate.gov/testimony.cfm?wit_id=9991&id=5058.

35. Howard LaFranchi, "Gates, Clinton Oppose Cuts to State Department Budget," *Christian Science Monitor*, April 23, 2010, accessed February 2, 2012, http://www.csmonitor.com/USA/Foreign-Policy/2010/0423/Gates-Clinton -oppose-cuts-to-State-Department-budget.

36. Robert M. Gates, "A Balanced Strategy: Reprogramming the Pentagon for a New Age," *Foreign Affairs* 88, no. 1 (2009), accessed December 26, 2012, http:// www.foreignaffairs.com/articles/63717/robert-m-gates/a-balanced-strategy.

37. Gates, "A Balanced Strategy."

38. Sarah Kenyon Lischer, "Humanitarian Aid Is Not a Military Business," *Christian Science Monitor*, April 15, 2003, accessed March 5, 2012, http://www .csmonitor.com/2003/0415/p09s02-coop.html; "Aid Groups Urge NATO to Separate Military and Humanitarian Activities to Protect Civilians in Afghani- stan," International Rescue Committee, May 20, 2012, accessed May 25, 2012, http://www.rescue.org/news/aid-groups-urge-nato-separate-military-and -humanitarian-activities-protect-civilians-afghanista-4463.

39. *The U.S. Army/Marine Corps Counterinsurgency Manual* (Chicago: University of Chicago Press, 2007).

40. Craig Collier, *Leaders' Perceptions of the Commander's Emergency Response Program in Iraq* (Arlington VA: Special Investigator General for Iraq Reconstruc- tion, April 2012), accessed May 17, 2012, http://www.sigir.mil/files/lessonslearned/ SpecialReportLeadersPerceptions.pdf#view=fit.

41. Kevin Baron, "Brass Tone Down the Ask for Foreign Aid," *Foreign Policy*, accessed May 3, 2013, http://e-ring.foreignpolicy.com/posts/2013/03/06/brass _tone_down_the_ask_for_foreign_aid.

42. "Questionnaire: American Public Opinion on Foreign Aid," *World Public Opinion*, November 30, 2010, accessed May 17, 2012, http://www.worldpublicopinion .org/pipa/pdf/nov10/ForeignAid_Nov10_quaire.pdf.

43. "More Blame Wars Than Spending or Tax Cuts for Nation's Debt: Jobs Are Top Economic Worry, Deficit Concerns Rise," Pew Research Center, June 7, 2011, accessed May 17, 2012, http://pewresearch.org/pubs/2017/poll-what-created-the -national-debt-wars-spending-tax-cuts-deficit-reduction-proposals.

44. Meghan O'Sullivan, *Shrewd Sanctions: Statecraft and State Sponsors of Terrorism* (Washington DC: Brookings Institution Press, 2003).

45. Karel Bryukhanov, "House GOP FY2012 Budget: Crazy?" *The Global Citizen* (blog), Global Solutions, April 7, 2011, accessed December 11, 2012, http:// globalsolutions.org/blog/2011/04/house-gop-fy2012-budget-crazy.

46. Russell Rumbaugh, "Shell Games," *The Will and the Wallet* (blog), December 15, 2011, accessed February 2, 2012, http://thewillandthewallet .squarespace.com/blog/2011/12/15/shell-games.html.

47. Lawrence Korb and Max Hoffman, "New Ryan Plan Hurts U.S. Foreign

Policy Budget Increases Defense Spending While Reducing Development and Diplomacy Spending," Center for American Progress, March 22, 2012, accessed May 8, 2012, http://www.americanprogress.org/issues/2012/03/ryan_budget _foreign_policy.html.

48. Michael Mandelbaum, *The Frugal Superpower: America's Global Leadership in a Cash-Strapped Era* (Jackson TN: Public Affairs, 2010), 184.

49. John Mearsheimer, *The Tragedy of Great Power Politics* (New York: Norton, 2003).

50. F. Gregory Gause III, "Don't Just Do Something, Stand There!" *Argument* (blog), *Foreign Policy*, December 21, 2011, accessed February 3, 2012, http://www .foreignpolicy.com/articles/2011/12/21/america_arab_spring_do_nothing?page=0,3.

51. Justin Logan and Christopher Preble, *Failed States and Failed Logic: The Case against a Standing Nation-Building Office* (Washington DC: CATO Institute, January 2006), accessed February 23, 2012, www.cato.org/pubs/pas/pa560.pdf.

52. Logan and Preble, *Failed States and Failed Logic*.

53. U.S. Agency for International Development, *Sudan, Monthly Update: Sudan* (Washington DC, February 2011), accessed March 15, 2012, http://www.genocide watch.org/images/Sudan_11_02_xx_USAID_Sudan_report.pdf.

54. U.S. Department of State, Offices of the Deputy Secretary of State for Management and Resources, *Quadrennial Diplomacy and Development Review: Fact Sheet* (Washington DC, 2010), accessed March 16, 2012, http://www.state.gov/s/ dmr/qddr/.

55. James Traub, "Nation-Building in Yemen?" *Foreign Policy*, May 18, 2012, accessed May 25, 2012, http://www.foreignpolicy.com/articles/2012/05/18/nation _building_in_the_yemen?page=0,1.

56. Chuck Spinney, "The Heritage Foundation, Then and Now," *Time*, January 10, 2012, accessed May 25, 2012, http://battleland.blogs.time.com/2012/01/10/the -heritage-foundation-then-and-now/.

4. Building States

1. Daniel Serwer, "A Bosnian Federation Memoir," in *Herding Cats: Multiparty Mediation in a Complex World*, ed. Chester A. Crocker, Fen O. Hampson, and Pamela R. Aall (Washington DC: United States Institute of Peace Press, 1999), 549–86.

2. Max Weber, "Politics as Vocation," in *Max Weber: Essays in Sociology*, ed. and trans. H. H. Gerth and C. Wright Mills (New York: Oxford University Press, 1946), 77–128, accessed March 19, 2012, http://www.sscnet.ucla.edu/polisci/ethos/ Weber-vocation.pdf.

3. Congressional Research Service, *The Cost of Iraq, Afghanistan, and Other Global War on Terror Operations since 9/11* (CRS Report RL33110, March 29, 2011), by Amy Belasco, accessed February 26, 2012, http://www.fas.org/sgp/crs/natsec/ RL33110.pdf.

4. Kurt Bassuener and Bodo Weber, "House of Cards: The EU's 'Reinforced Presence' in Bosnia and Herzegovina: Proposal for a New Policy Approach," Democratization Policy Council, May 2013, accessed May 21, 2013, http:// democratizationpolicy.org/images/policybriefs/may.pdf.

5. Edward Newman and Roland Rich, eds., *The UN Role in Promoting Democracy: Between Ideals and Reality* (New York: United Nations University Press, 2004).

6. Seth Jones, *In the Graveyard of Empires: America's War in Afghanistan* (New York: Norton, 2009).

7. Williamson Murray and Robert H. Scales Jr., *The Iraq War: A Military History* (Cambridge: Belknap Press of Harvard University, 2005).

8. *Agreement on Provisional Arrangements in Afghanistan Pending the Re-Establishment of Permanent Government Institutions ("Bonn Agreement")* [Afghanistan], s/2001/1154, December 5, 2001, accessed May 15, 2012, http://www.unhcr.org/refworld/ docid/3f48f4754.html. For a detailed account of the first year after the war, see J. Alexander Thier, "The Politics of Peace-Building: Year One: From Bonn to Kabul," in *Nation-Building Unraveled? Aid, Peace and Justice in Afghanistan*, ed. Antonio Donini, Morah Niland, and Karin Wermester (Bloomfield CT: Kumarian Press, 2004).

9. Jones, *In the Graveyard of Empires*, 115–32.

10. Thomas E. Ricks, *Fiasco: The American Military Adventure in Iraq* (New York: Penguin Press, 2006).

11. Christina Caan, Beth Cole, Paul Hughes, and Daniel Serwer, "Is This Any Way to Run an Occupation?" in *Interim Governments: Institutional Bridges to Peace and Democracy?*, ed. Karen Guttieri and Jessica Piombo (Washington DC: United States Institute of Peace Press, 2007), 319–43.

12. Fourth Geneva Convention Relative to the Protection of Civilian Persons in Time of War, August 12, 1949, 6 U.S.T. 3516, 75 U.N.T.S. 287, art. 6, accessed March 26, 2012, http://www.icrc.org/ihl.nsf/full/380.

13. "October 11, 2000 Debate Transcript," Commission on Presidential Debates, October 11, 2000, accessed March 19, 2012, http://www.debates.org/index.php ?page=october-11-2000-debate-transcript.

14. James Dobbins, Laurel Miller, et al., *Overcoming Obstacles to Peace: Local Factors in Nation-Building"* (Santa Monica CA: RAND, 2013), provides a good catalog of the evidence.

15. OECD, *Supporting Statebuilding in Situations of Conflict and Fragility: Policy Guidance* (Paris: OECD Publishing, 2011), accessed February 13, 2012, http://browse .oecdbookshop.org/oecd/pdfs/free/4311031e.pdf; I am indebted to Geoffrey Curfman for a timely and eloquent reminder of these points.

16. See, for example, Reidar Visser, "The Western Imposition of Sectarianism on Iraqi Politics," *Arab Studies Journal* 15, no. 2 (2007): 83–99.

17. Daniel Serwer, "Victory Is Just the Beginning," *Los Angeles Times*, October 28, 2002, accessed February 13, 2012, http://articles.latimes.com/2002/oct/28/ opinion/oe-serwer28.

18. Special Inspector General for Iraq Reconstruction (SIGIR), *Hard Lessons: The Iraq Reconstruction Experience* (Baghdad: SIGIR, 2009), accessed March 5, 2012, http://www.sigir.mil/files/HardLessons/Hard_Lessons_Report.pdf.

19. Robert Perito, *Establishing the Rule of Law in Iraq* (Washington DC: United States Institute of Peace, April 2003), accessed March 5, 2012, http://www.usip.org/publications/establishing-rule-law-iraq.

20. James Dobbins, Seth Jones, Benjamin Runkle, and Siddharth Mohandas, *Occupying Iraq: A History of the Provisional Authority* (Santa Monica CA: RAND Corporation, 2009).

21. SIGIR, *Hard Lessons,* vii.

22. Daniel Serwer, "State-Building in Iraq: An American Failure, Lately Redeemed," in *The International Community and State-Building: Getting Its Act Together?* ed. Patrice McMahon and Jon Western (New York: Routledge, 2012), 169–83.

23. For my own view of Iraq at the end of 2012, see Daniel Serwer, "Iraq Untethered," *Current History*, December 2012, 344–49. For a more jaundiced view from someone who has spent a lot of time there, see Emma Sky, "Iraq in Hindsight: Views on the U.S. Withdrawal," Center for a New American Security, December 14, 2012, accessed December 26, 2012, http://www.cnas.org/files/documents/publications/CNAS_IraqInHindsight_Sky_0.pdf.

24. For a Washington-focused view of what went wrong in the Bush administration's mismanagement of the reconstruction effort, see Dov Zakheim, *A Vulcan's Tale: How the Bush Administration Mismanaged the Reconstruction of Afghanistan* (Washington DC: Brookings Institution Press, 2011). For the foreign policy perspective of an insider, see James F. Dobbins, *After the Taliban: Nationbuilding in Afghanistan* (Dulles VA: Potomac Books, 2008).

25. Patrick Devenny, "Legal Advice from the Taliban," *Foreign Policy*, May 29, 2009, accessed February 13, 2012, http://experts.foreignpolicy.com/posts/2009/05/29/legal_advice_from_the_taliban.

26. Joel Migdal, *Weak States, Strong Societies* (Princeton NJ: Princeton University Press, 1988). For recent thinking on how to handle rule of law in such societies, see Rachel Kleinfeld, *Advancing the Rule of Law Abroad* (Washington DC: Carnegie Endowment for International Peace, 2012).

27. The "gacaca" courts in Rwanda are a particularly interesting case, as they were used in cases of interethnic crimes. See David Bamford, "Rwanda Sets up Genocide Courts," *BBC News,* November 25, 2002, accessed March 5, 2012, http://news.bbc.co.uk/2/hi/africa/2510971.stm; and William Schabas, "Genocide Trials and *Gacaca* Courts," *Journal of International Criminal Justice* 3 (2005), accessed October 24, 2012, http://english.konferenz-nuernberg08.de/Schabas_Genocide_Trials_and_Gacaca_Courts.pdf.

28. We have come late to recognize the importance of local conflicts in Aghanistan. See, for example, Ryan Evans, "The Micro-Level of Civil War: The

Case of Central Helmand Province," *CTC Sentinel* 5, no. 9 (2012), accessed October 29, 2012, http://www.ctc.usma.edu/posts/the-micro-level-of-civil-war-the-case-of -central-helmand-province. American efforts to shift gears after 2009 were over-ambitious for the local context. See Frances Z. Brown, "The U.S. Surge and Afghan Local Governance: Lessons for Transition," United States Institute of Peace Special Report No. 316 (September 2012), accessed December 27, 2012, http:// www.usip.org/files/resources/SR316.pdf.

29. The World Bank National Solidarity Program, *Afghanistan: Building an Effective State* (Washington DC: The World Bank, June 2008), accessed February 13, 2012, http://sitercsources.worldbank.org/AFGHANISTANEXTN/Resources/ 305984-1213128265371/50908551213128292963/AFstatebuildingsummary.pdf.

30. See, for example, "MoPH Launches First Community Female Nurses Training Program in Afghanistan," Ministry of Public Health, Islamic Republic of Afghanistan, July 5, 2011, accessed February 13, 2012, http://moph.gov.af/en/ news/2062; John A. Nagl, Andrew M. Exum, and Ahmed A. Humayun, "A Pathway to Success in Afghanistan: The National Solidarity Program," Center for New American Security, March 16, 2009, accessed March 19, 2012, http://www .cnas.org/node/768; Leonard S. Rubenstein and William Newbrander, "Militarizing Afghan Health Care," *Washington Post*, November 29, 2009, accessed May 8, 2012, http://www.washingtonpost.com/wp-dyn/content/article/2009/11/27/ AR2009112702454.html.

31. "Take context as the starting point," say the OECD Principles for Good International Engagement in Fragile States and Situations," accessed May 16, 2013, http://www.oecd.org/dac/incaf/38368714.pdf.

32. Daron Acemoglu and James Robinson, *Why Nations Fail: The Origins of Power, Prosperity and Poverty* (New York: Crown, 2012).

33. Valerie Hudson, Bonnie Ballif-Spanvill, Mary Capriolo, and Chad Emmett, *Sex and World Peace* (New York: Columbia University Press, 2012), 114.

34. *Guiding Principles for Stabilization and Reconstruction* (Washington DC: United States Institute of Peace, 2009), accessed February 13, 2012, http://www .usip.org/publications/guiding-principles-stabilization-and-reconstruction.

35. U.S. Department of Defense, *Military Support for Stability, Security, Transition, and Reconstruction (SSTR) Operations* (Washington DC, November 28, 2005), accessed February 13, 2012, www.fas.org/irp/doddir/dod/d3000_05.pdf.

36. The White House, *Management of Interagency Efforts concerning Stabilization and Reconstruction* (Washington DC, December 7, 2005), accessed February 13, 2012, http://www.fas.org/irp/offdocs/nspd/nspd-44.html.

37. U.S. Department of State, Civilian Response Corps, Coordinator for Reconstruction and Stabilization, *The Civilian Response Corps* (Washington DC, 2011), accessed February 13, 2012, http://www.civilianresponsecorps.gov/documents/ organization/156921.pdf.

38. U.S. Department of State, Deputy Secretary of State for Management and

Resources, *Quadrennial Diplomacy and Development Review* (Washington DC, 2010), accessed February 2, 2012, http://www.state.gov/s/dmr/qddr/; U.S. Department of Defense, Secretary of Defense, *Sustaining U.S. Global Leadership: Priorities for 21st Century Defense* (Washington: DC, 2012), accessed March 29, 2012, http://www.defense.gov/news/Defense_Strategic_Guidance.pdf.

39. This question is also discussed, with similar conclusions, in Rory Stewart and Gerald Knaus, *Can Intervention Work?* (New York: Norton, 2011).

40. UN Security Council, *Security Council Resolution 1244 (1999) [On the Deployment of International Civil and Security Presences in Kosovo]*, June 10, 1999, S/RES/1244 (1999), accessed March 16, 2012, http://www.unhcr.org/refworld/docid/3b00f27216.html.

41. Michael Dziedzic, "Kosovo," in *Twenty-First Century Peace Operations*, ed. William Durch (Washington DC: United States Institute of Peace Press, 2006), 319–88.

42. Michael Malley, "Inchoate Opposition, Divided Incumbents: Muddling toward Democracy in Indonesia, 1998–99," in Guttieri, and Piombo, *Interim Governments*, 147–69; see also Aurel Croissant, "International Interim Governments, Democratization, and Post-Conflict Peace Building: Lessons from Cambodia and East Timor," in Guttieri and Piombo, *Interim Governments*, 217–38.

43. Dobbins, Miller, et al., *Overcoming Obstacles to Peace*, xxxiv.

44. Richard Kaplan, ed., *Exit Strategies and State Building* (New York: Oxford University Press, 2012). But "wars are difficult to close out even when they are started well." Gideon Rose, *How Wars End: Why We Always Fight the Last Battle* (New York, Simon and Schuster, 2010), 11.

45. Congressional Research Service, *The Cost of Iraq, Afghanistan, and Other Global War on Terror Operations since 9/11* (CRS Report RL33110, March 29, 2011), by Amy Belasco, accessed March 5, 2012, http://www.fas.org/sgp/crs/natsec/RL33110.pdf.

46. Thomas S. Szayna, Nora Bensahel, Terrence K. Kelly, Keith Crane, David E. Mosher, and Beth E. Lachman, "Shifting Terrain: Stabilization Operations Require a Better Balance between Civilian and Military Effort," *RAND Review* 33, no. 3 (2009–10). See also Todd D. Calogne, "Secretary Clinton Announces Civilian Response Corp Reaches 1,000 Members," *DipNote* (blog),U.S. Department of State, July 15, 2010, accessed February 5, 2012, http://blogs.state.gov/index.php/site/entry/civilian_response_corps_1000_members: "Secretary of State Hillary Rodham Clinton *announced* the Civilian Response Corps, a group of civil federal employees who are trained to deploy to areas of crisis to provide prevention, reconstruction, and stabilization assistance, has reached 1,000 members at its two-year anniversary mark."

47. Rusty Barber, "Peace Initiative in the Triangle of Death," in *Facilitating Dialogue: USIP's Work in Conflict Zones*, ed. David R. Smock and Daniel Serwer (Washington DC: United States Institute of Peace Press), 9–30.

48. Hans Binnendijk and Patrick M. Cronin, eds., *Civilian Surge: Key to Complex Operations* (Washington DC: National Defense University Press, 2009), 30–31 and 213–30.

49. Nicholas J. Armstrong, "Afghan Security Force Assistance or Security Sector Reform? Despite Recent Improvements in the Afghan Security Forces, More Emphasis on Ministerial Development and Police Reform Is Needed," *Insct on Security* (blog), December 21, 2011, accessed May 22, 2012, http://insct.org/ commentary-analysis/2011/12/21/afghan-security-force-assistance-or-security -sector-reform-despite-recent-improvements-in-the-afghan-security-forces-more -emphasis-on-ministerial-development-and-police-reform-is-needed/.

5. Who Contributes to This Work?

1. "Kidnapped Aid Workers Rescued in Somalia," Danish Demining Group, January 25, 2012, accessed February 21, 2012, http://www.danishdemininggroup .dk/news/news/artikel/kidnapped-aid-workers-rescued-in-somalia-1/.

2. The number in 2008 was about 210,000, increasing at a rate of 6 percent per year. Paul Harvey, Abby Stoddard, Adele Harmer, and Glyn Taylor, *The State of the Humanitarian System: Assessing Performance and Progress* (London: Overseas Development Institute, January 2010), accessed March 19, 2012, http://www.alnap .org/pool/files/alnap-sohs-final.pdf.

3. E-mail from Sloan Mann to Daniel Serwer, January 18, 2012.

4. E-mail from A. Heather Coyne to Daniel Serwer, January 25, 2012.

5. Rory Stewart and Gerald Knaus, *Can Intervention Work?* (New York: Norton, 2011).

6. Mary B. Anderson, Dayna Brown, and Isabella Jean, *Time to Listen: Hearing People on the Receiving End of International Aid* (Cambridge MA: CDA Collaborative Learning Projects, 2012).

7. E-mails from Jeremiah Pam to Daniel Serwer, March 20, July 20, 2012.

8. Jeremiah Pam, "The Paradox of Complexity: Embracing Its Contribution to Situational Understanding, Resisting Its Temptation in Strategy and Operational Plans," in *Complex Operations: NATO at War and on the Margins of War*, ed. Christopher M. Schnaubelt (Rome: NATO Defense College, July 2010), accessed May 8, 2012, http://www.usip.org/files/Grants-Fellows/Paradox%20of%20 complexity%20in%20strategy%20-%20J%20Pam%20chapter%20in%20 NATO%20Defense%20College%20forum%20paper%20on%20Complex%20 Operations%20%28Jul%202010%29.pdf.

9. United States Office of the Special Inspector General for Iraq Reconstruction, *Hard Lessons: The Iraq Reconstruction Experience* (Washington DC, 2009), 151–52, accessed April 12, 2012, http://www.sigir.mil/publications/hardLessons.html.

10. Nadia Gerspacher, "In Afghanistan, Creating Effective Advisers for Times of Crisis," United States Institute of Peace, March 2012, accessed May 14, 2012, http://

www.usip.org/publications/the-value-advising-help-the-afghan-ministries; "Training U.S. Advisers, Building Afghan Ministries," *In the Field* (blog), United States Institute of Peace, April 7, 2011, accessed May 14, 2012, http://www.usip.org/in-the-field/training-us-advisers-building-afghan-ministries; Gordon Lubold, "Getting to 'Afghan Good Enough,'" United States Institute of Peace, August 19, 2011, accessed May 14, 2012, http://www.usip.org/publications/getting-afghan-good-enough.

11. Sloan Mann and James Derleth, "Unschooled: How to Better Train Our Nation Builder," *World Affairs Journal,* March/April 2011, accessed February 10, 2012, http://www.worldaffairsjournal.org/article/unschooled-how-better-train-our-nation-builders.

12. Peter Van Buren, *We Meant Well* (New York: Metropolitan Books, 2011), http://us.macmillan.com/wemeantwell/PeterVanBuren.

13. Dan Green, *The Valley's Edge* (Dulles va: Potomac Books, 2012).

14. E-mail from A. Heather Coyne to Daniel Serwer.

15. David H. Bayley and Robert M. Perito, *The Police in War: Fighting Insurgency, Terrorism and Violent Crime* (Boulder co: Lynne Rienner, 2010).

16. Dr. Patrick Cronin and Dr. Kristin M. Lord, "Deploying Soft Power: Restructured, Larger Civilian Force Needed for Crises," *Defense News*, April 12, 2012, accessed February 13, 2012, http://www.cnas.org/node/4331.

17. Humanitarian Outcomes, *Aid Worker Security Report 2012* (New York: Humanitarian Outcomes, August 2011), accessed May 8, 2013, http://www.humanitarianoutcomes.org/sites/default/files/resources/AidWorkerSecurityReport20126.pdf.

18. See, for example, the efforts of Nonviolent Peaceforce, "np Work in the Field," accessed May 8, 2013, http://www.nonviolentpeaceforce.org/fieldwork.

19. Beth Ellen Cole and Michael Dziedzic, *Guidelines for Relations between us Armed Forces and nghos in Hostile or Potentially Hostile Environments* (Washington dc: United States Institute for Peace, July 2007), accessed February 3, 2012, http://www.usip.org/publications/guidelines-relations-between-us-armed-forces-and-nghos-hostile-or-potentially-hostile-envi.

20. "About the Coalition," Coalition of International Development Companies, accessed February 20, 2012, http://www.americaningenuityabroad.org/about-the-coalition/.

21. "About the Corporation," Corporation for National and Community Service, accessed February 20, 2012, http://www.nationalservice.gov/about/overview/index.asp.

22. Julian Vasquez Heilig and Su Jin Jez, *Teach for America: A Review of the Evidence* (East Lansing mi: Great Lakes Center for Education Research and Practice, June 2010), accessed February 10, 2012, http://greatlakescenter.org/docs/Policy_Briefs/Heilig_TeachForAmerica.pdf.

23. Barack Obama and Michelle Obama, "Remarks by the President and First Lady on the End of the War in Iraq" (speech, The White House, Washington dc,

December 14, 2011), accessed February 13, 2012, http://www.whitehouse.gov/
the-press-office/2011/12/14/remarks-president-and-first-lady-end-war-iraq.

24. "New Opinion Research Shows American Voters Reject 'Going It Alone'
and Embrace International Cooperation," United Nations Foundation, November
13, 2007, accessed April 12, 2012, http://www.unfoundation.org/news-and-media/
press-releases/2007/going-it-alone-new-opinion-research.html.

25. "Mariam," accessed May 8, 2013, http://www.kiva.org/lend/389730.

26. Kiva, "About Us," accessed May 8, 2013, http://www.kiva.org/about.

27. Ushahidi, "About Us," accessed May 8, 2013, http://ushahidi.com/about-us.

28. "Syria Tracker: Crowdsourcing Crisis Information," *Ushahidi* (blog),
accessed February 13, 2012, http://blog.ushahidi.com/index.php/2011/05/24/
syria-tracker-crowdsourcing-crisis-information/; "What Are Stock-outs?" Stop
Stock-outs, accessed February 13, 2012, http://stopstockouts.org/stop-stock outs
-campaign/what-are-stock-outs/.

29. http://samasource.org/home/.

30. Soldiers of Peace, accessed May 21, 2013, http://soldiers-of-peace.com.

31. See http://globalvoicesonline.org/.

32. Ed Pilkington, "Avaaz Faces Questions over Role at Center of Syrian Protest
Movement," *The Guardian*, March 2, 2012, accessed March 16, 2012, http://www
.guardian.co.uk/world/2012/mar/02/avaaz-activist-group-syria.

33. "About I Paid a Bribe," I Paid a Bribe, Janaagraha Centre for Citizenship and
Democracy, accessed March 19, 2012, http://www.ipaidabribe.com/About-us.

34. Swanee Hunt, *Worlds Apart: Bosnian Lessons for Global Security* (Durham
NC: Duke University Press, 2011), illustrates this point beautifully, with contrasting
examples of "inside" and "outside" views.

35. Rebecca Hamilton, *Fighting for Darfur: Public Action and the Struggle to Stop
Genocide* (New York: Palgrave Macmillan, 2011).

36. "Questions and Answers," Invisible Children, http://invisiblechildren.com/
critiques/; Jack McDonald, "Joseph Kony and Crowdsourced Intervention," *Kings
of War* (blog), Department of War Studies, King's College London, March 7, 2012,
accessed December 3, 2012, http://kingsofwar.org.uk/2012/03/joseph-kony-and
-crowdsourced-intervention/.

37. Some praised *Kony 2012*: Curt Hopkins, "How Kony 2012 Campaign Went
Viral and Focused Rare Attention on Africa," *Christian Science Monitor*, March 9,
2012, accessed May 14, 2012, http://www.csmonitor.com/World/Africa/Africa
-Monitor/2012/0309/How-Kony-2012-campaign-went-viral-and-focused-rare
-attention-on-Africa. Others panned it: Max Fisher, "The Soft Bigotry of Kony
2012," *Atlantic*, March 8, 2012, accessed May 14, 2012, http://www.theatlantic
.com/international/archive/2012/03/the-soft-bigotry-of-kony-2012/254194/.

38. Eric Schmitt and Jared Cohen, *The New Digital Age* (New York: Knopf, 2013).

39. Anne-Marie Slaughter, "A New Theory for the Foreign Policy Frontier:
Collaborative Power," *Atlantic*, November 30, 2011, accessed February 20, 2012,

http://www.theatlantic.com/international/archive/2011/11/a-new-theory-for-the
-foreign-policy-frontier-collaborative-power/249260/.

40. But ended its publication in August 2012. For the typically two-sided explanation, see "Beyond Bitter Lemons," accessed October 30, 2012, http://www
.bitterlemons.org/index1.php.

6. Anticipation Is Cheaper and Better

1. Michael Lund, *Preventing Violent Conflict: A Strategy for Preventive Diplomacy* (Washington DC: United States Institute of Peace Press, 1996).

2. Congressional Research Service, *American War and Military Operations Casualties: Lists and Statistics* (CRS Report RL32492, February 26, 2010), by Hannah Fischer, accessed February 8, 2012, http://www.history.navy.mil/library/online/
american%20war%20casualty.htm#t2.

3. P. W. Singer, *Wired for War: The Robotics Revolution and Conflict in the Twenty-First Century* (New York: Penguin, 2009). For a drone-eyed view of the issues see @drunkenpredator, "Flying under the Influence," *Foreign Policy*, July 20, 2012, accessed October 30, 2012, http://www.foreignpolicy.com/articles/2012/07/
20/flying_under_the_influence?page=full.

4. "Obama Orders U.S. Troops to Help Chase Down African 'Army' Leader," CNN, October 14, 2011, accessed March 8, 2012, http://articles.cnn.com/2011–10
–14/africa/world_africa_africa-obama-troops_1_obama-orders-south-sudan
-central-african-republic?_s=pm:africa.

5. Congressional Research Service, *Kosovo and Macedonia: U.S. and Allied Military Operations* (CRS Issue Brief, IB10027, July 8, 2003), by Steven Bowman, 8–9, accessed May 9, 2012, http://www.au.af.mil/au/awc/awcgate/crs/ib10027.pdf; "Civilian Deaths in the NATO Air Campaign," *Human Rights Watch*, February 1, 2000, accessed August 1, 2012, http://www.hrw.org/legacy/reports/2000/nato/
Natbm200-01.htm.

6. Daniel Serwer, "American Support for Serbian Democracy," in *The Balkan Prism: A Retrospective by Policy-Makers and Analysts*, ed. Johanna Deimel and Wim van Meurs (Munich: Verlag Otto Sagner, 2007), 291–96.

7. Anne E. Kornblut, Scott Wilson, and Karen DeYoung, "During Marathon Review of Afghanistan Strategy, Obama Held Out for Faster Troop Surge," *Washington Post*, December 6, 2009, accessed February 8, 2012, http://www.washingtonpost
.com/wp-dyn/content/article/2009/12/05/AR2009120501376_pf.html.

8. I. William Zartman, *Preventive Negotiation: Avoiding Conflict Escalation* (Lanham MD: Rowman and Littlefield, 2001), 23.

9. Bruce Jentleson, ed., *Opportunities Seized, Opportunities Missed: Preventive Diplomacy in the Post–Cold War World* (New York: Rowman and Littlefield, 2000); Greg Austin, Emery Brusset, Malcolm Chalmers, and Juliet Pierce, *Evaluation of the Conflict Prevention Pools: Synthesis Report* (London: UK Department for International Development, March 2004), accessed December 11, 2012, http://

www.brad.ac.uk/acad/cics/publications/conflict_prevention/introduction/
synthesis_report_(EV647).pdf; Barry Leonard, *Investing in Prevention: An
International Strategy to Manage Risks of Instability and Improve Crisis Response*
(Darby PA: Diane Publishing, 2005).

10. Richard Haass, *War of Necessity, War of Choice: A Memoir of Two Iraq Wars*
(New York: Simon and Schuster, 2009); Bob Woodward, *Plan of Attack* (New York:
Simon and Schuster, 2004).

11. George W. Bush, *Decision Points* (New York: Broadway, 2011).

12. "Top Bush Officials Push Case against Saddam," CNN, September 8, 2002,
accessed February 8, 2012, http://articles.cnn.com/2002-09-08/politics/iraq
.debate_1_nuclear-weapons-top-nuclear-scientists-aluminum-tubes?_s=pm:
allpolitics.

13. David Kirkpatrick and Kareem Fahim, "Qaddafi Warns of Assault on
Benghazi as U.N. Vote Nears," *New York Times*, March 17, 2011, accessed February 8,
2012, http://www.nytimes.com/2011/03/18/world/africa/18libya.html?pagewanted
=all.

14. UN Security Council, *Security Council Resolution 1973 (2011) [on the Situation
in the Libyan Arab Jamahiriya]*, March 17, 2011, S/RES/1973(2011), accessed
February 8, 2012, http://www.unhcr.org/refworld/docid/4d885fc42.html.

15. *Conflict Prevention—A Strategic Framework* (Washington DC: United States
Institute of Peace, April 2009), accessed February 8, 2012, http://www.usip.org/
publications/conflict-prevention-strategic-framework.

16. Sanjeev Srivastava, "Indian Companies Face War Jitters," *BBC News*, June 6,
2002, accessed February 23, 2012, http://news.bbc.co.uk/2/hi/business/2029687
.stm; Ershad Mahmud, "Pak-India Peace Process: An Appraisal," *Policy Perspectives*
4, no. 2, accessed May 14, 2012, http://www.ips.org.pk/pakistan-and-its
-neighbours/1013-pak-india-peace-process-an-appraisal-.html.

17. Aditi Phadnis, "Parakram Cost Put at Rs 6,500 Crore," *Rediff India Abroad*,
January 16, 2003, accessed February 8, 2012, http://www.rediff.com/money/2003/
jan/16defence.htm.

18. Hugh White, "Why War in Asia Remains Thinkable," *Survival* 50, no. 6
(2008): 85–104.

19. The complex issues involved are treated in Michael Lund, "Engaging Fragile
States: An International Policy Primer," Woodrow Wilson International Center for
Scholars, accessed December 19, 2012, http://www.wilsoncenter.org/publication/
engaging-fragile-states-international-policy-primer.

20. Louis Sell, *Slobodan Milosevic and the Destruction of Yugoslavia* (Durham
NC: Duke University Press, 2002), 264–66.

21. Abiodun Williams, *Preventing War: The United Nations and Macedonia*
(Lanham MD: Rowman and Littlefield, 2000); Henryk J. Sokalski, *An Ounce of
Protection: Macedonia and the UN Experience in Preventive Diplomacy* (Washington
DC: United States Institute of Peace, 2003).

22. "Human Rights Council Opens Special Session on Human Rights in Syrian Arab Republic," United Nations Office of the High Commissioner for Human Rights, December 2, 2011, accessed February 8, 2012, http://www.ohchr.org/en/NewsEvents/Pages/DisplayNews.aspx?NewsID=11679&LangID=E.

23. Jane Perlez, "Kosovo Massacre Is Called Revenge," *New York Times*, January 22, 1999, accessed February 8, 2012, http://www.nytimes.com/1999/01/22/world/kosovo-massacre-is-called-revenge.html?scp=5&sq=Kosovo%20Verification%20Mission&st=cse.

24. "Paragraphs 138–139 of the World Summit Outcome Document," International Coalition for the Responsibility to Protect, accessed February 8, 2012, http://www.responsibilitytoprotect.org/index.php/component/content/article/35-r2pcs-topics/398-general-assembly-r2p-excerpt-from-outcome-document; and United Nations Security Council, *Report of the Secretary General 578 (2012) [Responsibility to Protect: Timely and Decisive Response]*, July 25, 2012, A/66/874–S/2012/578, accessed October 29, 2012, http://www.responsibilitytoprotect.org/UNSG%20Report_timely%20and%20decisive%20response%281%29.pdf.

25. Peter Gourevich, *We Wish to Inform You That Tomorrow We Will Be Killed with Our Families* (New York: Picador, 1999).

26. Daniel Serwer, "The Strikes on Libya: Humanitarian Intervention, Not Imperial Aggression," *Atlantic*, March 19, 2011, accessed February 8, 2012, http://www.theatlantic.com/international/archive/2011/03/the-strikes-on-libya-humanitarian-intervention-not-imperial-aggression/72740/.

27. Adam Nossiter, "Strikes by U.N. and France Corner Leader of Ivory Coast," *New York Times*, April 4, 2011, accessed February 23, 2012, http://www.nytimes.com/2011/04/05/world/africa/05ivory.html.

28. On the practical problems, see Lynn Pascoe, "The Practical Side of Protection" (speech, 53rd Strategy for Peace Conference, The Stanley Foundation, Warrenton VA, October 17, 2012), accessed October 29, 2012, http://www.stanleyfoundation.org/preview.cfm?ContentType=Article&ID=750.

29. Taylor Seybolt, *Humanitarian Military Intervention: The Conditions for Success and Failure* (Oxford: Oxford University Press, 2007).

30. Jacob D. Kathman and Reed M. Wood, "Managing Threat, Cost, and Incentive to Kill: The Short- and Long-Term Effects of Intervention in Mass Killings," *Journal of Conflict Resolution* 55, no. 5 (2011): 735–60.

31. Paul R. Williams, J. Trevor Ulbrick, and Jonathan Worboys, "Preventing Mass Atrocity Crimes: The Responsibility to Protect and the Syria Crisis," *Case Western Reserve Journal of International Law* 45 (Fall 2012): 473–503.

32. "Mass Atrocity Crimes Indices and Watch Lists," Genocide Prevention Project, accessed February 8, 2012, http://www.preventorprotect.org/overview/other-indices.html.

33. "Mass Atrocity Crimes Watch List," Genocide Prevention Project, accessed February 8, 2012, http://www.preventorprotect.org/overview/watch-list.html.

34. Stewart Patrick, *Weak Links: Fragile States, Global Threats, and International Security* (Oxford: Oxford University Press, 2011).

35. Roy Gutman argues this case persuasively for Afghanistan in *How We Missed the Story: Osama bin Laden, the Taliban, and the Hijacking of Afghanistan* (Washington DC: United States Institute of Peace Press, 2008).

36. It is arguable that social order, rather than states per se, should be the objective. See John Arquilla, "What the Vikings Can Teach Us about Terrorism," *Foreign Policy*, October 8, 2012, accessed October 30, 2012, http://www.foreignpolicy .com/articles/2012/10/08/what_the_vikings_can_teach_us_about_terrorism.

37. *Myanmar: Major Reform Under Way* (Washington DC: International Crisis Group, September 22, 2011), accessed February 8, 2012, http://www.crisisgroup .org/en/regions/asia/south-east-asia/burma-myanmar/B127-myanmar-major -reform-underway.aspx.

38. *Reconciliation in Sri Lanka: Harder Than Ever* (Washington DC: International Crisis Group, July 18, 2011), accessed February 8, 2012, http://www.crisisgroup.org/ en/regions/asia/south-asia/sri-lanka/209-reconciliation-in-sri-lanka-harder-than -ever.aspx.

39. "Peace Agreements: Sudan," Peace Agreements Digital Collection, United States Institute of Peace, March 2005, accessed February 2, 2012, http://www.usip .org/publications/peace-agreements-sudan.

40. Andrew Mack, "A More Secure World," in *Transatlantic 2020: A Tale of Four Futures*, ed. Daniel Hamilton and Kurt Volker (Washington DC: Center for Transatlantic Relations, 2011), 317.

41. Joshua Goldstein and Steven Pinker, "War Really Is Going Out of Style," *New York Times*, December 17, 2011, accessed December 11, 2012, http://www .nytimes.com/2011/12/18/opinion/sunday/war-really-is-going-out-of-style.html ?src=tp; Steven Pinker, *The Better Angels of Our Nature: Why Violence Has Declined* (New York: Viking, 2011); Joshua Goldstein, *Winning the War on War* (New York: Penguin Group, 2011).

42. Jacob Bercovitch, ed., *Resolving International Conflicts: The Theory and Practice of Mediation* (Boulder: Lynne Rienner, 1996), 19.

43. Sukyong Choi, "Divided States: Reunifying without Conquest," in Zartman, *Preventive Negotiation*, 91.

44. Terrence Hopmann, "Disintegrating States: Separating without Violence," in Zartman, *Preventive Negotiation*, 113; and J. Michael Greig, "Moments of Opportunity: Recognizing Conditions of Ripeness for International Mediation between Enduring Rivals," *Journal of Conflict Resolution* 45, no. 6 (2001): 691.

7. Five Missing Pieces

1. Dambisa Moyo, *Dead Aid: Why Aid Is Not Working and How There Is a Better Way for Africa* (New York: Farrar, Strauss and Giroux, 2009); William Easterly, *The*

White Man's Burden: Why the West's Efforts to Aid the Rest Have Done So Much Ill and So Little Good (New York: Penguin, 2006).

2. Christian Strohal, *Democratic Elections and Their Monitoring: Can This OSCE Success Story Be Sustained?* (Washington DC: Organization for Security and Cooperation in Europe, 2008), accessed February 13, 2012, www.osce.org/odihr/elections/41094; "Who We Are," International Foundation for Electoral Systems, accessed March 29, 2012, http://www.ifes.org/About/Who-We-Are.aspx; Daniel Serwer, "Benghazi Needs a Hug," *Foreign Policy*, July 11, 2012, accessed July 20, 2012, http://mideast.foreignpolicy.com/posts/2012/07/11/benghazi_needs_a_hug.

3. State Department, *"Interagency Conflict Assessment Framework,"* accessed March 17, 2013, http://www.state.gov/documents/organization/187786.pdf. USAID has its own "Conflict Assessment Framework 2.0," 2012, accessed March 17, 2013, http://www.usaid.gov/what-we-do/working-crises-and-conflict/technical-publications.

4. Executive Office of the President of the United States, Office of Management and Budget, *Fiscal Year 2012 Budget of the U.S. Government* (Washington DC: Government Printing Office, 2010), 115–20, accessed February 14, 2012, http://www.whitehouse.gov/sites/default/files/omb/budget/fy2012/assets/state.pdf. See also Congressional Research Service, *Building Civilian Interagency Capacity for Missions Abroad: Key Proposals and Issues for Congress* (CRS Report R42133, January 23, 2012), by Nina M. Serafino, Catherine Dale, and Pat Towell, accessed December 3, 2012, http://fpc.state.gov/documents/organization/183725.pdf.

5. Paul B. Stares and Micah Zenko, *Enhancing U.S. Preventive Action* (New York: Council on Foreign Relations Press, 2009), 19, accessed February 14, 2012, http://www.cfr.org/conflict-prevention/enhancing-us-preventive-action/p20378.

6. Specific proposals are in Paul B. Stares, *Policy Innovation Memorandum No. 5: Enhancing U.S. Crisis Preparedness* (New York: Council on Foreign Relations, June 21, 2011), accessed February 14, 2012, http://i.cfr.org/content/publications/attachments/Policy_Innovation_Memo5_Stares.pdf. Some have even proposed preventive deployments at the provincial level, though it is hard to imagine most at-risk countries agreeing to such a proposition. See Kevin D. Stringer and Katie M. Sizemore, "Provincial Reconstruction Teams for Select Partner Nations," *Interagency Journal* 3, no. 3 (2012), accessed December 18, 2012, http://thesimonscenter.org/wp-content/uploads/2012/08/IAJ-3-3-pg11-20.pdf.

7. Gail W. Lapidus, "The War in Chechnya: Opportunities Missed, Lessons Learned," in *Opportunities Seized, Opportunities Missed*, ed. Bruce W. Jentleson (Lanham MD: Rowman and Littlefield, 2000), 39–67.

8. Richard Clark, *Against All Enemies: Inside America's War on Terror* (New York: Free Press, 2004); Roy Gutman, *How We Missed the Story: Osama bin Laden, the Taliban, and the Hijacking of Afghanistan* (Washington DC: United States Institute of Peace Press, 2008); Peter L. Bergen, *The Longest War: The Enduring Conflict between America and Al-Qaeda* (New York: Free Press, 2011).

9. Amanda Hsiao, "Obama Administration Establishes Government Board to Prevent Genocide," *Christian Science Monitor*, August 8, 2011, accessed February 29, 2012, http://www.csmonitor.com/World/Africa/Africa-Monitor/2011/0808/ Obama-administration-establishes-government-board-to-prevent-genocide; *Presidential Study Directive on Mass Atrocities* (PSD-10, August 4, 2011), accessed February 29, 2012, http://www.whitehouse.gov/the-press-office/2011/08/04/ presidential-study-directive-mass-atrocities.

10. *Structuring the US Government to Prevent Atrocities: Considerations for an Atrocities Prevention Board* (Muscatine IA: The Stanley Foundation, October 18, 2011), accessed February 27, 2012, http://www.stanleyfoundation.org/spc2011/ SPC_2011_Atrocities_Policy_Memo.pdf.

11. "Fact Sheet: The Obama Administration's Comprehensive Efforts to Prevent Mass Atrocities over the Past Year," accessed May 22, 2013, http://www.whitehouse .gov/sites/default/files/docs/fact_sheet_-_administration_efforts_to_prevent _mass_atrocities5.pdf.

12. Barack Obama, *National Security Strategy*, May 2010, accessed February 13, 2012, http://www.whitehouse.gov/sites/default/files/rss_viewer/national_security _strategy.pdf.

13. George W. Bush, *National Security Strategy*, September 2002, accessed February 27, 2012, http://georgewbush-whitehouse.archives.gov/nsc/nss/2002/; George W. Bush, *National Security Strategy*, March 2006, accessed February 27, 2012, http://georgewbush-whitehouse.archives.gov/nsc/nss/2006/.

14. Woodrow Wilson, "Joint Address to Congress Leading to a Declaration of War against Germany" (speech, U.S. Congress, Washington DC, April 2, 1917), accessed October 31, 2012, http://www.ourdocuments.gov/doc.php?flash=true&doc =61&page=transcript.

15. Eliot Cohen, *Conquered into Liberty: Two Centuries of Battles along the Great Warpath That Made the American Way of War* (New York: Free Press, 2011).

16. John R. O'Neill and Bruce Russett, *Triangulating Peace: Democracy, Interdependence, and International Organizations* (New York: Norton, 2001).

17. "Measuring Systemic Peace," accessed December 11, 2012, http://www .systemicpeace.org/conflict.htm.

18. Thomas Carothers, *U.S. Democracy Promotion during and after Bush* (Washington DC: Carnegie Endowment for International Peace, 2007), accessed February 13, 2012, http://carnegieendowment.org/files/democracy_promotion _after_bush_final.pdf.

19. Barack Obama, "On a New Beginning" (speech, Cairo University, June 4, 2009), accessed February 27, 2012, http://www.whitehouse.gov/the-press-office/ remarks-president-cairo-university-6-04-09.

20. Erica Chenoweth and Maria J. Stephan, *Why Civil Resistance Works: The Strategic Logic of Nonviolent Conflict* (New York: Columbia University Press, 2011); Joerg Forbrig and Pavol Demes, *Reclaiming Democracy: Civil Society and Electoral*

Change in Central and Eastern Europe (Washington DC: German Marshall Fund, 2007).

21. Morton Abramowitz and Mark Lowenthal, "Restocking the Toolkit," *American Interest* 7, no. 3 (2012): 57–64.

22. Maytha Alhassen and Ahmed Shihab-Eldin, *Demanding Dignity: Young Voices from the Front Lines of the Arab Revolutions* (Ashland OR: White Cloud Press, 2012); and Robin Wright, *Rock the Casbah: Rage and Rebellion across the Arab World* (New York: Simon and Schuster, 2011). See also Cesare Merlini and Olivier Roy, *Arab Society in Revolt: The West's Mediterranean Challenge* (Washington DC: Brookings, 2012).

23. Nathan J. Brown, *When Victory Becomes an Option: Egypt's Muslim Brotherhood Confronts Success* (Washington DC: Carnegie Endowment for International Peace, January 2012), accessed November 28, 2012, http://www.carnegieendowment.org/files/brotherhood_success.pdf.

24. Richard LeBaron, "Talk to the Gulf about Leadership," Atlantic Council MENAsource, May 20, 2013, accessed May 22, 2013, http://www.acus.org/viewpoint/talk-gulf-about-leadership.

25. Many of the complexities are discussed in Salman Shaikh and Shadi Hamid, "Between Interference and Assistance: The Politics of International Support in Egypt, Tunisia, and Libya," Project on U.S. Relations with the Islamic World and the Brookings Doha Center, November 2012, accessed December 27, 2012, http://www.brookings.edu/~/media/Research/Files/Papers/2012/11/iwf%20papers/BDCweb.pdf.

26. For a summary of empirical evidence for democratization assistance, see Laurel E. Miller, Jeffrey Martini, F. Stephen Larrabee, Angel Rabasa, Stephanie Pezard, Julie E. Taylor, and Tewodaj Mengistu, *Democratization in the Arab World: Prospects and Lessons from around the Globe* (Washington DC: RAND, 2012), 27–33. Even in Iraq, some claim a measure of success; see Oussama Safa, "Against All Odds: An Assessment of the National Endowment for Democracy's Support to Iraqi Civil Society Organizations, 2003–2009," National Endowment for Democracy, June 2011.

27. Peter Burnell, "Does International Democracy Promotion Work?" (Discussion Papers Issue 17, German Development Institute, Bonn, Germany, 2007), accessed October 31, 2012, http://edoc.vifapol.de/opus/volltexte/2011/3094/pdf/BurnellPromotionWork.pdf; Thomas Carothers, *Revitalizing Democracy Assistance: The Challenge of USAID* (Washington DC: Carnegie Endowment for International Peace, 2009), accessed February 27, 2012, http://www.carnegieendowment.org/files/revitalizing_democracy_assistance.pdf.

28. Michael Cohen and Maria Figueroa Kupcu, *Revitalizing U.S. Democracy Promotion: A Comprehensive Plan for Reform* (Washington DC: Carnegie Endowment, 2009), accessed February 27, 2012, http://www.newamerica.net/files/nafmigration/Revitalizing_US_Democracy_Promotion.pdf.

29. Community of Democracies, "The Diplomat's Handbook for Democracy and Development Support," 2nd ed., 2008, accessed May 19, 2013, http://www .diplomatshandbook.org/pdf/Diplomats_Handbook.pdf .

30. David D. Kirkpatrick and Steven Lee Myers, "Egypt Raids Offices of Nonprofits, 3 Backed by U.S.," *New York Times*, December 29, 2011, accessed March 14, 2012, http://www.nytimes.com/2011/12/30/world/middleeast/egypts -forces-raid-offices-of-us-and-other-civil-groups.html?pagewanted=all.

31. Thomas Carothers and Diane De Gramont, *Development Aid Confronts Politics: The Almost Revolution* (Washington DC: The Carnegie Endowment for International Peace, 2013).

32. Mark J. Cohen and Tara R. Gingerich, *Protect and Serve or Train and Equip?U.S. Security Assistance and Protection of Civilians* (Washington DC: Oxfam America, 2009), accessed February 27, 2012, http://www.oxfamamerica.org/files/ protect-and-serve-or-train-and-equip.pdf; David H. Bayley and Robert M. Perito, *The Police in War: Fighting Insurgency, Terrorism, and Violent Crime* (Boulder: Lynne Rienner, 2010).

33. Colonel (Ret.) Dennis E. Keller, *U.S. Military Forces and Police Assistance in Stability Operations: The Least Worst Option to Fill the U.S. Capacity Gap* (Carlisle PA: Strategic Studies Institute, U.S. Army War College, 2010), 6, accessed March 19, 2012, http://www.strategicstudiesinstitute.army.mil/pubs/download.cfm?q=1013.

34. "About Us," Centre for Democratic Control of Armed Forces, accessed February 27, 2012, http://www.dcaf.ch/About-Us.

35. Special Inspector General for Iraqi Reconstruction, *Quarterly Report to the United States Congress* (Washington DC: Government Printing Office, October 30, 2011), 4, accessed March 29, 2012, http://www.sigir.mil/files/quarterlyreports/ October2011/Report_-_October_2011.pdf#view=fit; Special Inspector General for Iraq Reconstruction, *Hard Lessons: The Iraq Reconstruction Experience* (Washington DC: U.S. Independent Agencies and Commissions, 2009), accessed May 8, 2013, http://www.sigir.mil/files/HardLessons/Hard_Lessons_Report.pdf.

36. Nicholas J. Armstrong, "Afghan Security Force Assistance or Security Sector Reform?" *INSCT on Security* (blog), Institute for National Security and Counterterrorism, December 21, 2011, accessed March 19, 2012, http://insct.org/commentary -analysis/2011/12/21/afghan-security-force-assistance- or-security-sector-reform -despite-recent-improvements-in-the-afghan-security-forces-more-emphasis-on -ministerial-development- and-police-reform-is-needed/; Tim Arango, "U.S. May Scrap Costly Effort to Train Iraqi Police," *New York Times*, May 13, 2012, accessed May 23, 2012, http://www.nytimes.com/2012/05/13/world/middleeast/us-may -scrap-costly-effort- to-train-iraqi-police.html?pagewanted=all. See also David Rohde, *Beyond War: Reimaging American Influence in the Middle East* (New York: Viking Penguin, 2013).

37. Francis Fukuyama, *State-Building: Governance and World Order in the 21st Century* (Ithaca NY: Cornell University Press, 2004).

38. Alice E. Hunt, Kristin M. Lord, John A. Nagl, and Seth D. Rosen, eds., "Beyond Bullets: Strategies for Countering Violent Extremism," Center for New American Security, June 2009, accessed December 16, 2012, http://www.cnas.org/files/documents/publications/LordNaglRosen_Beyond%20Bullets%20Edited%20Volume_June09_0.pdf.

39. *U.S. Government Efforts to Counter Violent Extremism: Hearing before the Subcommittee on Emerging Threats and Capabilities of the Committee on Armed Services*, U.S. Senate, 111th Cong. (2010), accessed May 8, 2013, http://www.gpo.gov/fdsys/pkg/CHRG-111shrg63687/html/CHRG-111shrg63687.htm.

40. Frank Cilluffo, Scott Carpenter, and Matthew Levitt, *What's the Big Idea? Confronting the Ideology of Islamist Extremism* (Washington DC: Homeland Security Policy Institute and the Washington Institute for Near East Policy, February 4, 2011), accessed February 14, 2012, www.gwumc.edu/hspi/policy/issuebrief_confrontingideology.pdf.

41. *U.S. Government Efforts to Counter Violent Extremism*, 58.

42. Scott Atran, *Talking to the Enemy: Faith, Brotherhood, and the (Un)Making of Terrorists* (New York: Ecco, 2010).

43. Seth Jones and Martin Libicki, *How Terrorist Groups End: Lessons for Countering al Qa'ida* (Santa Monica CA: RAND Corporation, 2008), accessed February 16, 2012, http://www.rand.org/pubs/monographs/2008/RAND_MG741-1.pdf.

44. Jessica Stern, "Mind over Martyr: How to Deradicalize Islamist Extremists," *Foreign Affairs* 89, no. 1 (2010): 95–108.

45. Elizabeth Detwiler, *Iraq: Positive Change in the Detention System* (Washington DC: United States Institute of Peace, July 2008), accessed February 14, 2012, http://www.usip.org/files/resources/USIP_0708.pdf.

46. David Smock and Qamar ul Huda, *Islamic Peacemaking since 9/11* (Washington DC: United States Institute of Peace, January 2009), accessed February 14, 2012, http://www.usip.org/files/resources/islamicpeacemaking.pdf; Qamar ul Huda has delved deeper into specific cases in *Crescent and Dove: Peace and Conflict Resolution in Islam* (Washington DC: United States Institute of Peace Press, 2010).

47. Bergen, *The Longest War*.

48. J. Scott Carpenter, Matthew Levitt, and Michael Jacobson, "Confronting the Ideology of Radical Extremism," *Journal of National Security Law and Policy* 3 (2009): 301–27.

49. Neil J. Kressel, *Bad Faith: The Danger of Religious Extremism* (New York: Prometheus Books, 2007), 257.

50. The Global Counterterrorism Forum, accessed December 16, 2012, www.thegctf.org/web/guest/home; and Office of the State Department Spokesperson, "Ministerial Plenary Co-Chairs Fact Sheet: International Center of Excellence for Countering Violent Extremism," accessed December 16, 2012, http://www.state.gov/r/pa/prs/ps/2012/12/202089.htm.

51. *The Roots of Violent Islamist Extremism and Efforts to Counter It*, U.S. Senate, 110th Cong 2 (July 10, 2008), accessed February 14, 2012, www.fas.org/irp/congress/2008_hr/roots.pdf.

52. A. Lawrence Chickering, Isobel Coleman, P. Edward Haley, and Emily Vargas-Baron, *Strategic Foreign Assistance: Civil Society in International Security* (Stanford CA: Hoover Institution Press, 2006).

53. "MBTI Basics," The Myers & Briggs Foundation, accessed February 16, 2012, http://www.myersbriggs.org/my-mbti-personality-type/mbti-basics/.

54. "America's Greatest Asset: American Citizens Partnering with the World to Address Global Challenges in the 21st Century," U.S. Center for Citizen Diplomacy, accessed February 14, 2012, http://uscenterforcitizendiplomacy.org/summit/executive-summary.

55. James Marshall, "Citizen Diplomacy," *American Political Science Review* 43, no. 1 (1949): 83–90.

56. Benjamin Lough, Amanda McBride, and Margaret Sherraden, "The Estimated Economic Value of a US Volunteer Abroad" (CSD Working Paper 07-29, Center for Social Development, St. Louis MO, 2007), accessed February 14, 2012, http://csd.wustl.edu/Publications/Documents/WP07-29.pdf.

57. *FY 2010 Community Impact Summary* (Washington DC: National Council for International Visitors, March 16, 2011), accessed February 27, 2012, http://www.nciv.org/category/58-national-impact-summary-multi-year.html?download=1124.

58. U.S. Department of State, Secretary of State, *Congressional Budget Justification: Fiscal Year 2013*, Volume 1, Department of State Operations (Washington DC, February 13, 2012), 535, accessed December 4, 2012, http://www.state.gov/documents/organization/181061.pdf.

59. Rajika Bhandari and Raisa Belyavina, *Evaluating and Measuring the Impact of Citizen Diplomacy: Current Status and Future Directions* (New York: Institute of International Education, June 2011), accessed February 16, 2012, http://www.iie.org/~/media/Files/Corporate/Publications/ImpactofCitizenDiplomacyReport.ashx; U.S. Department of State, Bureau of Educational and Cultural Affairs, Office of Policy and Evaluation, *Outcome Assessment of the U.S. Fulbright Student Program* (Washington DC, June 2005), accessed March 19, 2012, http://exchanges.state.gov/media/pdfs/office-of-policy- and-evaluations/completed-program-evaluations/executive-summary/fulbright-us-student-ex-summary_june-2005.pdf.

60. The National Guard State Partnership Program, accessed May 8, 2013, http://www.nationalguard.mil/features/spp.

61. Office of the Special Representative for Global Intergovernmental Affairs, accessed May 8, 2013, http://www.state.gov/s/srgia/index.htm; and International Diaspora Engagement Alliance, "About Us," accessed May 18, 2013, http://diasporaalliance.org/about-us.

62. Michelle Acuto and Parag Khanna, "Around the World, Mayors Take Charge," *Atlantic*, April 26, 2013, accessed May 19, 2013, http://www.theatlantic

.com/international/archive/2013/04/around-the-world-mayors-take-charge/275335. The international role of mayors may be relatively new, but sister cities have long played a role in citizen diplomacy. See www.sister-cities.org, accessed May 19, 2013.

63. Richard T. Arndt, *The First Resort of Kings: American Cultural Diplomacy in the Twentieth Century* (Washington DC: Potomac Books, 2005).

64. Lewis Beale, "U.S. Students Hurting in Foreign Languages," *Miller-McCune*, May 17, 2010, accessed February 14, 2012, http://www.miller-mccune.com/culture-society/u-s-students-hurting-in-foreign-languages-13529/.

65. Nancy Rhodes and Ingrid Pufahl, *Executive Summary: Foreign Language Teaching in U.S. Schools: Results of a National Survey* (Washington DC: Center for Applied Linguistics, 2010), accessed February 14, 2012, http://www.cal.org/projects/executive-summary-08-09-10.pdf.

66. Anne-Marie Slaughter, "America's Edge: Power in the Networked Century," *Foreign Affairs* 88, no. 1 (2009): 94–113.

8. The Energy Conundrum

1. Keith Crane et al., *Imported Oil and U.S. National Security* (Santa Monica CA: RAND, 2009), 72.

2. "Venezuela Facts and Figures," OPEC, accessed February 2, 2012, http://www.opec.org/opec_web/en/about_us/171.htm.

3. Brenton Goldsworthy and Daria Zakharova, "Evaluation of the Oil Fiscal Regime in Russia and Proposals for Reform" (IMF Working Paper WP/10/33, International Monetary Fund, Washington DC, February 2010), accessed February 14, 2012, http://www.imf.org/external/pubs/ft/wp/2010/wp1033.pdf.

4. "Iran—Analysis," U.S. Energy Information Administration, accessed February 2, 2012, http://www.eia.gov/countries/cab.cfm?fips=IR.

5. Michael Eisenstadt, "The Pentagon's New Defense Strategic Guidance: Pivoting to Asia, But Still Stuck in the Middle East," Washington Institute for Near East Policy, January 6, 2012, accessed February 2, 2012, http://www.washingtoninstitute.org/templateC06.php?CID=1791.

6. Amy Myers Jaffe and Kelly Miller, "The Arab Awakening and the Pending Oil Pinch," *Whitehead Journal of Diplomacy and International Relations* 13, no. 1 (2012): 22, accessed December 4, 2012, http://www.bakerinstitute.org/publications/EF-pub-WhiteheadJaffeMillerArabAwakening-062912.pdf.

7. Daniel Serwer, "Iraq Untethered," *Current History* 111, no. 749 (2012): 345, accessed December 4, 2012, http://www.currenthistory.com/pdf_org_files/111_749_344.pdf.

8. "Oil: Crude and Petroleum Products Explained," U.S. Energy Information Administration, accessed February 2, 2012, http://www.eia.gov/energyexplained/index.cfm?page=oil_home#tab2.

9. International Energy Agency, *World Energy Outlook 2012 Executive Summary*

(Paris: OECD/IEA, 2012), 1, accessed December 4, 2012, http://www.iea.org/ publications/freepublications/publication/English.pdf.

10. Jordan Weissmann, "The Myth of Energy Independence: Why We Can't Drill Our Way to Oil Autonomy," *Atlantic*, February 9, 2012, accessed February 15, 2012, http://www.theatlantic.com/business/archive/2012/02/the-myth-of-energy -independence-why-we-cant-drill-our-way-to-oil-autonomy/252812/.

11. Liam Pleven and Russell Gold, "U.S. Nears Milestone: Net Fuel Exporter," *Wall Street Journal*, November 30, 2011, accessed December 4, 2012, http://online.wsj .com/article/SB10001424052970203441704577068670488306242.html.

12. "Oil: Crude and Petroleum Products Explained."

13. Paul Isbell, *Energy and the Atlantic: The Shifting Energy Landscapes of the Atlantic Basin* (Washington DC: German Marshall Fund of the United States and the OCP Foundation, 2012), accessed December 11, 2012, http://www.gmfus.org/wp-content/ blogs.dir/1/files_mf/1354225552Isbell_EnergySecurity_Aug12_web.pdf.

14. "Keystone Pipeline Map," TransCanada, accessed February 15, 2012, http:// www.transcanada.com/keystone_pipeline_map.html.

15. Daniel Yergin, "Oil's New World Order," *Washington Post*, October 30, 2010, B1.

16. "EIA Releases New Subsidy Report: Subsidies for Renewables Increase 186 Percent," Institute for Energy Research, August 3, 2011, accessed February 15, 2012, http://www.instituteforenergyresearch.org/2011/08/03/eia-releases-new-subsidy -report-subsidies-for-renewables-increase-186-percent/.

17. Congressional Research Service, *U.S. Oil Imports: Context and Consider- ations* (CRS Report R41765, April 1, 2011), by Neelesh Nerurkar, accessed February 15, 2012, http://www.fas.org/sgp/crs/misc/R41765.pdf.

18. The White House, The National Commission on Fiscal Responsibility and Reform, *The Moment of Truth: Report of the National Commission on Fiscal Responsibility and Reform* (Washington DC, December 2010), accessed February 2, 2012, http://www.fiscalcommission.gov/sites/fiscalcommission.gov/files/ documents/TheMomentofTruth12_1_2010.pdf.

19. I am indebted to Ambassador Tony Motley, whom I served with in Brasilia, for this cogent definition of diplomacy.

20. Arne Schröer, "European Energy Security: A New Pattern of External Stability and Internal Risks," *Transatlantic Perspectives* (blog), American Institute for Contem- porary German Studies, January 5, 2012, accessed February 15, 2012, http://www .aicgs.org/publication/european-energy-security-a-new-pattern-of-external -stability-and-internal-risks/. The IEA system for responding to an oil supply emergency is described in *IEA Response System for Oil Supply Emergencies* (Paris: International Energy Agency, 2012), accessed November 5, 2012, http://www.iea.org/ publications/freepublications/publication/EPPD_Brochure_English_2012_02-1.pdf.

21. "Releasing Crude Oil from the Strategic Petroleum Reserve," U.S. Depart- ment of Energy, accessed February 15, 2012, http://fossil.energy.gov/programs/ reserves/spr/spr-drawdown.html.

22. *Fueling the Niger Delta Crisis* (Brussels: International Crisis Group, September 28, 2006), accessed February 1, 2012, http://www.crisisgroup.org/~/media/Files/africa/west-africa/nigeria/Fuelling%20the%20Niger%20Delta%20Crisis.pdf.

23. For Norway see Thord Englund, "How to Invest $200 Billion . . . Ethically," Norway: The Official Site in the United States, accessed April 9, 2012, http://www.norway.org/ARCHIVE/business/businessnews/ethicoil/; for East Timor see "Quarterly Report," Central Bank of Timor-Leste, accessed April 9, 2012, http://www.bancocentral.tl/PF/Reports.asp.

24. "Middle East: GCC SA, UAE," *Migration News* 16, no. 1 (2009), accessed February 1, 2012, http://migration.ucdavis.edu/mn/more.php?id=3497_0_3_0.

25. See the Carnegie Endowment for International Peace's *Arab Reform Bulletin*, relaunched as "Sada," Carnegie Endowment for International Peace, accessed October 31, 2012, http://www.carnegieendowment.org/sada/.

26. Marina Ottaway and Marwan Muasher, *Arab Monarchies: Chance for Reform, Yet Unmet* (Washington DC: Carnegie Endowment for International Peace, December 2011), accessed February 1, 2012, http://carnegieendowment.org/2011/12/16/arab-monarchies-chance-for-reform-yet-unmet/8e7t.

27. Gregory Gause III, "Don't Just Do Something, Stand There!" *Argument* (blog), *Foreign Policy*, December 21, 2011, accessed February 1, 2012, http://www.foreignpolicy.com/articles/2011/12/21/america_arab_spring_do_nothing?page=0,3.

28. "SIPRI Arms Transfers Database," Stockholm International Peace Research Institute, accessed February 2, 2012, http://www.sipri.org/databases/armstransfer.

29. "UAE Opens Pipeline Bypassing Strait of Hormuz Oil Route," *BBC News Middle East*, July 15, 2012, accessed October 31, 2012, http://www.bbc.co.uk/news/world-middle-east-18848986.

30. Hamed Aleaziz and Robin Mills, "Do We Even Need the Strait of Hormuz?" *Atlantic*, January 13, 2012, accessed February 15, 2012, http://www.theatlantic.com/international/archive/2012/01/do-we-even-need-the-strait-of-hormuz/251348/.

31. Simon Henderson, "Facing Iran's Challenge: Safeguarding Oil Exports from the Persian Gulf," Washington Institute for Near East Policy, June 7, 2006, accessed February 15, 2012, http://www.washingtoninstitute.org/policy-analysis/view/facing-irans-challenge-safeguarding-oil-exports-from-the-persian-gulf. Dagobert L. Brito, "Revisiting alternatives to the Strait of Hormuz," James A. Baker III Institute for Public Policy, January 2012, accessed May 18, 2013, http://bakerinstitute.org/publications/BI-pub-RevisitingAltHormuz-012512.pdf. I am indebted to James Mina for drawing this paper to my attention.

32. Daniel Fineren, "Iran Plans Oil Export Terminal outside the Gulf," *Al Arabiya News*, May 22, 2012, accessed December 30, 2012, http://english.alarabiya.net/articles/2012/05/22/215664.html.

33. "Mission," European Union Naval Force Somalia, accessed February 1, 2012, http://www.eunavfor.eu/about-us/mission/.

9. Sharing the Burdens

1. Paul F. Horvitz, "Christopher Sees Sanctions in Place as Long as Saddam Stays in Power: U.S. Message to Iraq: Move Troops or Else," *New York Times*, October 17, 1994, accessed December 11, 2012, http://www.nytimes.com/1994/10/17/news/17iht-un_1.html.

2. *Conduct of the Persian Gulf War, Final Report to Congress* (Washington DC: Department of Defense, April 1992), accessed February 2, 2012, http://www.ndu.edu/library/epubs/cpgw.pdf.

3. Richard G. Lugar, "NATO: Out of Area or Out of Business" (speech, Overseas Writers Club, Washington DC, June 24, 1993).

4. Out-of-area contingencies are addressed explicitly in NATO's latest Strategic Concept, "Active Engagement, Modern Defense," 2010, accessed May 18, 2013, http://www.nato.int/strategic-concept/pdf/Strat_Concept_web_en.pdf, 21: "Crises and conflicts beyond NATO's borders can pose a direct threat to the security of the Alliance territory and its populations. NATO will therefore engage, where possible and when necessary, to prevent crises, manage crises, stabilize post-conflict situations and support reconstruction."

5. The former are described in detail in James Dobbins et al., *The UN's Role in Nation-Building: From the Congo to Iraq* (Santa Monica CA: RAND, 2005), accessed May 14, 2012, http://www.rand.org/pubs/monographs/MG304.html; the latter are described in Richard Gowan, *Review of Political Missions 2010* (New York: Center on International Cooperation, 2010), accessed May 14, 2012, http://www.cic.nyu.edu/politicalmissions/index_10.html. See also Richard Gowan, *Multilateral Political Missions and Preventive Diplomacy* (Washington DC: United States Institute of Peace, December 2011), accessed May 14, 2012, http://www.usip.org/publications/multilateral-political-missions- and-preventive-diplomacy.

6. "Financing Peacekeeping," United Nations, accessed February 16, 2012, http://www.un.org/en/peacekeeping/operations/financing.shtml#gadocs.

7. The much-debated rate is between one-third and one-half within five years, according to Charles T. Call and Elizabeth M. Cousens, "Ending Wars and Building Peace International Peace Academy" (CWC Working Paper Series, International Peace Institute, New York NY, 2007), 3, accessed November 6, 2012, http://www.ipinst.org/media/pdf/publications/cwc_working_paper_ending_wars_ccec.pdf.

8. Ian Martin, "All Peace Operations Are Political: A Case for Designer Missions and the Next UN Reform," in *Review of Political Missions 2010*, ed. Richard Gowan (New York: Center on International Cooperation, 2010), accessed May 14, 2012, http://www.cic.nyu.edu/politicalmissions/index_10.html.

9. Neil MacFarquhar, "Peacekeepers' Sex Scandals Linger, On Screen and Off," *New York Times*, September 7, 2011, accessed February 2, 2012, http://www.nytimes.com/2011/09/08/world/08nations.html?pagewanted=all.

10. Megan Gleason-Roberts, Richard Gowan, Alischa Kugel, and Morgan Hughes, "Political Missions 2012," Center on International Cooperation, New York University, December 17, 2012, accessed May 22, 2013, http://cic.nyu.edu/content/political-missions-2012.

11. "Peacekeeping Fact Sheet," United Nations, accessed March 1, 2012, http://www.un.org/en/peacekeeping/resources/statistics/factsheet.shtml.

12. Richard Gowan and Megan Gleason, "UN Peacekeeping: The Next Five Years," New York University Center on International Cooperation, 2012, accessed December 27, 2012, http://fnnewyork.um.dk/en/~/media/fnnewyork/Danish/Dokumenter/Nyheder/CIC-Denmark-peacekeeping-report-final.pdf.

13. Parts of this section were previously published as Daniel Serwer and Megan Chabalowski, "U.S.-EU Cooperation in Managing and Resolving Conflicts," in *Shoulder to Shoulder: Forging a Strategic U.S.-EU Partnership*, edited by Daniel S. Hamilton (Washington DC: Johns Hopkins University Center for Transatlantic Relations, 2010), 283–92. The text has been updated.

14. *Report on the Implementation of the European Security Strategy.*

15. European Union, "CSDP Mission Chart," accessed May 18, 2013, http://www.csdpmap.eu/mission-chart.

16. *European Security and Defence Policy: The Civilian Aspects of Crisis Management* (Brussels: European External Action Service, European Union, August 2009), accessed February 8, 2012, http://www.consilium.europa.eu/uedocs/cmsUpload/090702%20Civilian%20aspects%20of%20crisis%20management%20-%20version%203_EN.pdf.

17. *Bad Business: Billions of Taxpayer Dollars Wasted on Contractors* (Washington DC: Project on Government Oversight, September 13, 2011), accessed August 1, 2012, http://pogoarchives.org/m/co/igf/bad-business-report-only-2011.pdf.

18. "New Peacekeeping Force Staffed by Police Officers from across EU," *European Commission*, European Union, accessed June 1, 2009, http://ec.europa.eu/justice_home/fsj/police/peacekeeping/fsj_police_peacekeeping_en.htm.

19. This is the basis for the more skeptical view in Daniel Korski and Richard Gowan, *Can the EU Rebuild Failing States? A Review of Europe's Civilian Capacities* (London: European Council on Foreign Relations, October 2009), 11, accessed November 5, 2012, http://ecfr.eu/page/-/ECFR18_-_Can_the_EU_rebuild_failing__States_-_a_Review_of_Europes_Civilian_Capacities.pdf. The situation has improved since 2009.

20. Federiga Bindi, "Europe's Problematic Contribution to Policy Training in Afghanistan," *The Brookings Institution*, May 4, 2009, accessed February 18, 2012, http://www.brookings.edu/opinions/2009/0504_afghanistan_bindi.aspx.

21. *European Security and Defence Policy.*

22. "EULEX Kosovo," European External Action Service, European Union, accessed July 30, 2012, http://www.consilium.europa.eu/eeas/security-defence/eu-operations/eulex-kosovo.

23. *European Security and Defence Policy.*

24. Three documents serve as the basis for the EU SSR framework: *EU Concept for ESDP Support to Security Sector Reform* (Brussels: Council of the European Union, 2005), accessed November 19, 2012, http://register.consilium.europa.eu/pdf/en/05/st12/st12566-re04.en05.pdf; *Communication from the Commission to the Council and the European Parliament: A Concept for European Community Support for Security Sector Reform* (Brussels: Commission of the European Communities, European Union, 2006), accessed November 19, 2012, http://eurlex.europa.eu/LexUriServ/site/en/com/2006/com2006_0253en01.pdf; and *Council Conclusions on a Policy Framework for Security Sector Reform* (Luxembourg: 2736th General Affairs Council meeting, European Union, June 12, 2006), accessed November 19, 2012, http://www.eu2006.at/en/News/Council_Conclusions/1206SecuritySectorReform.pdf.

25. Maria Derks and Sylvie More, *The European Union and Internal Challenges for Effectively Supporting Security Sector Reform: An Overview of the EU's Set-up for SSR Support Anno Spring 2009* (The Hague: Netherlands Institute for International Relations—Clingendael, June 2009), accessed December 5, 2012, www.clingendael.nl/publications/2009/20090618_cru_ssr_derks_more.pdf.

26. *European Security and Defence Policy;* Daniel Flott, "European Union Security Sector Reform Missions: The Case of Guinea-Bissau," *European Security Review* 38, ISIS-Europe (May 2008), accessed December 6, 2012, http://isis-europe.eu/sites/default/files/programmes-downloads/2008_artrel_167_esr38-eussr-guinea-bissau.pdf.

27. OSCE *Guide to Non-military Confidence-Building Measures (CBMs)* (Vienna: Organization for Security and Co-operation in Europe, 2012), accessed August 2, 2012, www.osce.org/cpc/91082.

28. "Special Meeting of the Permanent Council (895th Plenary Meeting)" (PC.JOUR/895, OSCE, Vienna, December 22, 2011), accessed February 8, 2012, http://www.osce.org/pc/86720.

29. Dov Zakheim, *A Vulcan's Tale: How the Bush Administration Mismanaged the Reconstruction of Afghanistan* (Washington DC: Brookings Institution Press, 2011).

30. Julian Lindley-French, *Enhancing Stabilization and Reconstruction Operations: A Report of the Global Dialogue between the European Union and the United States* (Washington DC: Center for Strategic and International Studies, January 2009), accessed August 1, 2012, http://csis.org/publication/enhancing-stabilization-and-reconstruction-operations.

31. *Report on the Implementation of the European Security Strategy: Providing Security in a Changing World* (Brussels: European External Action Service, European Union, December 11, 2008), accessed August 1, 2012, http://www.consilium.europa.eu/ueDocs/cms_Data/docs/pressdata/EN/reports/104630.pdf.

32. U.S. Department of the Army, *Stability Operations, Field Manual 3–07* (Washington DC, October 2008), 16, accessed December 11, 2012, www.fas.org/irp/doddir/army/fm3-07.pdf.

33. International Dialogue on Peacebuilding and Statebuilding, *A New Deal for Engagement in Fragile States* (Dili, Timor-Leste: G7+, November 30, 2011), accessed February 16, 2012, http://www.g7plus.org/storage/New%20Deal%20English.pdf.

34. Daniel Serwer, "Post-Asad Syria," *Prism 3*, no. 4 (2012), accessed November 21, 2012, http://www.ndu.edu/press/lib/pdf/prism3-4/prism2-11_serwer.pdf.

10. Reorganizing for Hard Times

1. Mary L. Hinsdale, *A History of the President's Cabinet* (Ann Arbor: University of Michigan Historical Studies, 1911), 17, accessed March 23, 2012, http://archive .org/details/historyofpresideoohinsrich. Harry Kopp, in an e-mail dated February 4, 2013, notes that the full story is a bit more complicated: "At the first session of Congress under the Constitution, in 1789, James Madison, then a representative from Virginia, introduced a bill to establish a Department of Foreign Affairs, to succeed the one that functioned under the Articles of Confederation. The bill passed and was signed into law in July, but by September Congress, too parsimonious to establish other agencies, had added responsibilities and changed the name. Jefferson said that his responsibilities as the first Secretary included everything that did not fall to the attorney general or to War or Treasury."

2. Harry Kopp's "History of the Department of State" (unpublished lecture, Foreign Service Institute, Arlington VA, June 16, 2011) is the best I've seen, and I rely heavily on it, but Kopp tells the story straight, without the spin in my version. See also Harry W. Kopp and Charles A. Gillispie, *Career Diplomacy: Life and Work in the U.S. Foreign Service*, 2nd ed. (Washington DC: Georgetown University Press, 2011); and Nicholas Kralev, *America's Other Army: The U.S. Foreign Service and Twenty-First-Century Diplomacy*, 2012. On the broader foreign policy apparatus, see Charles Stevenson, *America's Foreign Policy Toolkit: Key Institutions and Processes* (Thousand Oaks CA: CQ Press, 2013).

3. Kopp and Gillispie, *Career Diplomacy*.

4. James Buchanan, secretary of state from 1845 to 1849, president from 1857 to 1861. William Howard Taft sometimes served as acting secretary of state before becoming president.

5. I've been surprised and pleased to discover that I am not the first former DCM in Rome to point out the excessive staffing there. See Peter Bridges, "Notes from Italy: The Oversized Embassy," *California Literary Review*, November 6, 2007, accessed March 14, 2012, http://calitreview.com/280.

6. *Foreign Service Act of 1980*, Public Law 96-465, *U.S. Statutes at Large* 94 (1980): 2071, accessed December 10, 2012, http://constitution.org/uslaw/sal/094 _statutes_at_large.pdf. Here is the specific language establishing the authority of the chief of mission: "(1) shall have full responsibility for the direction, coordination, and supervision of all Government executive branch employees in that country (except for employees under the command of a United States area military

commander); and (2) shall keep fully and currently informed with respect to all activities and operations of the Government within that country, and shall insure that all Government executive branch employees in that country (except for employees under the command of a United States area military commander) comply fully with all applicable directives of the chief of mission."

7. Christopher Lamb and Edward Marks, *Chief of Mission Authority as a Model for National Security Integration* (Washington DC: National Defense University Press, 2010), accessed March 14, 2012, http://www.ndu.edu/inss/docUploaded/ INSS%20Strategic%20Perspectives%202_Lamb%20.pdf. See also Edward Marks and Christopher Lamb, "Implementing the QDDR," *Interagency Journal* 3, no. 1 (2012): 8–14, accessed December 18, 2012, http://thesimonscenter.org/wp-content/ uploads/2012/02/IAJ-3-1-pg8-14.pdf.

8. Stephen Glain, *State vs. Defense: The Battle to Define America's Empire* (New York: Crown, 2011).

9. "The National Security Archive," George Washington University, accessed February 27, 2012, http://www.gwu.edu/~nsarchiv/; "Freedom of Information Act," U.S. Department of State, accessed March 13, 2012, http://www.state.gov/m/a/ips/.

10. Amb. Peter Bridges, "Streamline, Don't Swell, Our Foreign Affairs Machine," *Huffington Post*, November 19, 2008, accessed February 27, 2012, http:// www.huffingtonpost.com/amb-peter-bridges/streamline-dont-swell-our_b _144953.html.

11. Bridges, "Streamline, Don't Swell."

12. *European Recovery Act (Marshall Plan)*, Public Law 472, *U.S. Statutes at Large* 62 (1948): 137, accessed December 10, 2012, http://constitution.org/uslaw/sal/062 _statutes_at_large.pdf.

13. "Who We Are," USAID, accessed October 25, 2012, http://www.usaid.gov/ who-we-are.

14. "GAO Report Suggests That USAID Remains 'More of a Contracting Agency Than an Operational Agency,'" *Haiti: Relief and Reconstruction Watch* (blog), Center for Economic and Policy Research, November 21, 2011, accessed April 2, 2012, http://www.cepr.net/index.php/blogs/relief-and-reconstruction-watch/ usaid-more-of-a-contracting-agency-than-an-operational-agency.

15. "Frequently Asked Questions," USAID, accessed April 2, 2012, http://www .usaid.gov/faqs.htm; "Congressional Budget Justification," USAID, accessed April 2, 2012, http://www.usaid.gov/performance/cbj/.

16. John Norris and Connie Veillette, "Five Steps to Make Our Aid More Effective and Save $2 Billion," Center for American Progress, May 5, 2011, accessed March 13, 2012, http://www.americanprogress.org/issues/2011/05/foreign_aid_savings.html. The Obama administration is trying to move forward on some of these steps.

17. *The Development Response to Violent Extremism and Insurgency: Putting Principles into Practice* (Washington DC: USAID, September 2011), accessed February 27, 2012, http://pdf.usaid.gov/pdf_docs/PDACS400.pdf.

18. *Beyond Assistance: The HELP Commission Report on Foreign Assistance Program* (Washington DC: United States Commission on Helping to Enhance the Livelihood of People Living Abroad, December 7, 2007), accessed March 13, 2012, http:// www.americanprogress.org/issues/2007/12/pdf/beyond_assistence.pdf. A last-minute 923-page congressional proposal along these lines (accessed December 19, 2012, http://www.democrats.foreignaffairs.house.gov/112/GPA112/HR6644. pdf) died without being enacted at the end of the 112th Congress in January 2013.

19. *Leading through Civilian Power: The First Quadrennial Diplomacy and Development Review* (Washington DC: U.S. Department of State, 2010), accessed March 13, 2012, http://www.state.gov/documents/organization/153108.pdf.

20. *Leading through Civilian Power*, xix.

21. "Bureau of Conflict and Stabilization Operations," U.S. Department of State, accessed March 23, 2012, http://www.state.gov/j/cso/.

22. "State and USAID–FY 2013 Budget," U.S. Department of State, February 13, 2012, accessed March 23, 2012, http://www.state.gov/r/pa/prs/ps/2012/02/183808 .htm. The Defense Department, not surprisingly, is filling the gap with its own Civilian Expeditionary Workforce. See U.S. Department of Defense, "The Civilian Deployment Experience," accessed June 20, 2013, http://www.cpms.osd.mil/ expeditionary/.

23. Matthew 9:17.

24. This conclusion differs from the recommendations of Kori N. Schake, who argues that the problems of the State Department and USAID can be solved with reforms modeled on the successes of the Defense Department. I doubt such an overhaul within a long-established institutional framework will succeed. Kori N. Schake, *State of Disrepair: Fixing the Culture and Practices of the State Department* (Stanford CA: Hoover Institution Press, 2012). Ditto John Norris's different idea about copying Pentagon experience, "Please God, Not Another Blue-Ribbon Panel," *Foreign Policy*, October 24, 2012, accessed December 29, 2012, http://www.foreignpolicy .com/articles/2012/10/24/please_god_not_another_blue_ribbon_panel?page=0,1.

25. The institutional situation of peace-building in the U.S. government as of 2009 is described in detail in Dane F. Smith Jr., *U.S. Peacefare: Organizing American Peace-Building Operations* (Santa Barbara CA: Praeger, 2010).

26. *Diplomacy in a Time of Scarcity* (Washington DC: Stimson, October 2012), accessed October 25, 2012 http://www.stimson.org/images/uploads/research-pdfs/ AAD_10_23_12.pdf.

27. "Bureau of Resource Management," U.S. Department of State, accessed May 14, 2012, http://www.state.gov/s/d/rm/index.htm#mission.

28. "Ten Things You Should Know about the State Department and USAID," *DipNote* (blog), U.S. Department of State, accessed May 17, 2012, http://blogs .state.gov/index.php/site/entry/ten_things_state_department_usaid. This is odd, as the QDDR cites the following objectives, which are broadly consistent with what is proposed here: "protecting the security of the United States and its citizens, allies

and partners; promoting prosperity at home and abroad with a strong U.S. economy and an open international economic system that promotes opportunity; supporting the spread of universal values; and shaping a just and sustainable international order that promotes peace, security, and opportunity through cooperation to meet global challenges." *Leading through Civilian Power*, 9.

29. The role of strategy "is to co-ordinate and direct all the resources of a nation, or band of nations, toward the attainment of the political object of the war." B. H. Liddell Hart, *Strategy*, 2nd rev. ed. (London: Faber and Faber, 1967), 322. This refers to the combined diplomatic, economic, and military means used to attain a political goal. John Lewis Gaddis, director of the Grand Strategy Program at Yale University, defines "grand strategy" as the "calculated relationship of means to large ends," which allows the term to be used in both war and non-war scenarios. Gabe Starosta, "Cold War Historian Discusses Grand Strategy," Duke Sanford School of Public Policy, February 27, 2009, accessed July 20, 2012, http://news.sanford.duke.edu/news-type/news/2009/cold-war-historian-discusses-grand-strategy.

30. Chas W. Freeman Jr., "The Incapacitation of U.S. Statecraft and Diplomacy," *Hague Journal of Diplomacy* 6 (2011): 413–32.

31. Henry A. Kissinger, "The Age of Kennan," *New York Times*, November 10, 2011, accessed March 13, 2012, http://www.nytimes.com/2011/11/13/books/review/george-f-kennan-an-american-life-by-john-lewis-gaddis-book-review.html?_r=1&ref=review&gwh=a3a1147940f29016270281adc897a6f4.

32. Stephen M. Walt, "The End of the American Era," *The National Interest*, October 25, 2011, accessed March 13, 2012, www.nationalinterest.org/article/the-end-the-american-era-6037.

33. Andrew Krepinevich, "Strategy in a Time of Austerity," *Foreign Affairs* 91, no. 6 (2012): 58–69, accessed December 26, 2012, http://www.foreignaffairs.com/articles/138362/andrew-f-krepinevich-jr/strategy-in-a-time-of-austerity.

34. Richard N. Haass, "The Restoration Doctrine," *The National Interest* 7, no. 3 (2012), accessed March 19, 2012, http://www.the-american-interest.com/article.cfm?piece=1164.

35. James R. Clapper, *Unclassified Statement for the Record on the Worldwide Threat Assessment of the US Intelligence Community for the Senate Select Committee on Intelligence* (Washington DC: Office of the Director of National Intelligence, January 31, 2012), accessed March 13, 2012, http://s3.documentcloud.org/documents/288481/james-clapper-testimony-01-31-2012.pdf.

36. James R. Holmes and Toshi Yoshihara, "Why China's Navy Is a Threat," *The Diplomat*, September 17, 2010, accessed April 5, 2012, http://the-diplomat.com/2010/09/17/why-chinas-navy-is-a-threat. Others doubt China is a serious naval threat beyond its own environs: "China's Blue Water Navy Is Not a Threat," *Chicago Project on Security and Terrorism* (blog), University of Chicago, July 8, 2011, accessed April 5, 2012, http://cpost.uchicago.edu/blog/2011/07/08/chinas-blue-water-navy-is-not-a-threat.

37. The Project on National Security Reform has come to a similar conclusion. See Christopher Holshek, *America's First Quarter Millennium: Envisioning a Transformed National Security System in 2026* (Washington DC: Project on National Security Reform, February 8, 2012), accessed March 13, 2012, http://old.pnsr.org/data/images/pnsr_americas_first_quarter_millennium.pdf.

38. U.S. Department of State, Office of Inspector General, *Report of Inspection—Embassy Copenhagen, Denmark*, Report Number ISP-I-11-19A (Washington DC: United States Department of State and the Broadcasting Board of Governors, March 2011), accessed April 2, 2012, http://oig.state.gov/documents/organization/161345.pdf.

39. U.S. Department of State, Office of Inspector General, *Report of Inspection—Embassy Sarajevo, Bosnia, and Herzegovina*, Report Number ISP-I-09-55A (Washington DC: United States Department of State and the Broadcasting Board of Governors, September 2009), accessed April 2, 2012, http://oig.state.gov/documents/organization/132896.pdf.

40. U.S. Department of State, Office of Inspector General, *Report of Inspection—Embassy Kuala Lumpur, Malaysia*, Report Number ISP-I-10-74A (Washington DC: United States Department of State and the Broadcasting Board of Governors, August 2010), accessed April 1, 2012, http://oig.state.gov/documents/organization/147028.pdf.

41. *Fiscal Year 2011 Agency Financial Report: Leadership in a Time of Change* (Washington DC: United States Department of State Bureau of Public Affairs, November 2011), 8, accessed November 26, 2012, http://www.state.gov/documents/organization/177397.pdf.

42. Canada is already moving in this direction, by folding its development agency into its department of foreign affairs and international trade. Jennie Lei Revelo, "CIDA No More," Devex, accessed May 21, 2013, https://www.devex.com/en/news/blogs/cida-no-more?mkt_tok=3RkMMJWWfF9wsRonu6TPcu%2Fhmj TEU5z16e0tX6OwlMI%2F0ER3fOvrPUfGjI4ERcJgI%2FqLAzICFpZo2FFcH %2FaQZA%3D%3D.

43. Special Inspector General for Iraq Reconstruction, "Learning from Iraq" (Washington DC: Special Inspector General for Iraq Reconstruction, March 2013), accessed May 13, 2013, http://www.sigir.mil/learningfromiraq/index.html.

44. Christel Fonzo-Eberhard and Richard L. Kugler, "Sizing the Civilian Response Capacity for Complex Operations," in *Civilian Surge: Key to Complex Operations*, edited by Hans Binnendijk and Patrick M. Cronin (Washington DC: National Defense University Press, 2009), 11–32.

45. Nora Bensahel and Patrick M. Cronin, "America's Civilian Operations Abroad: Understanding Past and Future Requirements," Center for a New American Security, January 2012, accessed December 28, 2012, http://www.cnas .org/files/documents/publications/CNAS_AmericasCivilianOperationsAbroad _BensahelCronin_0.pdf.

46. There are, of course, non-American organizations involved as well. See, for

example, "Privatising Peace," *The Economist*, June 30, 2011, accessed May 24, 2013, http://www.economist.com/node/18895458. There are also substantial nongovernmental funders. See, for the United States, Peace and Security Funders Group, "Peace and Security Grantmaking by U.S. Foundations, 2009–2009," accessed May 24, 2013, http://peaceandsecurity.org/415/PSFGreport_Jan2011.pdf.

Suggested Reading

Acemoglu, Daron, and James Robinson. *Why Nations Fail: The Origins of Power, Prosperity and Poverty.* New York: Crown, 2012.

Annan, Kofi, and Nader Mousavizadeh. *Interventions: A Life in War and Peace.* New York: Penguin, 2012.

Arndt, Richard T. *The First Resort of Kings: American Cultural Diplomacy in the Twentieth Century.* Washington DC: Potomac Books, 2005.

Bacevich, Andrew. *Washington Rules: America's Path to Permanent War.* New York: Henry Holt, 2010.

Bayley, David H., and Robert M. Perito. *The Police in War: Fighting Insurgency, Terrorism and Violent Crime.* Boulder: Lynne Rienner, 2010.

Bilmes, Linda J., and Joseph E. Stiglitz. *The Three Trillion Dollar War: The True Cost of the Iraq Conflict.* New York: Norton, 2008.

Binnendijk, Hans, and Patrick M. Cronin, eds. *Civilian Surge: Key to Complex Operations.* Washington DC: National Defense University Press, 2009.

Bremmer, Ian. *Every Nation for Itself: Winners and Losers in a G-Zero World.* New York: Portfolio/Penguin, 2012.

Chenoweth, Erica, and Maria J. Stephan. *Why Civil Resistance Works: The Strategic Logic of Nonviolent Conflict.* New York: Columbia University Press, 2011.

Connable, Ben, and Martin Libicki. *How Insurgencies End.* Santa Monica CA: RAND Press, 2010.

Dobbins, James, et al. *The UN's Role in Nation-Building: From the Congo to Iraq.* Santa Monica CA: RAND, 2005.

Durch, William, ed., *Twenty-First-Century Peace Operations.* Washington DC: United States Institute of Peace Press, 2006.

Fukuyama, Francis. *State-Building: Governance and World Order in the Twenty-First Century.* Ithaca NY: Cornell University Press, 2004.

Gates, Robert M. "A Balanced Strategy: Reprogramming the Pentagon for a New Age." *Foreign Affairs* 88, no. 1 (2009): 22–40.

Glain, Stephen. *State vs. Defense: The Battle to Define America's Empire.* New York: Crown, 2011.

Goldstein, Joshua. *Winning the War on War.* New York: Penguin Group, 2011.

Gowan, Richard. *Review of Political Missions 2010*. New York: Center on International Cooperation, 2010.

Green, Dan. *The Valley's Edge*. Dulles VA: Potomac Books, 2012.

Guttieri, Karen, and Jessica Piombo, eds., *Interim Governments: Institutional Bridges to Peace and Democracy?* Washington DC: United States Institute of Peace Press, 2007.

Haass, Richard N. *War of Necessity, War of Choice*. New York: Simon and Schuster, 2009.

Hampson, Fen Osler, and I. William Zartman. *The Global Power of Talk: Negotiating America's Interests*. Boulder: Paradigm, 2012.

Huda, Qamar al, ed., *Crescent and Dove: Peace and Conflict Resolution in Islam*. Washington DC: United States Institute of Peace Press, 2010.

Hunt, Swanee. *Worlds Apart: Bosnian Lessons for Global Security*. Durham NC: Duke University Press, 2011.

Jentleson, Bruce, ed. *Opportunities Seized, Opportunities Missed: Preventive Diplomacy in the Post–Cold War World*. New York: Rowman and Littlefield, 2000.

Jones, Seth. *In the Graveyard of Empires: America's War in Afghanistan*. New York: Norton, 2009.

Kagan, Robert. *The World America Made*. New York: Knopf, 2012.

Kopp, Harry W., and Charles A. Gillispie. *Career Diplomacy: Life and Work in the U.S. Foreign Service*. 2nd ed. Washington DC: Georgetown University Press, 2011.

Korski, Daniel, and Richard Gowan. *Can the EU Rebuild Failing States? A Review of Europe's Civilian Capacities*. London: European Council on Foreign Relations, October 2009.

Kupchan, Charles A. *The End of the American Era*. New York: Knopf, 2002.

Logan, Justin, and Christopher Preble. *Failed States and Failed Logic: The Case against a Standing Nation-Building Office*. Washington DC: CATO Institute, January 2006.

Luce, Edward. *Time to Start Thinking: America in the Age of Descent*. New York: Atlantic Monthly Press, 2012.

Lund, Michael. *Preventing Violent Conflict: A Strategy for Preventive Diplomacy*. Washington DC: United States Institute of Peace Press, 1996.

Maddow, Rachel. *Drift: The Unmooring of American Military Power*. New York: Crown, 2012.

Mahnken, Thomas G. *Competitive Strategies for the Twenty-First Century: Theory, History and Practice*. Stanford CA: Stanford University Press, 2012.

Mandelbaum, Michael. *The Frugal Superpower: America's Global Leadership in a Cash-Strapped Era*. Jackson TN: Public Affairs, 2010.

McMahon, Patrice, and Jon Western, eds. *The International Community and State-Building: Getting Its Act Together?* New York: Routledge, 2012.

Merlini, Cesare, and Olivier Roy. *Arab Society in Revolt: The West's Mediterranean Challenge*. Washington DC: Brookings Institution Press, 2012.

Migdal, Joel. *Weak States, Strong Societies*. Princeton NJ: Princeton University Press, 1988.

Newman, Edward, and Roland Rich, eds. *The UN Role in Promoting Democracy: Between Ideals and Reality*. New York: United Nations University Press, 2004.

Nye, Joseph S., Jr. *The Future of Power*. New York: Public Affairs, 2011.

OECD. *Supporting Statebuilding in Situations of Conflict and Fragility: Policy Guidance*. Paris: OECD, 2011.

O'Neill, Jim. *The Growth Map: Economic Opportunity in the BRICs and Beyond*. New York: Portfolio/Penguin, 2011.

Pinker, Steven. *The Better Angels of Our Nature: Why Violence Has Declined*. New York: Viking, 2011.

Priest, Dana, and William Arkin. *Top Secret America: The Rise of the New American Security State*. New York: Little, Brown, 2011.

Schake, Kori N. *State of Disrepair: Fixing the Culture and Practices of the State Department*. Stanford CA: Hoover Institution Press, 2012.

Serwer, Daniel. "A Bosnian Federation Memoir." In *Herding Cats: Multiparty Mediation in a Complex World*, ed. Chester A. Crocker, Fen O. Hampson, and Pamela R. Aall, 547–86. Washington DC: United States Institute of Peace Press, 1999.

Singer, P. W. *Wired for War: The Robotics Revolution and Conflict in the Twenty-First Century*. New York: Penguin, 2009.

Slaughter, Anne-Marie. "A New Theory for the Foreign Policy Frontier: Collaborative Power." *Atlantic*, November 30, 2011.

Smith, Dane F., Jr. *U.S. Peacefare: Organizing American Peace-Building Operations*. Santa Barbara CA: Praeger, 2010.

Smock, David, and Daniel Serwer, eds. *Facilitating Dialogue: USIP's Work in Conflict Zones*. Washington DC: United States Institute of Peace Press, 2012.

Special Inspector General for Iraq Reconstruction. *Hard Lessons: The Iraq Reconstruction Experience*. Baghdad: SIGIR, 2009.

Stares, Paul B., and Micah Zenko. *Enhancing U.S. Preventive Action*. New York: Council on Foreign Relations Press, 2009.

Stewart, Patrick. *Weak Links: Fragile States, Global Threats, and International Security*. New York: Oxford University Press, 2011.

Stewart, Rory, and Gerald Knaus. *Can Intervention Work?* New York: Norton, 2011.

United States Institute of Peace and Army Peacekeeping and Stability Operations Institute. *Guiding Principles for Stabilization and Reconstruction*. Washington DC: United States Institute of Peace Press, 2009.

U.S. Department of State. *Leading through Civilian Power: The First Quadrennial Diplomacy and Development Review*. Washington DC: U.S. Department of State, 2010.

Van Buren, Peter. *We Meant Well*. New York: Metropolitan Books, 2011.

Wirls, Daniel. *International Security: The Politics of Defense from Reagan to Obama*. Baltimore: Johns Hopkins University Press, 2010.

Wright, Robin. *Rock the Casbah: Rage and Rebellion across the Arab World*. New York: Simon and Schuster, 2011.

Zakaria, Fareed. *From Wealth to Power: The Unusual Origins of America's World Role*. Princeton NJ: Princeton University Press, 1998.

Zakheim, Dov. *A Vulcan's Tale: How the Bush Administration Mismanaged the Reconstruction of Afghanistan*. Washington DC: Brookings Institution Press, 2011.

Zartman, I. William, ed. *Preventive Negotiation: Avoiding Conflict Escalation*. Lanham MD: Rowman and Littlefield, 2001.

Zenko, Micah, and Michael Cohen. "Clear and Present Safety: The United States Is More Secure Than Washington Thinks." *Foreign Affairs* 91, no. 2 (2012): 79–93.

Index